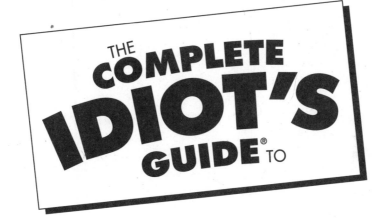

THE COMPLETE IDIOT'S GUIDE® TO

Knitting and Crocheting
Illustrated

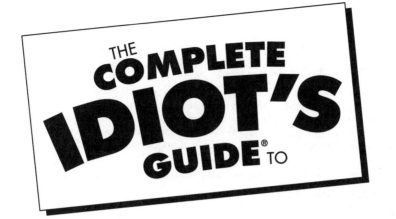

Knitting and Crocheting

Illustrated

Second Edition

by Barbara Breiter and Gail Diven

ALPHA

A member of Penguin Group (USA) Inc.

International Standard Book Number: 1-59257-089-5
Library of Congress Catalog Card Number: 2003108338

05 04 03   8 7 6 5 4 3 2 1

Interpretation of the printing code: The rightmost number of the first series of numbers is the year of the book's printing; the rightmost number of the second series of numbers is the number of the book's printing. For example, a printing code of 03-1 shows that the first printing occurred in 2003.

Printed in the United States of America

Note: This publication contains the opinions and ideas of its authors. It is intended to provide helpful and informative material on the subject matter covered. It is sold with the understanding that the authors and publisher are not engaged in rendering professional services in the book. If the reader requires personal assistance or advice, a competent professional should be consulted.

The authors and publisher specifically disclaim any responsibility for any liability, loss, or risk, personal or otherwise, which is incurred as a consequence, directly or indirectly, of the use and application of any of the contents of this book.

Most Alpha books are available at special quantity discounts for bulk purchases for sales promotions, premiums, fund-raising, or educational use. Special books, or book excerpts, can also be created to fit specific needs.

For details, write: Special Markets, Alpha Books, 375 Hudson Street, New York, NY 10014.

Publisher: *Marie Butler-Knight*
Product Manager: *Phil Kitchel*
Senior Managing Editor: *Jennifer Chisholm*
Senior Acquisitions Editor: *Randy Ladenheim-Gil*
Development Editor: *Lynn Northrup*
Senior Production Editors: *Katherin Bidwell, Christy Wagner*
Copy Editor: *Rachel Lopez Hohenshell*
Illustrator: *Chris Eliopoulos*
Cover/Book Designer: *Trina Wurst*
Indexer: *Julie Bess*
Layout/Proofreading: *Becky Harmon, Mary Hunt*

Contents at a Glance

Part 1: Begin at the Beginning 2

  1 Why Knit or Crochet? 4
      A look at what knitting and crocheting are all about and why you might want to join in.

  2 Choose Your Palette: A Yarn Primer 8
      To help you choose the best yarn for your projects, here's a look at the different types of yarns and fibers available.

  3 An Overview of Knitting and Crochet Tools...18
      This chapter sorts out the tools you'll need and demystifies needles and hooks.

  4 Why Gauge Is So Important 28
      You will not learn a more important concept in knitting and crocheting than measuring and verifying gauge.

Part 2: Learning to Knit...36

  5 Building the Foundation: Casting On Stitches 38
      All things must begin somewhere, and when you knit, you start a project by casting on stitches. This chapter tells you how.

  6 The Big Three: Knitting, Purling, and Binding Off 46
      Knit one, purl two ... you've probably heard that mysterious chant repeated in cartoons, films, or TV shows. But how? This chapter teaches you how to knit, how to purl, and how to end your work.

  7 Knitting Stitch Patterns 60
      A collection of common and helpful patterns, all using a combination of knits and purls.

  8 What Goes Up Must Come Down: Increasing and Decreasing............................66
      This chapter shows you how to increase and decrease stitches to shape your knitting.

  9 Beyond the Basics: Adding to Your Knitting Repertoire..74
      With the addition of a few simple moves, you can change the way your stitches— and your projects—look.

10 Making Your Knitting Colorful 82

Spice up your projects with a little zing. This chapter covers five ways to add color.

11 Knitting in the Round...90

You've been knitting back and forth; now try knitting in a circle to create a tube. This chapter tells you all about it.

12 Correcting Common Knitting Gaffes 98

Don't let a few common mistakes spoil your fun! A few easy tricks will help get your knitting back on track.

Part 3: Learning to Crochet 106

13 Getting Started: Basic Crochet Stitches..108

In this chapter you learn the basic stitches plus all about the importance of turning chains.

14 Shaping Your Work..124

Increases and decreases let you shape your fabric as well as work pretty stitch patterns.

15 Beyond the Basics: Adding to Your Crochet Repertoire 128

Slight changes to basic crochet alter the way these stitches look. You also learn about filet crochet and an entirely new concept called Afghan or Tunisian crochet.

16 Crocheting Around 142

You've been crocheting back and forth but now it's time to make circles and squares by crocheting around.

17 Colorful Crochet...148

In this chapter, you learn to add color to your projects by adding stripes and changing colors in the same row.

Part 4: Finishing Touches for Knitting and Crocheting...154

18 Finishing Your Work: Seaming and Blocking 156

This chapter teaches you how to seam and block for professional results.

19 Edgings 166

Edgings are often used around square or rectangular pieces for decoration or to help the piece lie flat. You learn all about them in this chapter.

20 Embellishments 170

Fringe, tassels, and pom poms add pizzazz to knit and crochet projects.

Part 5: **Knitting and Crocheting Patterns** 176

21 Talking the Talk: Reading a Knit or Crochet Pattern 178

This chapter helps you make sense of the code in which patterns are written.

22 Knitting Patterns 186

Five easy patterns to start you on your adventure in knitting.

23 Crochet Patterns 198

Enter the world of crochet with these four simple patterns.

Appendixes

A Resources 206

B List of Abbreviations 211

C Glossary 215

Index 219

Contents

Part 1: Begin at the Beginning 3

  1 Why Knit or Crochet? 5

     From Fundamental to Just Plain Fun 5

     Why Bother? 6

       Get Creative! 6

       Slow Down Your Hectic Pace 6

       Make Pieces for the Future 7

       Take It Along 7

     So What Exactly *Is* Knitting and Crocheting? 7

  2 Choose Your Palette: A Yarn Primer 9

     Put Up Your Yarn: Common Yarn Packaging 9

     Learning to Read Yarn Labels 10

     Selecting a Fiber 13

     Watching Your Weight: How Thick Is the Yarn? 15

     Substituting Yarn 16

  3 An Overview of Knitting and Crochet Tools 19

     Knitting Needles 19

       Straight or Circular? 19

       Is That American or English? 21

       Trekking Through the Material World 21

     Crochet Hooks 21

       Parts of a Crochet Hook 21

       Crochet Hook Sizes and Types 22

       Afghan Hooks 23

     Comparing Needle and Hook Sizes 23

     Gadgets Make the Job Easier 24

       Measuring Tools 25

       Stitch Markers 25

       Bobbins 25

       Finishing Accessories 26

     Just for Knitters 26

       Stitch Holders 26

       Row Counters 26

       Cable Needles 26

       Point Protectors 27

4	Why Gauge Is So Important	29
	Gauge? What's That?	29
	Some Examples of Gauge	30
	How Does Gauge Affect Size?	30
	How Do Patterns Specify Gauge?	31
	Is Gauge Ever Unimportant?	32
	Checking Your Gauge	32
	Measuring Gauge	32
	The Width's Okay, but the Length's a Bit Hefty	33
	The Advantages of Understanding Gauge	34
	What Do I Do with All These Little Squares?	34
Part 2:	**Learning to Knit**	**37**
5	Building the Foundation: Casting On Stitches	39
	Setting the Stage	39
	The Single Cast On	41
	The Double Cast On	42
	The Cable Cast On	43
	The Single Cast On for Lefties	44
6	The Big Three: Knitting, Purling, and Binding Off	47
	Same Stitch, Different Look: Knitting and Purling	47
	Knitting 101	48
	Continental Knitting	48
	English Knitting	49
	The Next Row	51
	Purls of Wisdom	51
	Continental Purling	52
	English Purling	53
	The Fabulous Two: Garter Stitch and Stockinette Stitch	54
	Bringing It to a Close	55
	Binding Off in Knit	56
	Binding Off in Purl	57
	Left-Handed Knitting	57
	The Knit Stitch	57
	The Purl Stitch	59
7	Knitting Stitch Patterns	61
	Combining Knits and Purls	61
	Understanding Stitch Multiples	62
	Ribbing	62
	Seed Stitch	63
	Checkerboard	64

8   What Goes Up Must Come Down: Increasing and Decreasing 67
     Common Increase and Decrease Abbreviations 67
     Adding Stitches: Increasing 68
       Yarn Over (yo) 68
       Bar Increase 68
       Make 1 (M1) 69
     Subtracting Stitches: Decreasing 70
       Knit 2 Together (k2tog) 70
       Knit 2 Together Through Back Loop (k2tog tbl) 70
       Purl 2 Together (p2tog) 71
       Purl 2 Together Through Back Loop (p2tog tbl) 71
       Slip Slip Knit (ssk) 71
       Slip, Knit, Pass Slipped Stitch Over (sl 1, k 1, psso) 72
     Going Left or Right 73
     When Increasing and Decreasing Don't Do Either 73

9   Beyond the Basics: Adding to Your Knitting Repertoire 75
     Knitting Through the Back Loop (tbl) 75
     Purling Through the Back Loop (tbl) 75
     Slip Stitch (sl) 76
     Cables 77
       Cable 4 Back (c4b) 77
       Cable 4 Front (c4f) 78
     How to Pick Up Stitches 78
     Buttonholes 81
       Horizontal Buttonhole 81
       Vertical Buttonhole 81

10 Making Your Knitting Colorful 83
     On Your Mark, Get Set, Stripe 83
     Slip Stitch and Color 84
     Intarsia Knitting 85
     Fair Isle Knitting 85
       Stranding from the Right Side 86
       Stranding from the Wrong Side 86
       Twisting Stitches 87
     Duplicate Stitch 87

11 Knitting in the Round 91
     Why Go 'Round and 'Round? 91
     Beware of Twisted Stitches 92
     Joining 93

Knitting with a Circular Needle 93
Knitting with Double Point Needles 95

12 Correcting Common Knitting Gaffes 99
Taking the Bull by the Horns: Preventing Mistakes 99
Turning Twisted Stitches 100
Catching Dropped Stitches 100
Picking Up a Dropped Knit Stitch in the Row Below *100*
Picking Up a Dropped Purl Stitch in the Row Below *101*
How to Become a Major Pick Up Artist *103*
Fixing Sloppy Stitches 103
When All Else Fails: Let 'Er Rip! 104
Taking Out Just a Few Stitches *104*
Going Wild! *104*
Extra, Extra! *104*

Part 3: Learning to Crochet 107

13 Getting Started: Basic Crochet Stitches 109
Holding the Hook 109
Making a Slip Knot *110*
Feeding the Yarn *111*
The Base of All Crochet: The Foundation Chain 112
Making the Chain *112*
Heads or Tails? *113*
Basic Stitches 113
Single Crochet (sc) *114*
Half Double Crochet (hdc) *114*
Double Crochet (dc) *115*
Triple Crochet (trc) *116*
Slip Stitch (sl st) *117*
The Next Row 117
Turning Chains *118*
The First or the Second Stitch? *119*
Practice Makes Perfect 119
Left-Handed Crochet 120
Left-Handed Basics *121*
Get Ready to Make Your First Chain *122*
Left-Handed Single Crochet (sc) *122*
Other Basic Stitches *123*

14 Shaping Your Work 125

   Common Abbreviations 125
   Upping the Ante: Increasing 125
   Subtracting Stitches: Decreasing 126
      Singles, Anyone? Decreasing in Single Crochet *126*
      Decreasing in Double Crochet *127*
      Decreasing in Triple Crochet *127*

15 Beyond the Basics: Adding to Your Crochet Repertoire 129

   Working Under One Loop 129
   Working Around the Post of a Stitch 130
      Front Post Double Crochet (fdpc) *130*
      Back Post Double Crochet (bpdc) *131*
   Working in a Space (sp) 132
   Reverse Single Crochet (reverse sc) 132
   Cluster Stitches 132
      Popcorn Stitch (pc st) *132*
      Bobble Stitch *133*
      Puff Stitch *133*
   Shell and V-Stitches 134
   Filet Crochet: Spaces and Blocks 134
      Creating Your First Mesh Piece *135*
      Filling in the Dots *136*
      Forming a Lacet *137*
      Increasing and Decreasing in Filet Crochet *137*
      Reading a Filet Crochet Chart *139*
   Afghan (Tunisian) Crochet 139
      Hooked on Afghans *140*

16 Crocheting Around 143

   Crocheting Around in Circles and Squares 143
      How to Make a Ring *143*
      Working into the Ring *144*
   Making a Circle or a Tube 145
   Working Rounds in Double and Triple Crochet 145
   Grannies Have More Fun 146

17 Colorful Crochet 149

   Scintillating Stripes 149
   Changing Colors in the Same Row 150
   Crocheting with Bobbins 151

Part 4:   Finishing Touches for Knitting and Crocheting 155

18   Finishing Your Work: Seaming and Blocking 157
    Final Call: Weaving in Ends 157
    Sewing Up the Seams 158
        Mattress Stitch *158*
        Backstitch *159*
        Overcast or Whip Stitch *160*
        Slip Stitch *161*
        For Knitters Only: Grafting *161*
    Blocking 163
        Wet Blocking and Washing *163*
        Pinning *164*
        Steaming *165*

19   Edgings 167
    The Finishing Touch: Crocheted Edgings 167
        Slip Stitch Edging *167*
        Reverse Single Crochet Edging *168*
        Picot Edging *168*
    Knit Edgings 168
        Creating Selvage Edges *168*
        Seed Stitch Edging *169*

20   Embellishments 171
    Fringe Is Fun 171
    Top It with a Tassel 172
    Puffy Pom Poms 173
    For Knitters: I-Cord 174

Part 5:   Knitting and Crocheting Patterns 177

21   Talking the Talk: Reading a Knit or Crochet Pattern 179
    Understanding the Basics 179
        Common Abbreviations *179*
        Yarn *180*
        Gauge *180*
        Suggested Needle or Hook Size *180*
        Other Materials *180*
        Stitch Multiples *180*
        Stitch Pattern *180*
    Which Size? 181
    What About Those Asterisks? 181
    And What About Parentheses? 181

Picture Perfect 182
Miscellaneous Considerations 182
   Work Even 182
   Ending on WS Row 182
   Reverse Shaping 183
   Decreasing or Increasing on Certain Rows 183
   Decrease or Increase Evenly 183
   Keeping to Pattern 184
   At the Same Time 184
   Knitters Only: Bind Off in Pattern 184
Reading Charts 184
Don't Skip the Instructions! 185

22 Knitting Patterns 187
Cotton Dishcloth 187
Simple Scarf 189
Felted Purse 190
Two Needle Hat 192
Short Sleeved Pullover 194

23 Crochet Patterns 199
Simple Scarf 200
Southwestern Stripes Afghan 201
Felted Crochet Purse 202
Easy Hat 204

Appendixes

A Resources 207

B List of Abbreviations 211

C Glossary 215

Index 219

Foreword

I've had a number of reincarnations in my life—some were knitting related and others weren't. After weaving in and out of various occupations and roles, I've come to my currently "very comfortable place." One thing has never changed during all the times and events, and that is I always knit. I consider this as an important part of me as the color of my hair and eyes. It's who I am. My friends and loved ones know me as a passionate knitter.

Granted I wasn't born with knitting needles in my hands. My knitting journey has been one of discovery and experience. With my father being an only child of Canadian descent, it was natural that I would look to my New Hampshire grandmother and my Canadian great-aunts for inspiration. They didn't just knit; they embroidered, crocheted, sewed, and quilted. For me, it was a very special classroom, and along with needlecraft lessons, I received a legacy far greater than diamonds or pearls. I learned early on that making things is simply a part of life. Once skilled in these needlearts, I have been able to use that knowledge throughout my changing life and have found great comfort in using my hands to create.

How do I find time to knit and crochet? I'm a very busy person; I multitask with the best of them. My usual goal is to knit or crochet in the evening while I gear down and watch a program or two on TV. I sometimes have to get creative about how to fit knitting time into my life. Fortunately, I have a loving husband who will drive the car on long and short journeys while I knit.

What do I knit? I love the portable nature of knitting and crocheting, and I find them both a sociable art form. I make lots of sweaters that I wear often, but I also make lots of gifts. I love to give a handmade item. It says that I care enough to spend time crafting a very personal piece just for the recipient. When my full-time workdays are gearing down, I fantasize about having the time to make lots of projects for charity efforts such as baby sweaters and mittens for kids in need.

My best memories involve knitting. I've circled the world in pursuit of knitting adventures. I've traveled and seen knitters in their natural settings. It didn't take long to learn that knitting is a universal language that needs very little translation. A few of my favorite destinations are the Shetlands, Iceland, Bolivia, and Peru. I encourage you to seek out knitting and crocheting experiences.

Along with my knitting journeys, a favorite part of my knitting life is the friendships I've made along the way. I've gotten to enjoy being with unbelievably talented and sharing people. Some of my best friendships came about in some knitting-related way. The husband of one of my best friends swears that we love to see each other just so we can spend hours "talking knitting."

Why do I tell you about my life and my personal history? It's not because what I've done is so extraordinary or special. It is simply for you to see how the knowledge you will gain from reading and using this book will bring you great satisfaction. It will enable you to enter into pursuits that are sure to bring you untold enjoyment in all of your life adventures.

Most likely the possibility that you will have a family mentor is not a reality, making *The Complete Idiot's Guide to Knitting and Crocheting Illustrated, Second Edition,* a vital helping hand. You can learn just as I did with expert help guiding you all the way. In a logical step-by-step fashion you'll be able to find out everything you need to know, from selecting the best yarns and tools to practicing basic stitches. It is helpful to have proven tips and tricks to turn you from novice to an experienced knitter and crocheter. You'll learn the language, terms, and abbreviations to guide you into this unique world.

Even after you learn, it's good to have a place to go for answers to questions that arise. This book will become your ultimate reference book.

I wish you much happiness and joy as you embark upon this incredible journey.

Nancy J. Thomas
Editorial director of Lion Brand Yarn Company; co-author of *A Passion for Knitting* and *Vogue Knitting: The Ultimate Knitting Book*; and former editor of *Knitter's Magazine*, *Vogue Knitting*, and *Family Circle Easy Knitting*

Introduction

We think of knitting and crocheting as an art. Some people use a blank canvas and oil paints to create something magnificent from essentially nothing at all. In turn, with the simple tools of yarn and needles or a hook, works of art take shape.

Like painting, learning to knit or crochet well takes time and patience. There is much to learn. But unlike painting, you can learn the necessary basic skills relatively quickly; you'll be creating lovely, usable items in no time at all. The more skills you learn and the better you become, the more elaborate the pieces you'll be able to make.

More and more people have turned to knitting and crocheting as not only a creative outlet, but as a relaxing escape from life's hectic pace. The repetitive nature can be soothing and calming and something to look forward to every day.

The Complete Idiot's Guide to Knitting and Crocheting Illustrated, Second Edition, will teach you the basics of knitting and crochet step by step. You'll then add additional skills to your repertoire, enabling you to make all the projects in this book and many, many more.

Even if you already know how to knit or crochet, there are many sections of this book you will find useful as a reference and from which, we hope, you can learn.

How to Use This Book

Knitting and crocheting involve only a handful of skills to begin. Once you get the basics down, you'll learn additional skills and how to combine them in new ways to create wearable art.

Part 1, "Begin at the Beginning," gives you an overview of knitting and crocheting. This part also discusses two very important concepts applicable to both crafts: choosing yarn and checking gauge.

Part 2, "Learning to Knit," takes you through the basics, step by step. You'll go on to learn additional skills, and you will be able to knit all the projects in the last chapters and many more.

Part 3, "Learning to Crochet," walks you through all the skills you'll need to begin crocheting fabulous pieces such as those at the end of this book. You'll learn the basics, plus you'll become skilled at how to work in rounds, change colors, increase and decrease, and much more.

Part 4, "Finishing Touches for Knitting and Crocheting," covers topics applicable to knitting and crocheting. You'll learn finishing skills such as seaming and blocking and how to work pretty edgings and embellishments.

Part 5, "Knitting and Crocheting Patterns," contains patterns for a variety of projects to try out your new skills. They are all easy enough to be worked as first projects, and there is extra help along the way.

You'll also find a list of helpful resources in Appendix A, a list of common abbreviations and their meanings in Appendix B, and glossary of common terms in Appendix C.

Extras

This book features a number of valuable sidebars that provide additional information about knitting and crocheting: definitions, historical anecdotes, potential pitfalls, and hints and tips.

Yarn Spinning

Knitting and crocheting have enjoyed long histories filled with interesting anecdotes. You'll read some of these compelling stories in the Yarn Spinning sidebars.

Tangles

Warning! You could hit a bump in the road if you don't watch out for the common errors explained in these sidebars.

Pointers

Is there a better way to do something? Are there variations to the common instructions? Check out the Pointers, where you'll learn valuable hints and tips.

Needle Talk

Many terms are defined in this book. Look to the Needle Talk sidebars for simple definitions. You'll also find these definitions in the Glossary.

Acknowledgments

From Barbara: Thank you from the bottom of my heart to my family of friends—Steve, Dan, Bill, and Leif—who have been there no matter what and have provided all the support and encouragement one human being could ever ask for.

My thanks go to Crystal Palace Yarns, Rowan, and Lion Brand for their support in this project.

I'm also grateful to Sandy Tracey for her excellent illustrations and patience and to Herb Stokes for his outstanding photography.

Trademarks

All terms mentioned in this book that are known to be or are suspected of being trademarks or service marks have been appropriately capitalized. Alpha Books and Penguin Group (USA) Inc. cannot attest to the accuracy of this information. Use of a term in this book should not be regarded as affecting the validity of any trademark or service mark.

In This Part

1 Why Knit or Crochet?

2 Choose Your Palette: A Yarn Primer

3 An Overview of Knitting and Crochet Tools

4 Why Gauge Is So Important

Part 1

Begin at the Beginning

As with any new hobby you pursue, if you learn a few key concepts before plunging in, your start will be much smoother. Knitting and crocheting are no exceptions.

This part begins with a look at what knitting and crocheting are all about and the differences between them. You'll learn the foundation for your new craft, including all the tools you'll use, how to choose yarn, and what *gauge* means and why it's important.

After you finish these chapters, you'll be ready to begin your adventure and learn how to knit and crochet.

In This Chapter

- ◆ Fundamental skills of long ago
- ◆ The modern popularity of knitting and crocheting
- ◆ Why learn these skills?
- ◆ The difference between knitting and crocheting

Chapter 1

Why Knit or Crochet?

Knitting? Crocheting? Didn't these skills die out some time ago along with butter churning? Absolutely not! Knitting and crocheting are alive and well and more popular than ever before.

You are about to join the millions of people who in recent years have learned the arts of knitting and crocheting. In this chapter you'll discover the joys of knitting and crocheting; while no longer necessary to daily life, they're creative, relaxing, and very fulfilling pastimes. You'll also learn the differences between them.

From Fundamental to Just Plain Fun

A long time ago, knitting and crocheting were skills as fundamental as breathing, particularly for young girls. They were practiced not only for practical reasons (you couldn't just run down to the store and buy a pair of socks) but for ornamentation such as lace collars.

As mechanism increased, the need for knitting and crocheting in many countries all but disappeared. People could buy sweaters, socks, and blankets. Even fancy crocheted lace items such as doilies, bedspreads, and tablecloths—once the sole property of the hand crocheter—are now produced by machine and sold in department stores.

You would think the automation that made these crafts unnecessary also would have deemed them extinct. Not so. Knitting and crocheting are gaining in popularity, and thousands of new enthusiasts learn every year. According to research conducted by Research Incorporated in the fall of 2000, more than 1 in 3—or 38 million—people in the United States knew how to knit or crochet. With the advent of the Internet, technology has allowed us to share our interest with others around the world. Clearly, knitting and crocheting are here to stay. And with the help of this book you'll be able to get in on the fun, too.

Yarn Spinning _____

Knitting dates very early in the history of man. Actual fragments can be traced only to 200 C.E. However, these fragments show great sophistication and understanding of the craft, causing historians to believe that the craft originated much earlier.

Interestingly enough, knitting started out as a craft mainly pursued by men and it remained predominately a man's craft for centuries. Sailors and traders from Arabia were instrumental in passing on this knowledge to the rest of world. Although today many men are accomplished knitters, considerably more women than men knit.

Yarn Spinning _____

Knitting and crocheting seem to have skipped a generation. They were tremendously popular with those born in the 1920s and 1930s, but experienced a sharp drop with the next generation. Today, one of the largest groups of people who knit or crochet is composed of people in their 20s or 30s. It's theorized that the first generation of women that didn't need to knit or crochet to keep their families warm chose not to. However, this generation's sons and daughters have found knitting and crocheting to be a source of relaxation, creativity, and fulfillment.

Why Bother?

What's the point? If you can walk into a store at any mall across America and buy a wool sweater, why spend valuable free time knitting or crocheting? By picking up this book you've shown that you believe, on some level, that pursuing this endeavor is worthwhile.

Some people enjoy the actual process the most, while others get the greatest satisfaction from what they produce at the end. Others still enjoy both equally.

Get Creative!

Knitting and crocheting are arts—generally a wearable or usable art—but still arts. When you knit or crochet, you are creating something from nothing but yarn and some needles or a hook. You are choosing the dimensions and how you want the finished product to look, and then executing the design. Think about wearing a beautiful hat or scarf you created yourself. You can wear it with an enormous sense of pride and accomplishment, and when a friend asks you where you got it, you can say with pride, "I made it."

Slow Down Your Hectic Pace

In a world full of cell phones, traffic jams, and the like, knitting and crocheting are not only fulfilling; the repetitive motion can be incredibly soothing as well. In fact, if done during quiet times it's meditative in nature. You might also find it fuels the creative process in other areas of your life. You could discover a solution to a problem at work, overcome writer's block, or perhaps come up with a new recipe.

Case in point: Writer Dorothy Parker was an avid knitter whose projects accompanied her _everywhere_. During Hollywood's heyday, Dorothy and husband Alan Campbell co-wrote award-winning screenplays for large film studios. Their writing method was simple and effective: After Alan blocked out the scenes Dorothy sat in a corner, knitting and spouting brilliant dialogue, while Alan typed up her words.

Tangles _____

Please don't let your knitting or crocheting become a task. This is something to do for enjoyment. If you find yourself feeling regimented, put your project away for a couple days so that taking it out again truly is a treat.

Make Pieces for the Future

Family heirlooms are precious. They make us feel like we own a piece of our own history. Are you lucky enough to perhaps have your great-grandmother's broach? Imagine how you would feel if you owned an afghan she had crocheted maybe 100 years ago. Your projects can become family heirlooms. Think of the next five generations in your family wearing a christening gown you created.

Take It Along

Knitting and crocheting are portable—you can take your project with you wherever you go. Heading on a family vacation where you'll spend 10 hours in the car on the way to Disneyland? Riding the train into the office? Waiting for your appointment in a doctor's office? Throw your knitting or crocheting in a bag; you can pull it out and work on it when time allows, turning down time into quality time. Women have even been known to spend time on their projects during labor!

Yarn Spinning

During World War I American citizens were asked to knit socks for the soldiers fighting in Europe. Several knitting bees in New York City's Central Park drew thousands of men, women, and children, all clicking needles in unison, working to clothe the troops.

So What Exactly *Is* Knitting and Crocheting?

You might already know how to knit or crochet—or perhaps both. In that case, this book will serve as a reference for you. Or maybe you learned many years ago and would like to begin again and need some help. However, if you're totally new to the worlds of knitting and crocheting, you might be asking, "What's the difference?"

Both knitting and crocheting involve creating a fabric made with interlocking loops—but that's where the similarity ends.

When you knit you use two needles (although there are other types of knitting, as you'll find out later in this book). You keep a whole row of loops, or *stitches*, active. You use one knitting needle to hold the stitches; another to work the new row of loops. When you crochet you use one hook, and keep only one loop at a time active. Each new stitch, created by catching the yarn with the hook and pulling it through a loop, seals off the last loop.

Crochet and knit stitches are shaped and sized differently; as a result, the fabrics you create knitting and crocheting look, feel, and behave very differently. Using identical yarn, crocheted fabric will be bulkier than knit fabric. Knitting will produce a piece that has more flow, or drape, to it.

Inch for inch, crocheting uses more yarn than knitting; crocheting is also generally much faster than knitting.

If you're not sure which you'd like to learn, try them both and see for yourself whether you have a preference. The only additional item you will need to purchase is a hook or a pair of needles. You might find that you enjoy both equally!

The Least You Need to Know

- Years ago, knitting and crocheting were considered essential skills, primarily for young women.

- Despite the machine age eliminating the necessity of knit or crocheted items, the popularity of knitting and crocheting continues.

- Both are portable, creative endeavors that are fulfilling and soothing.

- Knitting and crocheting involve making loops, but they are worked differently and the fabric you produce is not the same.

In This Chapter

- ◆ How yarn is packaged

- ◆ Gleaning valuable information from yarn labels

- ◆ Selecting a fiber

- ◆ Yarn weights and what they mean

- ◆ Substituting yarn

2

Choose Your Palette: A Yarn Primer

This chapter helps you wade through the mind-boggling number of yarn choices available. You'll learn about different fibers, what size hook or needle works with which thickness of yarn, and what to look for when selecting and substituting yarn.

Understanding different yarns will allow you to make wise choices and prevent you from throwing money away on yarn that won't work as intended for your project.

Put Up Your Yarn: Common Yarn Packaging

Walk into a yarn store and you'll be overwhelmed by the vast array of choices available for knitting and crocheting. Most of what you'll see is packaged—or "put up"—in one of four common ways:

◆ **Ball.** A ball is exactly what you would expect: yarn wound into a ball-like shape. You will begin working from the outside of the ball most of the time. Balls tend to roll around and get away from you; control them by placing them in a bag or other container.

◆ **Skein.** A skein is a bundle of yarn; some skeins are designed as *pull skeins*. An end will be sticking out of the center of the skein and you pull on this to begin working. Sometimes that end will be missing. All skeins have an outside end that allows you to work from that point as if it were a ball.

If you don't want to work from the outside and there is no visible end coming from the center, you can find an end by inserting your thumb and index finger into either end of the skein. Feel for the center; pull this out and the end should be with it. Extra yarn will come out with it but is quickly used up.

Unlike a ball, a skein won't roll around while you're working with it.

◆ **Hank.** A hank is a big circle of yarn twisted into a neat package. To knit or crochet a hank of yarn, you have to untwist the yarn and wind it into a ball. We've all seen images of a person holding yarn across his hands while another person wound it into a ball. That yarn came from a hank. If you don't have a friend available to hold the yarn you can drape the big circle over your knees or over the back of a chair. A contraption called an *umbrella swift* is also sold for this purpose.

◆ **Cone.** Cones come in one pound or greater quantities. They are most often used for machine knitting but can be used for hand knitting and crochet as well. They aren't commonly sold but are available.

Common yarn packaging: ball, skein, hank, and cone.

Although you can use balls and skeins just as they're packaged and wind hanks into balls by hand, a yarn winder (sometimes called a *wool winder*) is very handy. It's a small gizmo that attaches to any table and allows you to make pull skeins easily by cranking a handle. In addition

to the advantage of making a skein that won't roll away from you, as you wind you can check for any defects in the yarn. If you find them and cut them out now, it will save you from being in the middle of a row and finding a piece that is not spun properly or a knot in your yarn.

Pointers

Always cut out knots and imperfections. Occasionally you will find knots in your yarn. Yarn is spun and dyed in long lengths and then wound into whatever size ball, hank, or skein on which the yarn is sold. The length that was used to begin the process never works out exactly evenly to, say, 10 balls. After it's wound there might be 100 yards left over. If the ball that is sold is to contain 150 yards, the yarn is knotted at the point where the extra 50 yards are added on. It's too cost prohibitive to throw away the 100 yards that are left over; the price of yarn would rise dramatically.

Learning to Read Yarn Labels

The yarn label contains all the information you need to know about the yarn and whether it will work for a pattern you have in mind. Familiarize yourself with this information and what it means. Always ask the staff at the yarn shop for help if you're not sure. Choosing the right yarn can mean the difference between a successful and a failed project.

The yarn label speaks volumes about the yarn you're going to purchase.

Let's walk through what each of these items on a yarn label means:

- **Color name and number.** This is the name or number (or both) the company has given this color. An example might be 063067 Sunset Gold.

- **Dye lot number.** The dye lot number indicates the dye used for this package of yarn. There are noticeable color variations between dye lots, and it is difficult if not impossible to find more yarn of the same dye lot. Some synthetic yarns don't have a dye lot and this information is indicated on the label. Does a "no dye lot" yarn mean the color will match regardless of when you buy two skeins? Not necessarily. The yarn is dyed in much bigger batches but eventually it's sold out and additional yarn must be produced—in a different dye lot. *Always check the dye lot and be sure you purchase enough yarn in the same dye lot to complete your project!*

- **Manufacturer's name.** This is the name of the company that made the yarn. For example, Crystal Palace Yarns and Rowan are two yarn manufacturers.

- **Brand name.** This is the name the company assigned this line of yarn. Some examples are Fizz (by Crystal Palace Yarns) and Rowanspun Chunky (by Rowan).

- **Fiber content.** You guessed it: Here's where you'll learn what the yarn is made from. Examples are 100% wool, and 75% cotton / 25% silk.

Pointers

If you find some unlabeled yarn and you're not sure whether it's wool or synthetic, try this simple test. Use a match to light the end of the yarn. If it melts and leaves a ball on the end, it's synthetic. Wool (and cotton) will go out when the match is removed and leave an ash like burned paper. Wool will smell like burnt hair.

◆ **Yarn size or ply.** Yarn is classified by how thick it is; this is called the *yarn size* or *weight*. Examples of this are baby weight, sport weight, worsted weight, and bulky weight. This information isn't always included, and can vary from manufacturer to manufacturer and among countries, so be careful. It gives you only a general idea of the thickness of the yarn (there's more information on this later in this chapter).

In the United States, the term *ply* simply refers to the number of strands that make up the yarn. It does not indicate how thick or thin the yarn is. You can purchase a very bulky 2 ply yarn or a very thin 8 ply yarn.

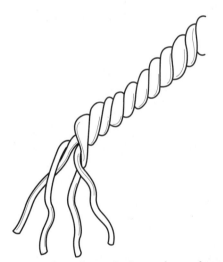

Ply is the number of strands that make up the yarn.

◆ **Weight.** This is the amount the package of yarn weighs. It's usually sold in packages weighing 50 or 100 grams, which is roughly equivalent to 1.75 ounces and 3.5 ounces.

◆ **Yarn length in yards or meters.** The yarn length is a more accurate indicator than weight of how much yarn the skein contains. Different fibers weigh different amounts; for example, cotton is heavier than wool. All things being equal, a

pound of cotton will have fewer yards than a pound of wool. When substituting yarn, pay special attention to yardage.

◆ **Suggested gauge.** You'll learn more about *gauge* (stitches required to make an inch of fabric) and what this means in Chapter 4. For now, just know that these small pictures depict what the yarn manufacturer believes will be the gauge if you use the size knitting needle or crochet hook shown on the label.

The suggested crochet gauge often is not given, as many yarns are marketed toward knitters only. There's more information to help you translate the suggested knit gauge into crochet later in this chapter and in Chapter 3.

◆ **Care instructions.** Here's where you're told how to care for the yarn. Let's walk through the four symbols you see here in the earlier figure that shows a yarn label. The first symbol shows that you can wash the wool in 40° Celsius / 104° Fahrenheit water; if the symbol has a × through it, you can't wash it in water. The second symbol indicates that you may wash the yarn in a washing machine. The third symbol indicates that you may not bleach the yarn; if this symbol doesn't contain a × you can bleach it. The final symbol shows that the garment may be dry cleaned using any dry cleaning solution; if the symbol has a × through it, it cannot be dry cleaned.

 Tangles

Always read the yarn label and follow the manufacturer's advice before you wash or dry clean your finished product. Your valuable time and effort have gone into your project, and you want the results to last.

Selecting a Fiber

There are many things to consider when choosing a yarn. The appearance and fiber content are major factors, just as when you are buying clothes. If you live in a temperate climate, you'll probably prefer lightweight cotton. A heavier wool is a better choice for a ski sweater. Some people like the easy care aspect of acrylic. Consider the properties of each fiber and what you'll be using it for when selecting yarn.

Many yarns are a blend of two or more fibers. The result is a combination of the properties of the fibers used. For example, yarn sold especially for socks might be 80% wool and 20% nylon; the resulting yarn combines the warmth of wool with the durability of nylon. Fiber is animal or protein based, plant based, or synthetic. Any yarn that is animal based is subject to moth invasions so use caution to protect your investment.

Here's an overview of some common fiber choices:

- **Sheep's wool.** This is a popular choice. Wool is elastic, durable, absorbs moisture, and insulates well. Not all wool is created equal; depending upon the breed of sheep, it can be soft and luxurious or harsh and itchy. Wool will shrink or felt if not washed gently by hand. *Superwash wool*, which can be machine washed, is now available; check the label carefully.

Needle Talk

Superwash wool is specially treated to be machine washed without shrinking or felting. It's a good choice for baby clothes: You get the warmth and comfort of wool without troubling a new mother with time-consuming hand washing.

- **Mohair.** Mohair is a longhaired yarn, spun from the fleece of the angora goat. The long hairs are what make mohair fuzzy. It can be difficult to see stitches, especially when you're learning, and the fuzziness obscures any fancy stitch patterns you might be working. It also has a tendency to shed. Mohair works up into lightweight yet warm garments. It's soft and lustrous.

- **Alpaca.** The alpaca is a member of the camel family and closely related to llamas. Alpaca feels very soft and silky, has a nice luster, and is durable. It's light yet warm. Considered a luxury fiber, it's actually the least expensive of the yarns in that class. A garment made from alpaca has a tendency to lose its shape over time so sometimes it is blended with wool to alleviate this problem.

- **Cashmere.** Expensive and luxurious describes the fiber that comes from the cashmere goat. This goat is not an actual breed but one that has been bred for its downy undercoat. Each goat yields only a small amount annually—about 3 to 8 ounces—which is why it's so costly. It's exceptionally soft and warm but tends to pill.

- **Angora.** Spun from the angora rabbit of which there are several breeds, this yarn is extremely soft, silky, and fine. It's also exceptionally warm. The down side is it sheds considerably and is expensive. Angora is often limited to small areas of trim such as collars to hold down the cost of completing a garment.

- **Silk.** Silk is wonderfully lustrous and soft. It comes from the cocoon of the silkworm. Like wool, it absorbs moisture and retains heat well. Silk dyes readily so you will find it in a range of colors. It's stronger than any other fiber. The negative side of silk is that it's not very elastic, and a garment knit or crocheted with silk might "grow" as you wear it.

- **Cotton.** Cotton is a plant fiber. It's usually soft but depending upon the type of cotton used, some cotton yarns are softer than others (Egyptian cotton is considered the softest and finest). It absorbs moisture into its center, so it is cooler to wear in the summer. It's very strong—actually stronger wet than dry—making it a great choice for dishcloths. Cotton is machine washable so it's easy to care for. *Mercerized cotton* has been treated to add luster to the yarn; it also dyes to more brilliant, jewel-like shades and won't shrink. Cotton is not elastic but with practice you will find it as easy to work with as wool. You can work elastic thread into the cuffs and bands of sweaters so they retain their shape.

- **Acrylic.** Acrylic is a common synthetic fiber that is easy to care for—it can be tossed in the washer and dryer. It's inexpensive and often used for baby clothes. Because acrylic is not animal based, moths will not attack it, and it's lightweight and strong. However, it often pills, doesn't insulate, and doesn't absorb or wick moisture—so you might find yourself sweating or cold in an acrylic sweater. Acrylic can be manufactured to resemble wool, cotton, and other natural fibers.

- **Nylon.** Nylon, also called *polyamide*, is extremely strong, durable, and elastic; it is another manmade fiber. It's often used blended with other fibers, both natural and synthetic, to add these positive characteristics. It doesn't insulate or "breathe" well.

- **Rayon.** Rayon, another synthetic fiber, is also known as *viscose*. It's strong, elastic, and absorbs water. It also dyes well so you will frequently find it blended with other fibers to add luster and dyeing capability.

- **Polyester.** Polyester is strong and durable but not absorbent. It's similar to nylon.

- **Novelty yarns.** Fun, funky yarns from manmade fibers, natural fibers, and blends are very popular. The yarn does all the work, and creates exciting textures in everything from pastels to the most vibrant of colors. There are eyelash yarns that can look furry, glittering metallics, slubbed yarns that periodically have a bigger piece of yarn in a different color, ribbons, and much, much more. Have fun experimenting with novelty yarns; they can make wonderful scarves, hats, purses, and even sweaters!

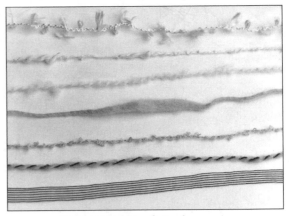

Some examples of novelty yarns.

You also might find yarn spun from camel hair, llama, quivit, yak, vicuña, linen, ramie, hemp, or jute. They are less common and some, such as quivit, are very expensive.

Yarn Spinning

By the fifteenth and sixteenth centuries, the art of knitting was widespread and well practiced, and silk knitting was introduced. The garments knitted at this time were so elaborate, laced with gold and silver threads, that they became garments for nobility.

Watching Your Weight: How Thick Is the Yarn?

As mentioned, yarn is classified by a system known as *weight* or *yarn weight*. The terms don't refer to how much the yarn literally weighs; rather, it's a system used to define how thick or thin the yarn is. Each weight of yarn works best to a particular number of stitches per inch with specific needle or hook sizes. When you stick to these recommendations, you will produce a fabric that is neither too loose and droopy, nor too tight and stiff.

It can be confusing because different countries have different terms for the same weight of yarn. Not all companies show the yarn weight on their labels and there is some variation between companies as to the terms they use.

The following table show the terms commonly used to refer to yarn weights as well as the suggested gauge, and needle or hook sizes. The recommended gauge shown is over 4 in or 10cm (you'll learn about gauge and what this means in Chapter 3). Please note that these are only suggested recommendations. There might be a time when the pattern calls for a larger or smaller gauge than you would normally use with a specific yarn. Always follow the gauge of the pattern.

Yarn Weights, Recommended Gauge, and Needle/Hook Size

Weight	Knit Gauge	Needle Size	Crochet Gauge	Hook Size
Fingering Baby Sock 4 Ply	28 to 32	0 to 3 US 2 to 3.25mm	22 to 28	B-1 to D-3 2.25 to 3.25mm
Sport 5 Ply	24	3 to 6 US 3.25 to 4.25mm	16 to 22	D-3 to G-6 3.25 to 4.25mm
DK 8 Ply	22	4 to 6 US 3.50 to 4.25mm	16 to 20	F-5 to 7 3.75 to 4.5mm
Worsted 10 Ply	18 to 20	6 to 9 US 4.25 to 5.50mm	14 to 16	H-8 to J-10 5 to 5.5mm
Heavy Worsted Aran 12 Ply	16 to 18	8 to 10.5 US 5 to 6.50mm	12 to 16	H-8 to L-11 5 to 8mm
Bulky Chunky 14 Ply	12 to 14	9 to 11 US 6 to 8mm	8 to 10	J-10 to M-13 6 to 9mm
Super Bulky Very Bulky	8 to 10	11 to 15 US 8 to 10mm	6 to 8	L-11 to P 8 to 11.5mm

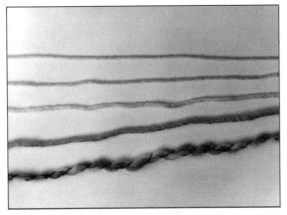

Various weights of yarn.

The thicker the yarn, the faster your project will work up because you need fewer stitches per inch of fabric produced. Thicker yarns are much warmer than thinner yarns and produce a heftier, bulkier fabric. Think of the difference between making a pair of socks with fine, thin cotton or thick, bulky wool. Although a sock made with a thick yarn will keep your feet toasty warm, the bulk of the fabric will likely prevent you from being able to get your shoes on over the socks. Choose your projects—and, thus, the yarn—keeping things like this in mind.

Cotton thread is generally used for very fine crochet projects, such as doilies, lace edgings for pillowcases, and the like. Thread is twisted much more tightly than yarn and consequently has less give than yarn. As a result, cotton thread is an exceptional choice for projects that require a piece to be taut and firm.

Cotton thread is sized according to numbers: The higher the number, the finer the thread. Numbers start with size 3 and go up to 100. The most common weight is bedspread weight, which is a size 10 weight.

Substituting Yarn

Most patterns will tell you the yarn that was used for the project, the amount needed, and the fiber content. If you're going to use the same yarn, you're in business. Be sure you buy enough of the same dye lot to complete your project. Nothing's worse than running out of yarn and being unable to get the last bit you need. If you end up with leftover balls, sometimes you can exchange them for other store merchandise or you can always use it for other projects.

All things are not created equal in the world of yarn. A very inexpensive acrylic is not the same as a fine silk. You will put many hours into your work, and after repeated use you want it to look as good as the day you finished it. Although the most expensive yarn in the store isn't necessarily the best—the term *best* being relative—you don't want to use a yarn made for dishcloths to make an heirloom christening gown.

Pointers

Buy the best yarn you can afford; you will enjoy knitting or crocheting with it more, and your projects will wear better and look nicer. If your yarn budget is limited, use more expensive yarn for smaller projects that don't require as much. Purchase single balls and experiment with them to appreciate the differences.

At times you'll find you want to substitute a different yarn. It might be that the yarn the project calls for is beyond your budget, no longer available, you just don't care for it, or a host of other reasons. Remember, if you substitute yarn your project is going to look different from the picture. This isn't necessarily bad—it's just a fact. Knitting a sweater in smooth wool will not look identical to the same sweater knit with a multicolored novelty yarn.

The suggested gauge of the yarn should match or be very, very close to the gauge of the pattern. You'll never get the gauge right if you try to substitute a bulky weight yarn for a sport weight yarn; it simply won't work. Although you probably could manage to squeeze in 6 stitches to the inch with a bulky yarn, the resulting fabric would be as stiff as cardboard.

Consider the fiber content of the original yarn. You've already learned that some fibers are heavier than others. Think about a long sweater coat that was originally made in wool. This same coat made in cotton would weigh considerably more; as a result it wouldn't hang in the same manner when you're wearing it. The fiber has an effect on how the final fabric you make will drape. Some projects, such as jackets, are designed to have body and perhaps even a little stiffness. A dressy lace shawl would likely have more of a fluid drape.

Is there a fancy stitch pattern you're going to use? A complex lace pattern will be obscured if you use a novelty yarn with lots of texture or a longhaired yarn such as mohair.

Once you've settled on which yarn you'd like to buy, it's time to figure out how much you'll need. If your pattern calls for 5 skeins, you can't simply buy 5 skeins of the alternate yarn you've selected. Substituting ounce for ounce won't work because again, some fibers weigh more than others.

Make sure that you match the total yardage of the yarn you are purchasing to the total yardage required by the original yarn. Your pattern should tell you the number of yards or meters per skein for the yarn that was used. Multiply this number by the total number of skeins required to find the total number of yards needed. Buy the equivalent number of yards of the new yarn, plus extra just to be safe. For example, if each skein in the pattern contains 100 yards and uses 9 skeins, you'll need 900 yards (100 yards per skein × 9 skeins = 900 yards).

Find the yardage of each skein of the yarn you want to substitute and divide the number of total yards you need by the number of yards in each skein. In this example, if the yarn you're substituting contains 150 yards per skein, you'll need 6 skeins (900 yards needed ÷ 150 yards per skein = 6 skeins). However, as this isn't an exact science, you should purchase 7 skeins to be on the safe side.

Don't hesitate to ask the folks at your yarn shop for help in matters like this. They have lots of experience and you'll benefit from their knowledge.

The Least You Need to Know

- Yarn options are limitless and exciting; no matter what thickness, fiber, color, or texture you desire, it's available.
- The label on yarn provides valuable information about the yarn you are purchasing.
- Different fibers have unique properties.
- Always check the dye lot and be sure you purchase enough yarn in the same dye lot to complete your project.
- Each weight of yarn works best to a particular number of stitches per inch with specific needle or hook sizes.
- Knowing the number of yards of yarn required to finish a project is much more accurate than knowing the number of ounces.

In This Chapter

- ◆ Knitting needles 101
- ◆ All about crochet hooks
- ◆ Understanding the sizing system
- ◆ Comparing needle and hook sizes
- ◆ Helpful accessories

Chapter 3

An Overview of Knitting and Crochet Tools

As you begin to explore knitting and crocheting, you'll find a mind-blowing array of needles, hooks, and accessories. This chapter explains how needles and hooks are sized and how tools and gadgets make needlework easier.

It might sound like you're about to break the bank. Don't worry, you don't need to buy everything right away. Experiment first with hooks and needles made from different materials.

Knitting Needles

Knitting needles are one of only two items necessary for successful knitting (the other being yarn). Walk into any yarn store and the number of options can be overwhelming. They come in many styles and materials.

Straight or Circular?

Knitting needles come in two varieties: straight and circular. Straight needles, in turn, come in two varieties: single pointed and double pointed.

Single point needles have a point at one end and a nub or knob at the other; the point is what you knit from and the nub is what keeps stitches from falling off the needle. These needles are sold in pairs and come in various lengths. You may find that a 12-inch long needle feels more balanced to you than a 14-inch long needle. They are used for knitting a flat piece of fabric.

With double point needles, you can knit tubular items such as socks.

Circular needles create tubes in the same way as double points. However, unlike double point needles, circular needles enable you to work on one needle only. They also allow you to knit larger items than double points. Circular needles have two short needles on each end that are attached by a flexible cord. Circular needles range in length from 8½ to 60 inches.

Single point needles are used for knitting a flat piece of fabric.

Double point needles, as you might guess, have points at both ends and also come in various lengths. Consequently, you can knit from both ends. As you'll learn in Chapter 11, you can use these needles to make tubular, seamless items such as socks. Double point needles are sold in sets of four or five needles. If you have a choice, always buy a set of five. Some patterns call for a set of five and some for a set of four; if you buy a set of five, you can always use four of them instead as required by the pattern.

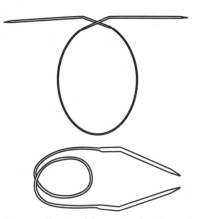

Circular needles enable you to knit in a circle.

Pointers _____

If a flat piece such as an afghan has more stitches than will fit on a pair of single point needles, you can use a circular needle to knit back and forth—rather than in a circle—to accommodate all the stitches. In addition, the flexibility of a circular needle means your work will lie in your lap; you don't have to support its full weight as you would with straight needles.

Is That American or English?

Knitting needles come in different sizes, which affect the size of the finished stitch. This is easy enough. But going by nothing but a number can get a little tricky because knitting needles can be sized using three different systems: U.S., English/U.K./Canadian, and metric.

The following table shows the needle equivalents among these three systems. Sizes vary slightly by brand so, for example, an American size 6 needle might be the equivalent of a 4mm or a 4.25mm. Always check patterns carefully to determine which sizing system was used for the suggested needle size.

Metric	U.K./Canadian	U.S.
2.00	14	0
2.25	13	1
2.75	12	2
3.00	11	
3.25	10	3
3.50		4
3.75	9	5
4.00	8	
4.25		6
4.50	7	7
5.00	6	8
5.25		
5.50	5	9
5.75		
6.00	4	10
6.50	3	10½
7.00	2	
7.50	1	
8.00	0	11
9.00	00	13
10.00	000	15
12.00		17
15.00		19
19		35

Trekking Through the Material World

Needles are available in a variety of materials such as plastic, aluminum, bamboo, birch, rosewood, ebony, and many more. If you don't already have needles, start with bamboo. Stitches slide around more on aluminum needles, and can cause trouble for new knitters. Aluminum conducts heat and cold. If you're knitting by a fire, the needles might get hot and uncomfortable to the touch; likewise, if you're sitting on the porch on a brisk autumn day, the needles could get cold. Wood and bamboo remain at a fairly constant temperature.

As you gain experience you might notice that some brands have blunt tips and others are pointier. Some are balanced at both ends and some are more top heavy. A particular yarn might move more smoothly over one type of needle than another. The needle you prefer might not be another knitter's first choice. Buy several different kinds and see which you like best before investing in an entire set.

Crochet Hooks

Crochet hooks come in sizes from tiny steel hooks used for crocheting with cotton thread to huge hooks as big as a broomstick. As you'd expect, they also are made from a host of materials.

Parts of a Crochet Hook

Let's take a look at what a crochet hook really looks like and the name of each part.

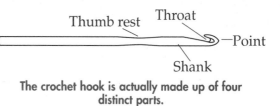

The crochet hook is actually made up of four distinct parts.

The four simple parts of the hook have been designed for comfort and to speed up your work. Each part has a unique function:

- The *point* goes into the stitch on the crocheted fabric.
- The *throat* catches the yarn. The throat needs to be large enough to accommodate the yarn being used.
- The *shank* holds the loops with which you're working. The shank is actually what determines the size of your stitches.
- The *thumb rest* is just that: a place to rest your thumb so you can rotate the hook with ease while working.

Crochet Hook Sizes and Types

Small hooks are generally made of steel, and used for crocheting intricate doilies and table runners with thread. Some are so fine you might mistake them for darning needles. Larger hooks are made from plastic, aluminum, bamboo, or other materials. The average length of a crochet hook is about 6 inches.

The size of the hook determines the size of the stitch—but here's where things get tricky. Crochet hooks can be sized using three different systems: U.S., English/U.K./Canadian, and metric. To complicate matters, some manufacturers produce their hooks in slightly different sizes. Take special note of the suggested hook size in your pattern and always be sure of the exact size hook you're using. The following tables show the hook equivalents among these three systems.

Steel Crochet Hook Conversion Chart

Metric	U.K./Canadian	U.S.
.6, .75	7	14
.75, .85	6½, 7	13
.75, 1	6, 6½	12
1.05, 1.1	5½, 6	11
1, 1.3	5, 5½	10
1.15, 1.4	4, 5	9
1.25, 1.5	3, 4½	8
1.5, 1.65	2½, 4	7
1.6, 1.8	2, 3½	6
1.7, 1.9	½, 3	5
1.75, 2	1, 2½	4
2.1	1/0, 2	3
2.25	2/0, 1½	2
2.35, 2.75	3/0, 1	1
2.55, 3.25	0	0
2.70, 3.5		00

Crochet Hook Conversion Chart

Metric	U.K./Canadian	U.S.
2.00	14	
2.25	13	B-1
2.5	12	
2.75		C-2
3.00	11	
3.25	10	D-3
3.50	9	E-4
3.75		F-5
4.00	8	
4.25		G-6
4.50	7	7
5.00	6	H-8
5.50	5	I-9

Metric	U.K./Canadian	U.S.
6.00	4	J-10
6.50	3	K-10½
7.00	2	
7.50	1	
8.00	0	L-11
9.00	00	M-13, N-15
10.00	000	N-15, P
11.50		P
13.00	0000	
15.00	00000	
15.75		Q
16.00		Q

With experience you will learn what type of hook you prefer. You might find you prefer wood to aluminum. Try hooks with a differently shaped point; perhaps one that's more round than sharply angled.

Afghan Hooks

One type of specialized crochet—called *Afghan* or *Tunisian crochet*—requires you to hold many stitches on the hook simultaneously. Afghan hooks are longer than regular crochet hooks and come in various lengths. You'll learn more about Afghan crochet in Chapter 16.

Needle Talk

Afghan (Tunisian) crochet is a special type of crochet that requires many stitches to be held on the crochet hook. Special afghan hooks that look like a cross between a crochet hook and a knitting needle are available for this purpose.

Afghan hooks are used to work Afghan crochet.

Afghan hooks also come in a version that has a long flexible cord on one end. The cord holds many stitches, and the flexibility of the cord means your work can more easily rest in your lap.

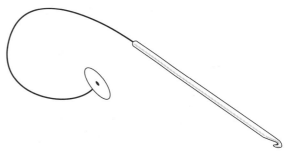

Flexible Afghan hooks make Afghan crochet even easier.

Comparing Needle and Hook Sizes

It's handy to know which knitting needle size compares to which crochet hook size. Knitters will find many uses for crochet hooks. You will need them for correcting problems, picking up stitches around necklines, adding a crochet edge to a knit piece, and much more. You'll want to use the equivalent size hook in most cases.

Although a crocheter won't find much of a need for a knitting needle, it's still useful to know the equivalent sizes. Armed with this knowledge, you will more easily be able to substitute yarn in your patterns. Most yarn is marketed toward knitters; thus the label might tell you only the suggested needle size and stitches per inch while knitting—for the yarn, not the suggested hook size.

If you know which needle size is equal to which hook size, you're in business. The gauge (stitches per inch) for knitting will be different than for crochet; you almost always will have fewer stitches per inch crocheting than knitting, even if you use the same size hook and needle. That's because a crochet stitch is a different shape and size than a knit stitch. Nonetheless, it will give you a good idea of what hook size will work well with that yarn.

Remember that hooks and needles are sized using three different systems. As you saw in the earlier table, the American system sizes hooks with numbers such as B-1, C-2, and so forth. The number after the letter is the same number used to size knitting needles in the American system. To make it even easier, the metric sizing is the same for hooks and needles; a 5mm hook is the same size as a 5mm needle. The following table shows the equivalent U.S. size hooks and needles, and the metric counterparts.

Equivalent Needle and Hook Sizes

Metric	U.S. Needles	U.S. Hooks
2.00	0	
2.25	1	B-1
2.75	2	C-2
3.25	3	D-3
3.50	4	E-4
3.75	5	F-5
4.25	6	G-6

Metric	U.S. Needles	U.S. Hooks
4.50	7	7
5.00	8	H-8
5.50	9	I-9
6.00	10	J-10
6.50	10.5	K-10.5
8.00	11	L-11
9.00	13	M-13
10.00	15	N-15
11.50		P
12.00	17	
15.00	19	
15.75		Q
19	35	

Gadgets Make the Job Easier

There's a gadget for just about anything you can imagine. Most aren't really necessary but they do make your life easier. Many are useful to both knitters and crocheters.

Small, sharp embroider scissors are a must. You'll be doing quite a bit of yarn cutting. Project bags are great for holding your work, yarn, and other necessary items when you're on the go. There are many on the market designed especially for this purpose; diaper bags work well, too! You might also want something to store all your hooks and needles. You'll find lots of pretty holders made of material with slots sewn in the fabric, which roll up and close with ribbon or Velcro. If you sew, you can easily make them yourself. Also consider potato chip cans (washed, please) or display them in a pretty vase.

Many of these gadgets are tiny and easily lost. Small tackle boxes and storage devices meant to hold nuts and bolts have lots of compartments to hold all these doo-dads. Check out hardware and sporting goods stores for some great storage ideas.

Measuring Tools

A good tape measure and gauge counter will help you immeasurably (no pun intended). You can use both to check your gauge (as you'll learn in Chapter 4), and you'll use the tape measure for a million other tasks: measuring the length of a sleeve, the waist size of your best friend to whom you promised a sweater, and so on. Although you can wait to purchase most of the accessories in this section, go out at lunch and buy yourself a good tape measure. You'll use it almost immediately.

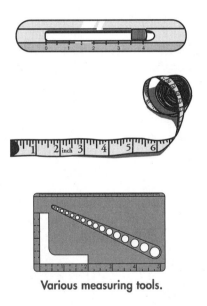

Various measuring tools.

Stitch Markers

Stitch markers are also handy. When you work certain patterns you need to keep track of information such as where to increase or when to repeat a particular stitch pattern. Stitch markers are little rings of plastic you use to mark a specific spot in a piece. They are also used to mark the right side or the wrong side of the fabric.

Stitch markers are available as solid rings or with slits in them. Knitters can use the solid rings to slip on the needle at a point where you need to remember something in your pattern. The type with slits can be affixed to knit or crochet fabric (and knitters can use this type to slip on the needle). A loop of contrasting yarn, a safety pin, or a paper clip can also be used as a stitch marker.

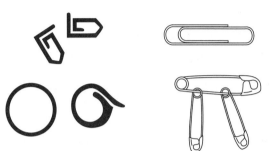

Stitch markers help you mark your place.

Bobbins

Bobbins are helpful accessories to have on hand when you're working in multiple colors. These little gems are made of plastic and look similar to bread bag tabs, only larger. To use a bobbin, wrap yarn around it and work from the bobbin, rather than from a ball of yarn. You can then unwind only what you need for the next few stitches, and you won't have to negotiate cumbersome amounts of yarn. You can make your own bobbins out of cardboard; just follow the shape of the illustration of any of the bobbins on this page.

Bobbins let you work in multiple colors without creating a tangled mess of yarn.

Finishing Accessories

Pins are irreplaceable when it comes time to finishing your work. You'll use straight, rust-proof pins to block your pieces and hold seams together as you sew or crochet them into place.

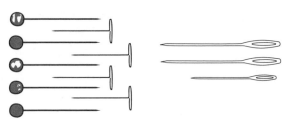

Needles and pins are used for finishing your work.

Yarn needles (also called *tapestry needles* or *weaving needles*) are used to weave in yarn ends and sew together seams. They have dull (rather than sharp) points and large eyes. These needles come in varying sizes to accommodate different thicknesses of yarn.

Just for Knitters

There are a few more gadgets that only knitters will use. They're handy helpers and the cost is minimal.

Stitch Holders

Stitch holders are exactly what the name implies: a place to hold stitches that you aren't currently using but will need later. Shaped like big safety pins, stitch holders come in a variety of lengths.

In a pinch, if you need to hold onto only a couple of stitches, you can use a safety pin. Or if you have a number of stitches, you can make your own stitch holder. Thread a strand of contrasting yarn into a yarn needle, and then thread the needle through the stitches you want to hold. Tie the yarn ends together to secure the stitch holder. When you want to use the stitches, cut the contrasting thread and place the stitches back on your needle.

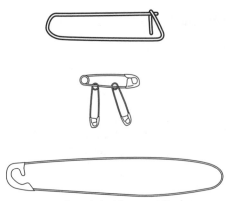

A variety of stitch holders in different sizes.

Row Counters

Row counters are useful for keeping track of rows. They slide on to the end of your needle so it's always handy. To use them, just turn the dial at the end of each row. They come in three sizes to accommodate different needle sizes. A row counter with a loop at the top is available to hang from circular needles. Of course, a tick mark made with pencil and paper works, too.

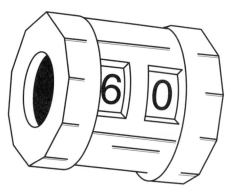

Row counters help you keep track of rows.

Cable Needles

Look at a Fisherman knit sweater and you'll probably be perplexed by the different patterns twisting and swirling up and through the garment. These details are courtesy of cable needles: small, double pointed needles that hold stitches and help you move stitches across a knitting piece. You'll learn a lot more about cables in Chapter 9.

The most common shapes are straight, straight with a bend in the middle, and U-shaped. The last two are especially handy, as the stitches do not slide off the cable needle. Like regular needles, cable needles are available in a variety of sizes. You can use a regular double point needle or a crochet hook as a cable needle, but these can be cumbersome and cause you to drop stitches.

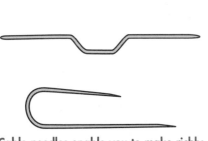

Cable needles enable you to make richly patterned designs.

Point Protectors

Point protectors are usually made of hard rubber and slip on the end of your needle when you're not knitting. If you have a large number of stitches and they're close to the end of the needle, they'll keep your work from falling off. (So will rubber bands wound around the end of your needle.) Point protectors also keep the points of needles from poking through bags when you're carrying your knitting with you. They come in various sizes to accommodate different needle sizes.

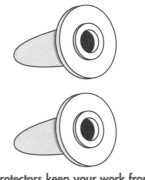

Point protectors keep your work from falling off the needle.

The Least You Need to Know

◆ Needles and hooks can be sized using three different systems: U.S., English/U.K./Canadian, and metric.

◆ Hooks and needles are made with various materials and have differing point shapes. Experiment to find the shape and material you like best.

◆ Understand which hook size is equal to which needle size and use that knowledge to help you select yarn.

◆ There are many inexpensive gadgets available to make your knitting and crocheting projects go more smoothly.

In This Chapter

◆ What is gauge?

◆ Examples of gauge

◆ How gauge affects size

◆ How patterns specify gauge

◆ Swatching and measuring gauge

◆ What to do if your gauge is wrong

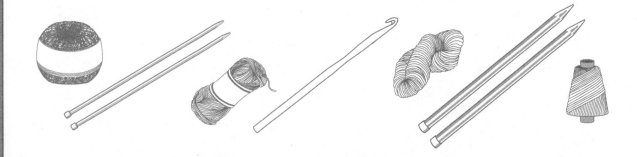

Chapter 4

Why Gauge Is So Important

What comes to mind when you think of gauge? A measure of tire pressure? Pounds per pressure when canning summer tomatoes? It's all these things, but gauge is also the most important concept you will learn in knitting and crocheting.

In this chapter, you'll discover how gauge affects the size of the piece you're making and how to be sure your work "measures up." Even though a pattern will suggest which needle or hook size to use, it's vital that you don't take that suggestion at face value.

Gauge? What's That?

Gauge is a measurement of how big or small each of your stitches are, based on several factors:

◆ The stitch
◆ How tightly or loosely you knit or crochet
◆ The yarn
◆ The size of the knitting needles or crochet hook

In addition, sometimes your mood can affect gauge. As you become more accustomed to knitting and crocheting, you might find that the stitches you knit in the evening after you've been stuck in a traffic jam for 90 minutes are tighter than those you make while sipping a margarita at Martha's Vineyard. There are two measurements to consider: the width, called the *stitch gauge*, and the length, called the *row gauge*.

Needle Talk

Gauge is the number of stitches and rows you need to complete to create a specified width and length of fabric. Gauge is measured by the inch over a specific number of stitches and rows, such as 5 stitches per inch and 7 rows per inch.

Some Examples of Gauge

Take a look at a T-shirt. Notice the tiny adjoining loops that make up the fabric? You're looking at a very tight-knit gauge. Now look at a sweater. Notice it still contains loops (just like the T-shirt) but the loops are larger. This is a looser gauge. Both items are knit, but the size of the stitches varies significantly. Think about it: If you're using a big hook or needles and thick yarn, it stands to reason that you'll get chunkier stitches.

Look at the following photo. These knit samples all are very different sizes. Guess what? All three were knit with the exact same number of stitches and rows—22 stitches and 26 rows! Only the size of the yarn and the needles were changed—and what a difference it made. The smallest sample was knit with a sport weight yarn on size 5 U.S. needles, the middle sample with a worsted weight yarn on size 8 U.S. needles, and the largest sample with a bulky yarn on size 11 U.S. needles. So you can see for yourself gauge truly does matter.

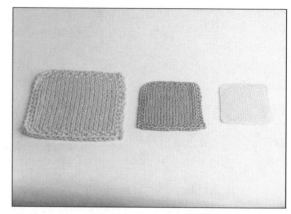

These samples show how gauge affects the size of your project.

How Does Gauge Affect Size?

Your pattern will tell you the gauge you'll need to work to and the needle or hook size used. If you buy the exact yarn specified, can you just hurry up and get started with the needle or hook the pattern told you to use? Sorry, you can't. Gauge affects everything you knit or crochet—absolutely everything. If you don't take time to measure your gauge, you're throwing caution to the wind.

Tangles

Knitting or crocheting without knowing your gauge is like sailing a boat without a compass: You'll get somewhere, but it might not be where you wanted to go. It's better to take the time to make a swatch and measure your gauge than to later regret it.

Everyone knits and crochets a little differently. The needle or hook size in the pattern is a suggestion of where to start—it's the size that the designer used. It doesn't mean you will get the exact same result.

If you want a project such as an afghan to be the size specified in the pattern, or if you want your sweater or hat to fit and not turn out big enough to cover a moose, you must work to the gauge of the pattern with whatever size needle or hook will get you there. There's just no getting around this!

Still not convinced? Wondering what possible difference a teensy little quarter of a stitch per inch can make? Let's look at an example. Suppose you're making something that is 40 inches wide. The stitch gauge of the pattern is 4 stitches per inch. The pattern would instruct you, in this case, to work over 160 stitches:

40 (width in inches) × 4 (stitches per inch) = 160 (total number of stitches)

Now let's say that instead of 4 stitches per inch, your gauge is 4.25 stitches per inch. What would the final size of your project be?

160 (total number of stitches) ÷ 4.25 (stitches per inch) = 37.65 (width in inches)

That teensy little quarter of an inch difference means that the piece you just worked so hard to create measures 37.65 inches wide instead of 40. Too many stitches per inch means your piece will be too small.

What happens if your gauge has too few stitches per inch? Let's use the same example but this time you're working to a gauge of 3.75 stitches per inch:

160 (total number of stitches) ÷ 3.75 (stitches per inch) = 42.67 (width in inches)

As you can see, now your piece is too big.

The bigger the variation between the gauge you're actually working at and the gauge of the pattern, the more it affects the final size of the piece. The more stitches worked on every row, the more your actual gauge will affect the width of the piece.

Tangles

Needles and hooks are sized according to U.S., U.K., and metric standards. Be sure the pattern you're using specifies which system of measurement it's using.

How Do Patterns Specify Gauge?

Almost all patterns specify gauge. It might be called something else such as "stitch measurement" or "tension," but the information is the same. Sometimes patterns will give you the gauge over 4 inches and at other times over a fewer number of inches. A 1-inch sample isn't really big enough to get a good measurement so you should convert the information they've given you into at least 4 inches.

Suppose, for example, that a pattern shows the following:

Gauge: 20 stitches equal 4 inches (10 centimeters)

This means the pattern assumes that for every 20 stitches you complete, your fabric will be 4 inches wide. If you divide the 20 stitches by 4 (the number of inches), you'll see that every inch will equal 5 stitches:

20 (number of stitches) ÷ 4 (number of inches) = 5 stitches per inch

This is a gauge of 5 stitches per inch.

Conversely, suppose the pattern shows the following:

Gauge: 5 stitches equal 1 inch (2.5 centimeters)

To determine what your gauge should be over 4 inches, multiply 5 (stitches per inch) by 4 (the number of inches needed for your swatch):

> 5 (number of stitches per inch) × 4 (number of inches) = 20 stitches per 4 inches

There are many combinations of knit and crochet stitches that create an almost infinite number of looks. These are called *stitch patterns.* Sometimes a pattern will instruct you to measure your gauge over a specific stitch pattern. If you see those instructions please follow them, as they're as important to the final size of your project as gauge itself. If the instructions don't specify, test your gauge by making a *swatch* of *stockinette stitch* (knit one row and purl the next) if you're knitting, or over single crochet if you're crocheting.

Needle Talk

A **swatch** is a sample you knit or crochet to determine whether the gauge you're achieving is correct. It also helps you decide if you like the yarn you're using and how it looks with the stitch pattern.

Is Gauge Ever Unimportant?

The short answer is no. Gauge is never unimportant. It impacts the finished size of your project.

But is gauge ever not vital? The answer to that question is sometimes. Is it absolutely imperative that your afghan, placemat, dishcloth, or scarf be the exact width and length of your pattern? Likely not.

That doesn't mean you can start working on that new scarf with the yarn you picked out and any old size needle or hook. You wouldn't want to end up with a scarf that's 20 inches wide.

Remember, different weights of yarn work best at a particular range of gauges with certain sized hooks or needles. If you deviate too far, you'll end up with fabric that feels as stiff as cardboard or is so loose that it looks as holey as Swiss cheese.

Checking Your Gauge

Now that you know how important gauge is, let's get down to making a swatch and measuring it. Make a good size sample—at least 4 inches by 4 inches. You can't accurately measure gauge over a single inch of fabric because your stitches are going to vary somewhat from one another.

Start by working at least the number of stitches that are supposed to equal 4 inches in width in the pattern stitch. Continue until the swatch is at least 4 inches long. Don't worry—you'll learn how to get started, and knit and crochet in a bit. In fact, after you've learned the basics, please come back and read this chapter again.

If you're knitting, take the yarn off the needles by binding off. You'll learn how to do that later, too. Don't leave your swatch on the needles as it will distort your measurements. Let your swatch sit and rest for a bit. All that pulling and tugging traumatized the yarn. Give it some time to bounce back to its natural state.

Don't try to make the swatch something it isn't. Don't squish it together trying to make it narrower. Don't stretch it in an attempt to make it wider. It is what it is. When you wear a sweater, you don't walk around pulling and tugging on it all day trying to make it fit. The sweater drapes over your body at the size it was made. The same is true for your swatch.

Measuring Gauge

To measure your swatch, you can use either a good old-fashioned measuring tape or a commercial *gauge counter.*

Needle Talk

Gauge counters are tools for measuring gauge. You lay the counter over your knitting or crocheting and count the number of stitches that appear in the window.

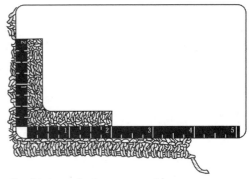

Checking crocheting gauge with a gauge counter.

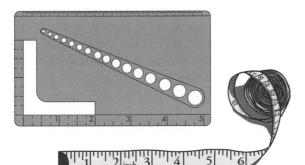

Two tools for measuring swatches: a gauge counter and a measuring tape.

To measure your gauge, whether knitting or crocheting, measure straight across. Going off on an angle will give you an inaccurate measurement. Double and triple check your measurement; then check it again. Now check it in different spots throughout your swatch. Measure straight across toward the bottom, in the middle, and toward the top.

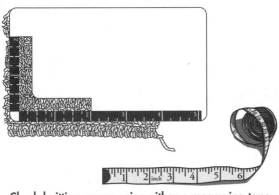

Check knitting gauge using either a measuring tape or gauge counter.

Do you have more stitches per inch than the pattern specifies? Try a larger needle or hook. Do you have fewer stitches per inch than the pattern requires? Try a smaller needle or hook. Continue moving up or down one size until your swatch matches the gauge indicated in the pattern.

Unless you're using a yarn that isn't compatible with what gauge you're trying to achieve, the gauge will come out correctly after you fiddle a bit with different sizes. However, if you're trying to use a bulky yarn for a pattern that features fine baby yarn, you're probably barking up the wrong tree.

Now measure your row gauge. Patterns don't always include a row gauge so don't be alarmed if it's absent. The row gauge is measured the same way: straight across (turn your swatch) in several different positions. Or feel free to measure up and down if you prefer.

The Width's Okay, but the Length's a Bit Hefty

In some cases you'll be able to get either the stitch gauge or the row gauge correct, but both won't cooperate at the same time. What to do?

In most cases it's more important that you get the stitch gauge or width right. Look through the rest of the pattern. Does it tell you to knit or crochet in inches rather than rows, like this: "Continue until piece measures 5 inches from beginning"? Generally, your row gauge will be close enough to that of the pattern if you've gotten the stitch gauge correct. You should be fine with the rows in most cases.

Pointers _____

You might need additional yarn to finish the project if your row gauge is smaller than that of the pattern, because you'll have to work more rows.

The Advantages of Understanding Gauge

If all of this seems like too much work, think of the time it'll take you to make an item at the wrong gauge, rip it apart, and then make it again. Or think of how heartbreaking it would be to see an ill-fitting item you've tenderly made for a loved one stuffed at the bottom of a drawer because you didn't check your gauge. Checking your gauge is worth every second you spend on it. And don't forget, it gives you a sneak preview of what your project will look like when you're done.

Although making swatches and checking your gauge might seem like a big pain, understanding gauge is incredibly important when you want to break away from a pattern and forge your own path. For instance, yarns are discontinued all the time. Suppose you come across a beautiful pattern you want to try but the yarn is no longer available? What if you find a pattern you love but in your opinion the yarn specified is frightfully ugly? Or prohibitively expensive?

By understanding gauge, you can substitute another yarn. You just need to make sure the new yarn works up to the gauge in the pattern and that the resulting fabric is neither too stiff nor too loose. What if you have a gorgeous yarn in your stash that you want to try on a pattern you've found? Stitch up a swatch and see whether the yarn can be used in that pattern.

Although yarn labels have a suggested gauge (sometimes just for knitting but some yarn has a suggested gauge for both knitting and crochet), it's just that: a suggestion. Remember, everyone knits and crochets a little differently, which is why measuring your gauge is so important. The suggested gauge is a starting point for you; it suggests what hook or needle size you might use and how many stitches you might expect per inch. Does that mean you'll get the same results? Nope.

If the suggested gauge of the yarn is a teensy bit off from the gauge specified in your pattern, you can usually fiddle with needle and hook sizes to get the gauge you need. For example, if the yarn label specifies that the gauge is 18 stitches to 4 inches and you need 16 stitches to 4 inches, you can probably use larger needles and get the correct gauge. However, if the yarn specifies 20 stitches to 4 inches and you need 12 stitches to 4 inches, pick another yarn. When in doubt, never hesitate to ask the people at your local yarn shop for help and advice.

What Do I Do with All These Little Squares?

While swatches help you determine gauge and give you a preview of the pattern and fabric, they can also serve other purposes. After you work up a swatch, you can throw it in the washer and dryer to test for shrinkage and how well it holds up. You can see whether the color bleeds or rub on it a bit to see whether it has a tendency to pill.

You could also save all your swatches and sew them into a crazy-quilt afghan. If you don't have quite enough swatches for a whole afghan, you can make placemats or pillow covers. Keep your swatches and use them for future reference; start a needlecraft diary of sorts. And you never know—you just might run a tad short of yarn and need to use the yarn from your swatch to finish your project.

The Least You Need to Know

- The stitch, yarn type, and needle or hook size determine gauge, as well as how loosely or tightly you work.
- Always check your gauge; you'll save yourself lots of time and effort in the end.
- Use the needle or hook sizes indicated in patterns or on yarn labels as a guide, but determine the size you should use by working a swatch and measuring your gauge.
- To determine gauge, work a swatch and measure to determine whether the stitches and rows you make per inch match the number specified in the pattern.
- To change gauge, change the needle or hook size: bigger for a looser gauge, smaller for a tighter gauge.

In This Part

5 Building the Foundation: Casting On Stitches

6 The Big Three: Knitting, Purling, and Binding Off

7 Knitting Stitch Patterns

8 What Goes Up Must Come Down: Increasing and Decreasing

9 Beyond the Basics: Adding to Your Knitting Repertoire

10 Making Your Knitting Colorful

11 Knitting in the Round

12 Correcting Common Knitting Gaffes

Part 2

Learning to Knit

This part takes you through the basics of learning to knit and much more. You'll discover how to begin by casting stitches on your needle using different methods, knit and purl two ways, and bind off your stitches so they won't unravel.

We'll then move on to the next level of skills. You'll learn various ways to increase and decrease, how to knit in the round, make cables, make small changes to the way stitches are worked to change the way they look, and knit with color. When you're done, you will have the ability to knit just about any project you desire.

In This Chapter

- ◆ What is casting on?
- ◆ The single, double, and cable cast on methods
- ◆ The single cast on for left-handed knitters
- ◆ Practice makes perfect

Building the Foundation: Casting On Stitches

If you're building a house, you can't begin with the roof; you must first lay the foundation. The same is true with knitting. Before you can begin knitting, you need a foundation row of stitches from which to knit. You create this row by casting on stitches.

This chapter walks you through three cast on methods. Two methods involve casting on by winding yarn around your thumb: the single cast on and the double cast on. The third method, called the cable cast on, actually uses a form of knitting to place the stitches on the needle. In addition, a special section helps those who are left handed make sense of the process.

Many other cast on methods exist; however, the three methods you will learn in this chapter will serve you well and meet about any knitting need you'll have in the future. Once you get the hang of casting on you can move on to the next chapter where you'll learn to work from those stitches to make knitted fabric.

Setting the Stage

You have to *cast on* before you knit, and to begin casting on, you have to tie a slip knot. This slip knot is how you attach the yarn to the needle and is the first stitch, regardless of the type of cast on you use.

Depending on the method of casting on you choose, you will have either a long or short *tail* of yarn before you tie the slip knot—but we'll get to that soon enough. For now, tie the slip knot about 4 inches from the end of the yarn.

Needle Talk

Casting on (abbreviated CO) is creating the foundation row of stitches from which you will knit by tying a slip knot, attaching the knot to your needle, and adding stitches. The **tail** is the amount of yarn between the end of the yarn and the slip knot. The length of the tail you leave (before tying the slip knot to cast on) differs based on the cast on method you choose. It is woven in later so it doesn't show.

For practice, select wool yarn that knits to 4 or 4.5 stitches to the inch (commonly called *worsted weight*) and size 8 U.S. needles. Wool is very elastic and forgiving, and you will find it much easier to work with than say, cotton, which is stiff and not elastic at all. Choose a smooth yarn, not a novelty yarn full of loops or eyelashes. They look pretty and you can knit with them soon enough but using them will only confuse you as you begin.

The following three figures show a simple three-step method for tying a slip knot:

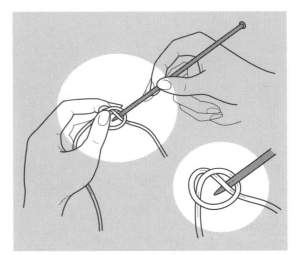

Slip the yarn from your finger, and hold the loop between your thumb and index finger.

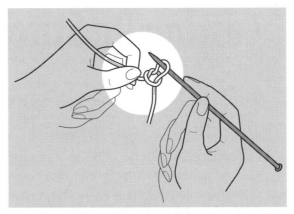

Use the needle, held in your right hand, to draw the loop up and tighten around the needle.

After the knot is on the needle, you can gently tug at both ends of the yarn to lightly tighten the knot. Don't pull too tightly, however. You want the slip knot to be loose enough to move freely on your needle.

Loop the yarn around your left index finger.

Pointers

Each of the cast on methods covered in this chapter creates an edge that differs slightly in appearance and elasticity. Choose the method to use depending on your particular project.

The Single Cast On

The *single cast on* is the easiest way to cast on, making it ideal for beginners and children. The single method creates a fairly elastic edge so it's perfect for sweaters, jackets, and hats—items for which you want some give at the bottom. However, it can look sloppy and the double cast on described later in this chapter is usually the better choice.

To cast on using the single method, begin with the slip knot on your needle. With your right hand, grip the needle that holds the slip knot as you would a wooden spoon. Then follow the steps in the following figures:

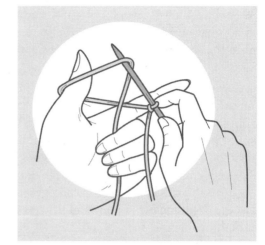

Insert your right needle upward through the strand of yarn facing you at the base of your left thumb.

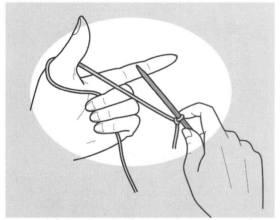

In your left hand, wrap the yarn that is coming from the skein around your thumb from front to back. Close your left fingers over the yarn in your palm to keep it in place.

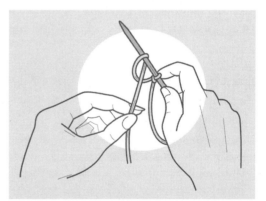

Slip the loop off your thumb onto your needle. Gently pull down on the long strand to tighten the yarn.

 Tangles _____

Be sure when using both the single method and cable cast on you'll learn later in this chapter, that you use the yarn feeding from the skein or ball, not the tail of yarn, to cast on stitches.

Beautiful! You've just cast on your first stitch. You now have two stitches on the needle. Remember, the slip knot counts as your first stitch.

Continue casting on using this method until you feel comfortable. Try to keep all the stitches uniform by gently pulling down the long strand of yarn after you make each loop. Initially, your stitches will look fairly uneven: Some will be tight and pinched while others will be loose. Just keep practicing. It takes time to get the tension even in all the stitches, and you won't get it right the first time out of the gate. Rome was not built in a day.

You can reuse the yarn and start over while practicing if you wish by taking all your stitches off the needle and pulling on them (gently, please). If the yarn starts to look frayed, cut the yarn at the point.

Tangles

If you cast on your stitches too tightly, you'll end up with a pinched bottom edge on your finished piece. After you practice knitting a bit, check to see whether the cast on row is tighter and less elastic than the knitted stitches. If so, you'll need to cast on more loosely. To help you make a looser foundation row, cast on stitches using a needle one or two sizes bigger than the size you will use for knitting. For example, if you're going to use size 6 U.S. needles to knit with, use a size 7 U.S. or 8 U.S. needle to cast on.

The Double Cast On

Now that you feel comfortable with the single cast on, it's time to learn the *double cast on*. The double cast on involves two ends of yarn. Your thumb is still a big player here but you will add a few fingers to expedite the procedure. Like the single cast on, this method creates a fairly elastic edge, so it's perfect for sweaters, jackets, and hats. It looks neater than the single cast on method.

Start with the same slip knot you used for the single cast on. This time, though, the length of the yarn tail before you tie the slip knot is important; you use the tail to cast on stitches. The easiest way to determine where to tie the slip knot is to allow 1 inch of yarn for each stitch you will be casting on. Add an extra 4 inches so that after you finish casting on, you'll still have a little tail. You'll weave in this tail after you finish knitting. If you want to cast on 20 stitches, start your slip knot 24 inches from the end of the yarn: 20 inches (20 stitches) + 4 inches (tail) = 24 inches.

To cast on using the double method, follow the steps shown in these figures:

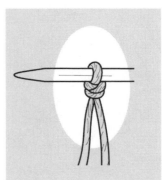

Make a slip knot far enough from the end of the yarn to accommodate 1 inch per stitch you'll cast on, plus 4 inches.

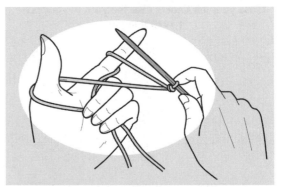

Grasp the shorter end of yarn with your left hand as you did for the single method; wrap it around your thumb and secure it against your palm. Now wrap the yarn from the skein over your right index finger and hold the yarn against your right palm.

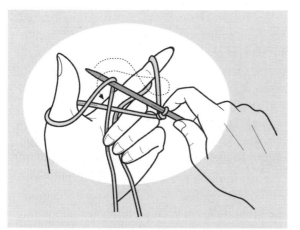

Insert your needle upward at the base of your left thumb, as you did for the single method. Bring the yarn from your index finger over the point of the needle from the back to the front.

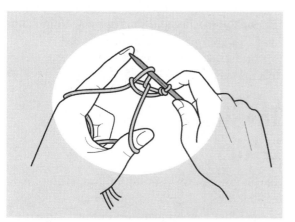

With the yarn over the needle, pull the needle through the loop made by your thumb so that the new loop you created is on the needle.

Now gently pull the short end of the yarn to tighten the stitch on the needle. Nice work! You have just completed a double cast on. You now have two stitches on the needle; the slip knot counts as your first stitch.

Keep practicing until you feel comfortable. When you run out of yarn from the tail, just pull out the stitches, tie another slip knot, and start again. Initially, the tension on your stitches is going to vary quite a bit. No big deal. Just keep practicing and soon the stitches will be fairly even.

The Cable Cast On

The last method of casting on is the *cable cast on*. This method requires two needles; you'll actually knit your stitches onto the needle. The cable cast on creates a fairly firm edge, so it works best for items that need a straight, firm edge, such as scarves and afghans. It is also decorative. Look closely and you'll see a nice little ridge that almost looks braided. Be sure you use the yarn feeding from the skein or ball, not the tail of yarn, to cast on stitches.

Pointers

Sometimes a pattern calls for adding more stitches to the edge of a piece, such as the sleeve of a sweater. A pattern might also ask you to cast on stitches in the middle of a row (buttonholes sometimes require this). In these cases use the cable cast on to add the necessary stitches.

To begin, tie a slip knot, leaving about a 4-inch tail; then follow the steps in these figures:

Insert the tip of your right needle into the slip knot on your left needle, from front to back, under the left needle.

With your right hand, bring the yarn under and then over the point of the right needle and pull the loop through; you now have a loop on the right needle.

Use the right needle to slide the new loop onto the left needle. You now have two loops on the left needle; the slipknot counts as your first stitch.

Insert the right needle between the two stitches on your left needle. Be sure you insert the right needle *between* stitch loops on the left needle, rather than *through* the loops.

Again loop the yarn around the point of the right needle as you did before and pull the stitch through.

Whew! You not only mastered the cable cast on; you also just learned the basic process of knitting! You now have two stitches on the needle; the slip knot counts as your first stitch.

If you hold the yarn in your right hand, it's called the *English* or *American* method. If you hold the yarn in your left hand, it's known as the *Continental* or *German* method. (We'll discuss English and Continental knitting methods in detail in the next chapter.) Because you held the yarn in your right hand, you just learned the English cable cast on method.

To try the Continental cable cast on method, follow the same procedures as outlined, but with the yarn in your left hand lay it over the needle (away from you). There is no need to bring the yarn under the right needle first.

Both methods produce the same results, but it's a good idea to try both of them and decide which you're most comfortable with.

There is a variation of the cable cast on called the *knit cast on.* It creates an edge that is a little less firm. Begin by inserting the needle into the slip knot and casting on one stitch like you did before. For the next stitch, instead of inserting your needle *between* the two stitches, insert it into the front loop (the loop closest to you) of the next stitch, loop the yarn around in the same way, and finally place your new cast on stitch on the left needle. In other words, cast on all your stitches as you did with the first slip knot.

Go ahead and keep practicing. If you have more stitches on the needle than it can hold, rip out the stitches and start again with the slip knot. It's going to feel a little awkward at first, but pretty soon you'll notice you feel comfortable and your stitches look more even.

The Single Cast On for Lefties

The single cast on is the simplest method for left-handed knitters, but you can also use any of the other cast on methods in this chapter (and see the next chapter for more on left-handed knitting in general). Just reverse the instructions so that if the instructions say to do something with your right hand, do it with your left.

Casting on for left-handed knitters starts with a slip knot just like it does for right handed knitters. Leave about a 4-inch tail. You're now ready to cast on a stitch. With your left hand, grip the needle that holds the slip knot as you would hold a wooden spoon. Then follow these steps:

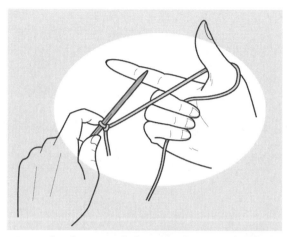

Grasp the shorter end of yarn with your right hand and wrap it around your thumb from front to back. Then wrap the yarn from the skein over your left index finger and hold both yarn ends with your right palm.

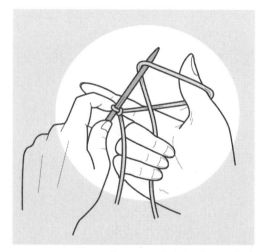

Now insert your needle upward at the base of your right thumb into the loop around your thumb.

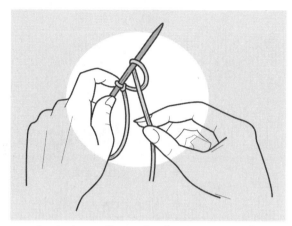

Slip the loop off your thumb onto your needle. Gently pull on the long strand to tighten your stitch.

Great! You've just cast on a stitch using the single method. You now have two stitches on the needle; the slip knot counts as your first stitch. Cast on some more stitches, trying to keep them even. Initially, your stitches are going to vary somewhat; some will be tight while others will be loose. Just keep practicing. After a bit, your stitches will even up and you'll feel more comfortable with casting on.

The Least You Need to Know

- Casting on means building a foundation of stitches from which you'll knit.
- There are several methods of casting on, using either one needle or two.
- Lefties can use any cast on method by reversing instructions.
- It takes practice to get even stitches.

In This Chapter

- ◆ The knit stitch

- ◆ The purl stitch

- ◆ Garter stitch and stockinette stitch

- ◆ Binding off

- ◆ Left-handed knitting

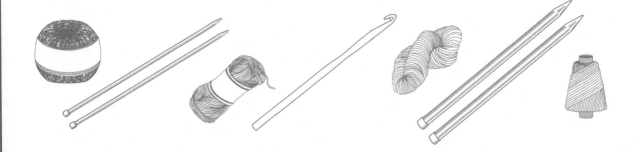

Chapter **6**

The Big Three: Knitting, Purling, and Binding Off

In Chapter 5, you learned to cast on stitches to get ready to knit. In this chapter, you'll actually learn to knit. You'll also learn how to purl and bind off stitches. With these three skills, and the cast on methods you learned in the previous chapter, you'll know everything necessary to create scarves, afghans, and much more.

So what are you waiting for? Let's start knitting!

Same Stitch, Different Look: Knitting and Purling

Knitting creates fabric of interlocking loops. Knitting and its best buddy *purling*, which you'll also learn about in this chapter, are two complementary ways to create and join these loops. You knit or purl in rows, using the stitches you cast on the needle.

Here's where things get interesting: Knitting and purling are actually the same stitch. The only difference lies in whether you pull a loop toward you or move it away from you. When you look at a knit stitch on the reverse side of the fabric, it looks exactly like a purl stitch; when you look at a purl stitch on the reverse side of the fabric, it looks exactly like a knit stitch.

If you purl every row, you'll ultimately end up with a fabric that looks exactly the same as if you knit every row. This concept might sound confusing, but as you begin watching what your hands are doing, you'll understand how knitting and purling interact to create interesting patterns and effects.

Needle Talk _____

Knitting (abbreviated k) forms rows of interconnecting loops in which the ends of the loops face away from you as you work. **Purling** (abbreviated p) forms rows of interconnecting loops in which the ends of the loops face toward you as you work.

The fabric you create will have a *right side* and a *wrong side*. The right side is the side that will show on the outside while the wrong side will not. Think of wearing a shirt or sweater inside out. Sometimes it will look exactly the same on both sides, which is wonderful for items such as afghans, scarves, and baby blankets. These are called *reversible stitch patterns*. Your pattern will always specify which is the right side and which is the wrong side (although many times it's obvious). Sometimes the first row you work will be the wrong side and sometimes the right side.

Needle Talk _____

The **right side** (abbreviated RS) of knitted fabric is the side that will be showing, such as the outside of a sweater. The **wrong side** (abbreviated WS) is the side that faces inward.

Knitting 101

There are two methods of knitting: Continental (sometimes called German) and English (sometimes called American). Both create exactly the same stitch; the only difference is in how you execute it. In Continental knitting, you "catch" the yarn using the needle; in English knitting, you "throw" the yarn with your hand.

Continental knitting is generally considered faster and more efficient. But there is no right way or wrong way. Practice both and see which feels more comfortable to you. In fact, with a certain type of knitting where you work with more than one color, it will benefit you to learn how to knit both ways.

Continental Knitting

It's time: You're going to knit! Follow along by casting on about 20 stitches with a smooth wool yarn that knits to 4 to 4.5 stitches to the inch and size 8 U.S. needles. The needle with the cast on stitches is held in your left hand. Your right hand will hold the other needle you'll use to form stitches.

There are as many ways to hold the needles as there are knitters. It's important that you find what's comfortable for you. Follow these instructions to begin; if you need to make adjustments and find holding either needle slightly differently works better, by all means do so.

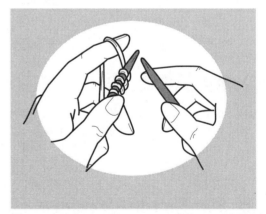

Hold the needle with the cast on stitches in your left hand as shown. The yarn that you'll be knitting from is draped over your index finger and held at the back of your work. In your right hand, hold the second needle as you would a pencil.

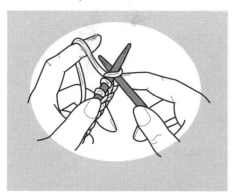

Insert the tip of the right needle from left to right (front to back) through the front loop (nearest you) of the stitch on the left needle. Keep the yarn in your left hand at the back of the needles. The left needle is on top of the right needle.

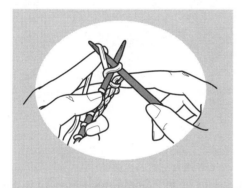

Lay the yarn on top of the right needle (wrapped from you moving away from you). Use the middle finger of your left hand if that feels comfortable. It's very important that the yarn is moving away from you and not toward you; otherwise your stitches will be twisted.

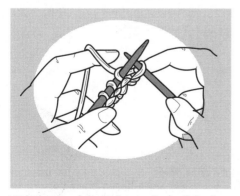

With the tip of the right needle, pull the loop through and keep it on the right needle.

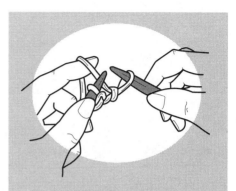

Pull the stitch off the left needle. You've completed 1 knit stitch. You might need to give the yarn a slight tug to tighten the stitch. The objective is to obtain an even tension throughout without tugging.

Congratulations! Now keep going. Keeping that new stitch you just formed on the right needle, insert the right needle into the first stitch on the left needle and knit it. You'll have two stitches on the right needle. Continue across the row and keep practicing. Remember, it feels awkward for everyone at first but you'll soon get the hang of it and be able to knit in the dark!

English Knitting

Now we're going to learn the English knitting method. It produces exactly the same stitch; it's just done in a little different way. As with Continental knitting, getting a comfortable grip is important. But again, it's not how you hold the needles or yarn that's important; it's how you form the stitches. So find what is most comfortable for you.

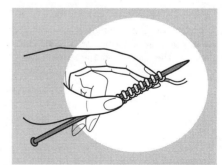

With your left hand, grip the needle with the cast on stitches, lightly holding the first stitch on the needle with your index finger near the pointed end of the needle.

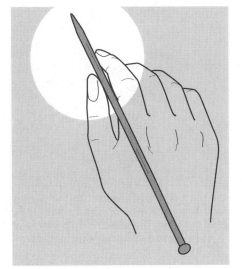

In your right hand, hold the second needle as you would a pencil.

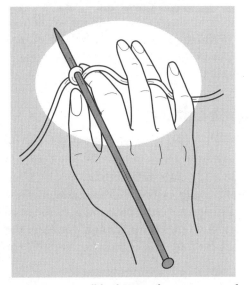

Place the yarn you'll be knitting from over your first finger, under your second, over your third, and under your fourth. This controls the tension of the yarn.

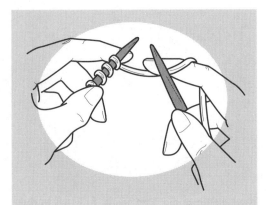

Move your hands closer together and you're ready to begin.

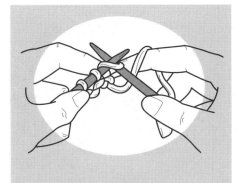

Insert the tip of the right needle from left to right (front to back) through the front loop (nearest you) of the stitch on the left needle. The right needle will be under the left needle.

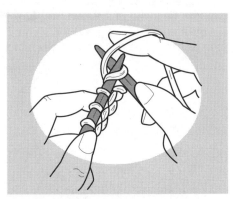

Rest the right needle on top of your left index finger. With your right index finger, bring the yarn under and then over the right needle. It is very important that the yarn is moving away from you and not toward you; otherwise your stitches will be twisted.

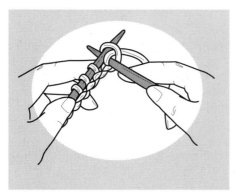

With the help of your left index finger, slide the point of the right needle back toward you and catch the loop made by the yarn over the needle.

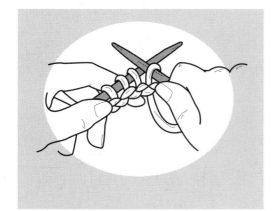

Pull the stitch off the left hand needle. You now have a stitch on the right needle.

Beautiful! You have just knit your first stitch using the English method. Continue across the row by inserting the right needle into the first stitch on the left needle again. Work the entire row. And keep practicing until knitting becomes second nature!

Yarn Spinning

Many years ago, when children were routinely taught to knit, a wonderful phrase helped to make the process easier. Try chanting it to help you remember the steps: "in, over, through, and off."

The Next Row

Regardless of whether you're knitting Continental or English, when you have completed the first row, you'll run out of stitches on the left needle and you'll have a fresh new row of stitches on the right needle. You are now ready to turn your work so you can knit the second row.

Transfer the needle with the stitches from your right hand to your left hand. You will be looking at the back of the stitches you just knit. In this case, because you knit the stitches and the ends of the loops were pointed away from you when you worked the row, they will now be pointed toward you when you turn the stitches; this is why the stitches look bumpy. What you are looking at are purl stitches!

Now you are starting over with the empty needle in your right hand and the needle with the stitches in your left. You knit this second row of stitches exactly the same way you knit the first row. That's all there is to it! You now know how to knit. Can you see how this can become addictive?

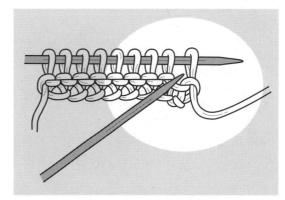

Knitting into a stitch on the second row.

Purls of Wisdom

It's time to learn the ying to knitting's yang: the purl stitch. Purling is knitting in reverse: You pull the end of the loop toward you so that the end of the loop faces you. Consequently, the row you are looking at while working will have a bumpy texture.

There are two major differences between a knit and a purl stitch. The first is the position of your yarn while you work the stitch. In knitting, the yarn is held to the back of the work. In purling, the yarn is held to the front of the work. The second difference is where you insert the needle. In knitting, you insert the needle front to back; in purling, you insert it back to front.

Just as with knitting, there is a Continental and an English method of purling. Practice along by using the same fabric you created while learning to knit or cast on with 20 new stitches. Each stitch is created the same way, regardless of whether it's the first row or the hundredth row.

Continental Purling

Begin by holding the needles and yarn the same way you did for Continental knitting. The difference is that the yarn is held to the front of the work.

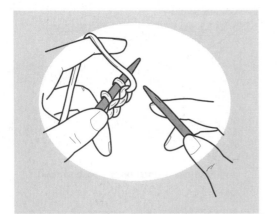

Hold the needle with the stitches in your left hand as shown. The yarn that you'll be knitting from is draped over your index finger and held at the front of your work. In your right hand, hold the second needle as you would a pencil.

Insert the tip of the right needle from right to left (back to front) through the front loop (nearest you) of the stitch on the left needle. Keep the yarn in your left hand at the front of the needles. The right needle is on top of the left needle.

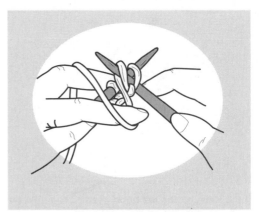

Lay the yarn over the right needle from front to back. A common mistake is to lay the yarn from back to front and pick it; if you do this, your stitches will be twisted. Hold the yarn taut as shown.

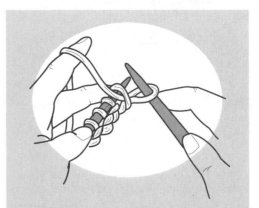

With the tip of the right needle, pull the loop through back toward you and keep it on the right needle.

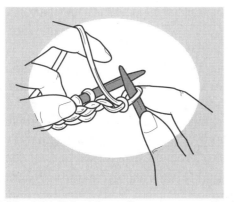

Pull the stitch off the left needle. You've completed 1 purl stitch. You might need to give the yarn a slight tug to tighten the stitch. The objective is to obtain an even tension throughout without tugging.

Way to go! You know how to purl! Keep practicing. Most people find purling a bit more awkward than knitting so don't be alarmed if you find this to be the case. Complete the row and turn your work. What do you notice? The purl stitches look like knit stitches on the other side!

English Purling

Begin by holding the needles and yarn the same way you did for English knitting. However, the yarn is now held at the front of your work.

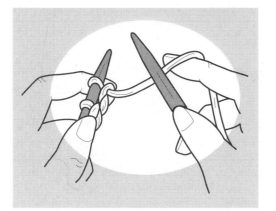

Hold the needle with the stitches in your left hand and the empty needle in your right hand. Keep the yarn at the front of your work.

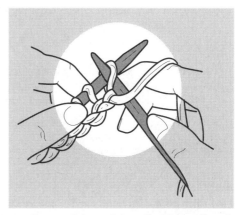

Insert the tip of the right needle from right to left (back to front) through the front loop (nearest you) of the stitch on the left needle. Keep the yarn in your left hand at the front of the needles. The right needle is on top of the left needle.

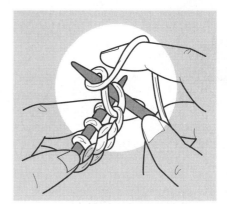

With your right hand, bring the yarn over, under, and then over the right needle as shown. It is very important that the yarn is initially moving away from you and not toward you in a counterclockwise direction, otherwise your stitches will be twisted.

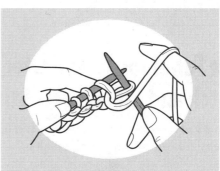

With the tip of the right needle, pull the loop through back toward you and keep it on the right needle.

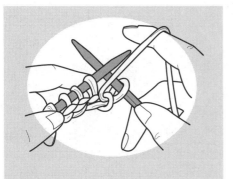

Pull the stitch off the left hand needle. You've completed 1 purl stitch. You may need to give the yarn a slight tug to tighten the stitch. The objective is to obtain an even tension throughout without tugging.

Wonderful! You've now learned how to purl using the English method.

Pointers

Unless you're knitting something small, usually you'll need more than one ball of yarn to complete a project. What if you run out of yarn and need to start a new ball? Simply start working with the new ball at the beginning of a row, leaving a 4-inch length of yarn you will weave in the seam later. It takes approximately three times the width of a project to complete one row; this will give you a good estimate of if you have enough left to complete the row. You can begin working with the new ball in the middle of a row but you will have ends to weave in the middle of your fabric.

The Fabulous Two: Garter Stitch and Stockinette Stitch

With these two simple stitches—knit and purl—you can create many different, fabulous stitch patterns, which you'll learn more about in Chapter 7. These will ask you to knit and purl at different times on the same row. However, there are two basic patterns you can create while working entire rows in either knit or purl: *garter stitch* and *stockinette stitch*.

Knitting every row creates garter stitch. Because a knit stitch looks like a purl on the other side, you can also purl every row to produce garter stitch. However, because most people find purling a little slower than knitting, knitting every row is more common.

Garter stitch produces a fabric with horizontal ridges. If you look closely, you'll see a smooth row followed by a bumpy row. Ridges are the bumpy rows you see on both sides the fabric. Each ridge represents two rows of knitting. Garter stitch lies flat so it's an appropriate and easy way to create a scarf.

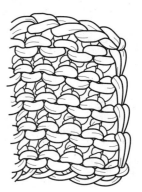

Knitting every row creates garter stitch.

Needle Talk

Knitting every row creates **garter stitch**; the fabric has horizontal ridges and lies flat. **Stockinette stitch** (abbreviated St st and sometimes called *stocking stitch*) creates a fabric that is smooth on one side and bumpy on the other by alternating knit and purl rows. The smooth side is called "stockinette"; the bumpy side is called **reverse stockinette** (abbreviated rev St st).

Stockinette stitch really defines knitting. T-shirts, socks, and sweatshirts are made using stockinette. Look closely and you'll notice the side facing out is smooth, whereas the inside is composed of tiny bumps.

Alternating one row of knitting with one row of purling creates stockinette stitch. The result is a fabric that is smooth on one side (the knit side) and bumpy on the other (the purl side). The bumpy side is known as *reverse stockinette stitch.*

It is the nature of stockinette to curl. This happens because the knit stitches are slightly thinner and shorter than the purl stitches, so the piece rolls toward the knit side.

If you are making something that will be seamed such as a sweater, curling isn't cause for alarm because seaming will take care of the problem. But if you try to make a scarf of stockinette, you'll find it will roll into a tube all by itself. To keep it from curling, you'll need to use an edging, which you'll learn more about in Chapter 19. Some designs incorporate this natural curling tendency to make sweaters with rolled collars or hats with rolled brims.

The knit side of stockinette stitch.

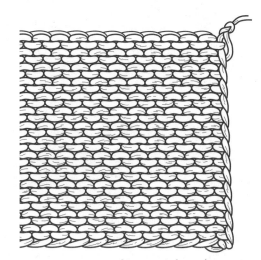

Reverse stockinette stitch.

 Pointers

If you get confused about what row you are on when working stockinette, look at your stitches and work them as they appear. If the smooth side is facing you, then you knit. If the bumpy side is facing you, then you purl.

Bringing It to a Close

Okay, so you can now knit and purl, using two different methods. How do you get your work off the needles so all your hard work doesn't unravel?

Just as you had to work a special row to get ready to knit, you have to work a special row to finish your piece. This row is worked following a procedure called *binding off.* Binding off actually creates a final row of fabric so, as you might expect, when you are knitting you bind off differently than when you are purling.

Needle Talk

Binding off (abbreviated BO) is the process in which you "lock up" all active stitches on the needle so that they can't unravel. You bind off stitches when you're finished with a piece or want to shape an area (such as the armhole in a sweater). It's sometimes called *casting off.*

Always bind off loosely. Otherwise, you'll end up with a knitted piece that looks pinched or a sweater that won't fit over your head. If you find you are binding off too tightly, use needles one or two sizes larger than the size you used to knit the piece.

Binding Off in Knit

If the next row calls for you to knit but instead it's time for you to bind off, you'll bind off in knit. To begin, loosely knit the first 2 stitches in the row; you now have 2 stitches on the right needle. Then follow these steps:

Insert the point of the left needle into the first stitch on the right needle from left to right.

Using the left needle, lift the stitch up and over the second stitch, and off the point of the right needle. You have bound off 1 stitch.

Do you see what you just did? You had 2 stitches on the needle and you looped one over the other to end up with only 1 stitch. If you ever made potholders as a kid using those looms with colored nylon loops, you've bound off stitches before, just in a different context.

Here's how to continue binding off across the row:

1. Knit the next stitch on the left needle. You again have 2 stitches on the right needle.

2. Following the preceding illustrations, use the left needle to lift the stitch up and over the second stitch, and off the point of the right needle.

3. Repeat steps 1 and 2 until you have bound off all but 1 stitch.

4. Cut the end of your yarn at least 3 inches from the needle; pull the yarn end through the last remaining stitch and pull.

You have just secured the last stitch. Your knitted piece now can't unravel.

You'll find many situations in which you bind off only part of the stitches across a row, such as shaping the armhole or the neck of a sweater. For example, the instructions might tell you to bind off 5 stitches at the beginning of the next two rows. To continue working across the row and have your yarn in the appropriate place, you can bind off stitches only at the beginning of a row.

To bind off 5 stitches, you're actually knitting 6 stitches; the last stitch will remain on the right needle and end up as the first stitch of the row. Remember, after you've lifted the first stitch up and over the second stitch on the right needle, this counts as 1 bound off stitch.

Binding Off in Purl

If the next row calls for you to purl but instead it's time for you to bind off, you'll bind off in purl. Follow the same procedure you learned in the preceding section with one difference: Purl the stitches rather than knit them. Once you have bound off all but 1 stitch, cut your yarn like you did before, leave a tail, and pull the end of the yarn through your last stitch. That's it!

Pattern instructions will often state, "Bind off in pattern." This means you should bind off using whatever stitch you would use to continue the established pattern. Pretend you are going to continue to work the row as you have been. Knit or purl each stitch before it's bound off as appropriate to the pattern. If the next stitch would have been a purl, purl that stitch and bind off. If the next stitch would have been a knit, knit that stitch and bind off.

Left-Handed Knitting

Knitting is an ambidextrous task: The left hand and right hand are equally important. If you are left handed, first try to learn using either the English or Continental method discussed earlier in this chapter. The awkwardness you might be feeling isn't necessarily because you are left handed; we all feel awkward when beginning. The procedures in this section are specifically geared toward left handers using the English method, but you will forevermore have to reverse instructions and it can cause a great deal of confusion.

Patterns and stitch instructions are always written assuming you are knitting right handed, as in the beginning of this chapter. If you are going to learn to knit left handed, you *must* substitute the words *right* for *left*, and *left* for *right*. To avoid confusion as you work, use two different colors to highlight the words *right* and *left* in your patterns.

Pointers

If you need clarification on how to do a procedure left handed, hold a mirror next to the right-handed illustrations so that you can see the image reversed. The reversed image will give you the necessary information you need to work left handed.

This section discusses those steps that differ from right-handed knitting. Therefore, it's important to read all the instructions at the beginning of this chapter before you begin.

The Knit Stitch

Comfortable knitting begins with properly positioning the yarn and the needles. Follow these instructions:

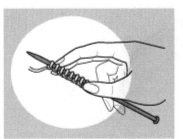

With your right hand, grip the needle that contains the cast on stitches, lightly holding the first stitch on the needle with your index finger near the point end of the needle.

In your left hand, hold the second needle as you would a pencil.

Place the long end of the yarn over your first finger, under your second, over your third, and under your fourth.

Okay. You're sitting there holding the needle, the yarn twisted around your fingers at the ready. Now what? You're ready to knit your first stitch! Here's how:

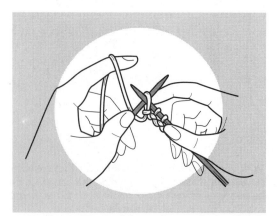

Insert the tip of your left needle into the first stitch on your right needle from front to back. The left needle should be under the right needle.

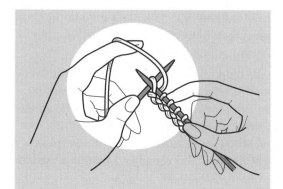

Rest the right needle on top of your left index finger. The yarn is at the left of your work in your left hand. Using your left hand, bring the yarn under and then over the point of the left needle.

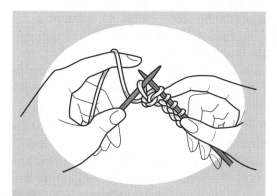

With the help of your right index finger, slide the point of the left needle back toward you. Using the point of the left needle, catch the loop made by the yarn over the needle.

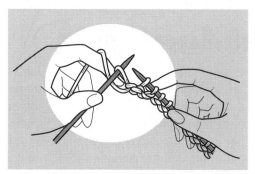

You now have a stitch on the left needle. Pull the original stitch off the right needle.

You just produced your first knit stitch! The process might seem awkward. Try another stitch … and then another. The process gets easier as you move across the row.

The Purl Stitch

Begin by holding the needles and yarn the same way you did for knitting. The difference is that the yarn is held to the front of the work:

Bring the yarn forward in front of your left needle.

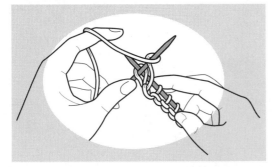

From the left side, insert the point of the left needle into the first stitch on the right needle from back to front. The left needle should be in front of the right needle. Using your left index finger, wrap the yarn around the left needle clockwise.

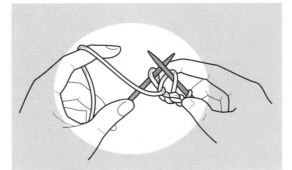

Keeping the new loop on the left needle, slide the point of the left needle back toward you, down, and out. You now have a new loop on the left needle. Slide the original stitch off the right needle.

Wonderful! You have just completed your first purl stitch. That's it—you're a knitter!

The Least You Need to Know

- The knit and purl stitches are really the same stitch, but the method used to create them is different.
- The Continental method and the English method produce exactly the same stitches, just in different ways.
- Alternating knit and purl rows creates stockinette stitch. Knitting every row creates garter stitch.
- Binding off is a way to lock up your stitches when you finish a piece so it doesn't unravel. Always bind off loosely in the correct pattern stitch.
- Left-handed knitting is a reverse image of right-handed knitting. If you learn to knit left handed, you will always need to reverse instructions.

In This Chapter

- ◆ How to combine knits and purls
- ◆ Exploring stitch multiples
- ◆ Create an elastic fabric with ribbing
- ◆ Dressing up your work with seed stitch
- ◆ Working a checkerboard pattern

Chapter 7

Knitting Stitch Patterns

Knitting and purling open the door to creating all types of stitch patterns. Up until now, you have knit or purled the entire row.

Now you'll learn to combine knit and purl stitches in the same row. By using them in different combinations, you can create an almost limitless number of different patterns, from simple ribbing at the bottom of a sweater to the most intricate of patterns.

Combining Knits and Purls

In the previous chapter you learned that if you knit every row you create garter stitch; both sides look the same. If you knit one row and purl the next, you create stockinette stitch (and the other side, which looks bumpy, is called reverse stockinette). The manner in which you arrange rows of knitting and purling creates these stitch patterns. Now you're going to learn more stitch patterns, made by arranging combinations of knit and purl stitches in the same row.

Become familiar with and practice these easy stitch patterns. They are common and you will find many uses for them. For example, seed stitch (which you'll learn later in this chapter) lies flat and a border of 3 seed stitches around a stockinette scarf will keep it from rolling in.

When you work knit and purl stitches on the same row, pay special attention to the position of the yarn before you start the next stitch. You'll need to move the yarn into position to get ready for the next stitch. Remember: yarn in back for knitting, yarn in front for purling.

Understanding Stitch Multiples

A *stitch multiple* is the number of stitches necessary to complete a pattern stitch. A pattern of knit 2, purl 2 requires 4 stitches, so it would have a stitch multiple of 4. Often a stitch multiple includes an extra stitch or two. For example, a stitch multiple of "4 plus 2" means you can start by casting on a number divisible by 4, plus an extra 2 stitches. For this example, you could use 14:

4 (stitch multiple) × 3 (number of times you want to repeat the stitch) + 2 = 14

This means you can work the pattern 3 times, plus have the extra 2 stitches required.

Stitch multiples aren't always included in project patterns because the number of stitches you'll be working has already been determined for you. But understanding how they work will allow you to resize patterns as your knowledge increases. You can make a simple scarf from any stitch pattern that lies flat once you grasp how they work. If a stitch pattern has a multiple of 4, cast on 16, 20, or 24 stitches depending on how wide you want the scarf to be and the gauge you're working to; then repeat the stitch pattern until the scarf is the length you want.

Ribbing

Ribbing is made by combining knit and purl stitches to form an elastic fabric. This fabric stretches and then returns to its original shape. Ribbing uses a knit and purl combination; the knit and purl stitches are aligned to create a vertical texture. It often begins and ends sweater projects, as well as hats, mittens, and socks. Being snug and elastic, ribbing keeps edges from rolling and provides snug openings.

In this section you'll learn two variations of the basic rib.

Pointers

When an asterisk (*) appears, repeat the directions that appear after the asterisk across the row. There might be additional instructions before or after the asterisk, or sometimes both. For more help, see Chapter 21.

Knit 1, purl 1 ribbing.

Stitch multiple: 2 plus 1

Row 1: K1, *p1, k1; rep from * across.

Row 2: P1, *k1, p1; rep from * across.

Repeat Rows 1 and 2 for pattern.

The same pattern can also be worked over an even number of stitches.

Stitch multiple: 2

Row 1: *K1, p1; rep from * across.

Repeat Row 1 for pattern.

Pointers _____

When working in rib, work your stitches as they appear. In other words, if you're about to work into a knit stitch (a smooth stitch that faces you), you knit this stitch. If you are about to work into a purl stitch (a bumpy stitch that faces you), you purl this stitch. In ribbing, the knit stitches are prominent and the purl stitches recede between the knit stitches.

The elasticity of ribbing is determined by how far apart you place the knit and purl stitches: the farther apart, the less "give" in the ribbing. Now try a ribbing with a little less give, such as knit 2, purl 2 ribbing. This creates ribs that are, as you might expect, twice as wide as knit 1, purl 1 ribbing.

Knit 2, purl 2 ribbing.

Stitch multiple: 4 plus 2

Row 1: K2, *p2, k2; rep from * across.

Row 2: P2, *k2, p2; rep from * across.

Repeat Rows 1 and 2 for pattern.

The same k2, p2 ribbing can also be worked over 4 stitches instead of 4 plus 2.

Stitch multiple: 4

Row 1: *K2, p2; rep from * across.

Repeat Row 1 for pattern.

Seed Stitch

Seed stitch is a wonderful basic pattern that dresses up plain sweaters or jackets. The pattern has the same texture on both sides, so you can use seed stitch to make beautiful scarves, afghans, or washcloths. It's also great as an edging.

The seed stitch pattern.

This pattern, when completed, resembles little seeds scattered across the fabric. It uses a knit 1, purl 1 combination like the first ribbing pattern you learned. But here's the trick: Instead of aligning the knits and purls, you knit the purl stitch as it faces you and purl the knit stitch as it faces you. Here's how:

Stitch multiple: 2

Row 1: *K1, p1; rep from * across.

Row 2: *P1, k1; rep from * across.

Repeat Rows 1 and 2 for pattern.

Guess what? You can also work seed stitch over an odd number of stitches!

Stitch multiple: 2 plus 1

Row 1: P1, *k1, p1; rep from * across.

Repeat Row 1 for pattern.

Yarn Spinning

Barbara Walker spent more than a decade chronicling hundreds of knitting patterns. The sources for her work came from vintage knitting instruction books, her own ideas, and patterns sent in from readers. The result was a trio of wonderful knitting stitch pattern encyclopedias.

Checkerboard

When you work the checkerboard pattern, you form blocks or squares. It's a visually interesting pattern that looks the same on the front and back of the fabric. It also lies flat.

Once you understand how it works, it can be made in blocks of 3, 4, or more stitches over various numbers of rows, making it a very versatile pattern stitch.

The versatile checkerboard pattern.

Stitch multiple: 4 plus 2

Row 1: K2, *p2, k2; rep from * across.

Row 2: P2, *k2, p2; rep from * across.

Row 3: Repeat Row 1.

Row 4: Repeat Row 1.

Row 5: Repeat Row 2.

Row 6: Repeat Row 1.

Repeat Rows 1–6 for pattern.

The Least You Need to Know

◆ You can create numerous stitch patterns by changing the combination of knit and purl stitches in a row.

◆ How stitches are placed determines their final appearance. They can lie flat like the checkerboard pattern or appear alternately raised and recessed like ribbing.

◆ Ribbing generally edges the bottom, neck, and cuffs of sweaters and other items because it provides an elastic edge.

◆ Using stitch patterns as an edging will prevent stockinette from rolling in.

In This Chapter

- ◆ Common increase and decrease abbreviations
- ◆ Adding stitches by increasing
- ◆ Removing stitches by decreasing
- ◆ Choosing the correct decrease
- ◆ Using increase and decrease stitches decoratively

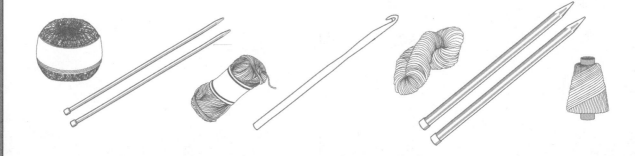

Chapter 8

What Goes Up Must Come Down: Increasing and Decreasing

By knowing how to knit and purl you can create beautiful scarves, ornamental afghans, and a host of other projects. But, as you might have guessed, knitting isn't limited to making only squares and rectangles. Instead, your knitted pieces can take nearly any form by shaping them through increasing and decreasing stitches.

In this chapter, you'll learn the basic procedures for increasing and decreasing. In addition, you'll learn how to select the correct increase or decrease and how they can add decorative effects.

Common Increase and Decrease Abbreviations

The following abbreviations are commonly used to indicate increasing and decreasing stitches. (You'll find a full list of common abbreviations in Appendix B.)

Abbreviation	What It Means
dec	Decrease
inc	Increase
k2tog	Knit 2 together
p2tog	Purl 2 together
k2tog tbl	Knit 2 together through back loop
p2tog tbl	Purl 2 together through back loop
sl	Slip
psso	Pass slipped stitch over
ssk	Slip Slip Knit
yo	Yarn over
M1	Make 1

Adding Stitches: Increasing

You'll often find yourself increasing the number of stitches on your needles: A sleeve knit from the wrist up will instruct you to increase stitches to widen the sleeve to fit your arm. There are several methods of increasing and each looks different. Increases can be worked at any point in a row.

Tangles

If a pattern instructs you to use a specific increase or decrease, be sure to follow the instructions. Using a different type of increase or decrease can change the entire look of the project.

Yarn Over (yo)

Yarn over creates a lacy hole in the fabric. Obviously, you only want to use a yarn over increase if you want a lacy hole in the fabric. And don't worry—the hole won't unravel. The dishcloth pattern in Chapter 22 is an excellent

example of using a yarn over to increase the number of stitches on your needle and create a decorative edge at the same time.

To yarn over when knitting, get ready to knit the next stitch, but don't insert the right needle into the stitch on the left needle. Wrap the yarn over the needle, away from you. The needle now has an extra loop on it.

Complete a yarn over by wrapping the yarn over the needle away from you, creating an extra stitch and a lacy hole.

Continue working the row as instructed. On the next row, when you knit or purl into the extra loop, the hole will appear. You work into this extra loop just as if it were a stitch. It's very important to watch for this extra loop while working the next row, and make sure you knit or purl it as the case may be. The loop is easily dropped off your needle without working it. If you find this has happened, you will need to rip back your work and correct the problem.

To make a yarn over when purling, wrap the yarn from the front of the needle to the back, under the needle, and back to the front. Then continue purling.

Bar Increase

A bar increase literally creates a visible "bar" of yarn where you increase. The bar increase is fairly unnoticeable and creates no decorative hole, making it perfect for increasing when you want to discreetly add stitches without calling attention to the increases.

The bar increase is the default increase. If a pattern indicates that you should increase stitches, but it doesn't indicate which type to use, you can safely use the bar increase.

Here's how to make a bar increase:

1. Knit a stitch as you normally would; insert the right needle into the front loop of the next stitch on the left needle and pull the new stitch through, but don't yet slide the stitch off the left needle. Remember, the front loop of the stitch is the loop closest to you on the needle.

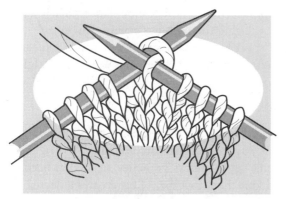

Beginning a bar increase by knitting into the front of a stitch.

2. Now insert the point of the right needle into the back of the same stitch on the left needle and complete another knit stitch. The back loop of the stitch is the loop farthest from you on the needle.

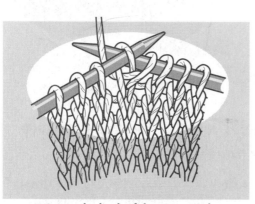

Knit into the back of the same stitch.

3. Now slide the stitch off the left needle. You'll have 2 stitches on the right needle for the 1 stitch you had on the left needle when you started.

Pointers

Patterns will often instruct you to "knit into the front and back of the next stitch" instead of telling you to work a bar increase. They mean the same thing.

If you need to increase a stitch while purling a row, simply purl into the back and front of the stitch. The principle of the front and back loops is exactly the same.

Make 1 (M1)

Make 1 is the trickiest of the increase stitches, but also the most versatile. This stitch creates a nearly invisible increase if done one way, or a decorative hole if done another way. The idea behind M1 is that you are making a stitch from the knitted fabric where one didn't exist.

Here's how to work M1:

1. Find the horizontal strand of yarn between the stitch on the left needle and the stitch on the right needle.

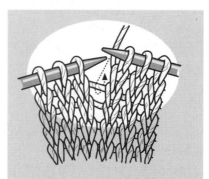

Finding the horizontal strand between the stitches on the right and left needles.

2. Insert the tip of the right needle under this strand of yarn from front (closest to you) to back; then pull the strand onto the left needle, making an extra stitch on that needle.

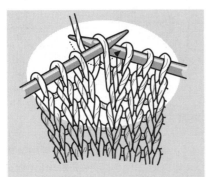

Pulling the horizontal strand onto the left needle.

3. If you want to create a decorative hole, knit into the front of this new stitch and slide the stitch off the left needle onto the right needle. If you don't want a hole, knit into the back of this new stitch and slide the stitch off the left needle onto the right needle. If the pattern instructions don't specify which to do, you should knit into the front of the new stitch.

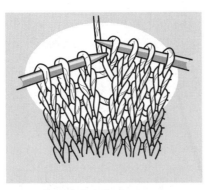

Completing the increase.

There is a third way to M1. Insert the right needle from the back (farthest from you) to the front under the horizontal strand. Place it on the left needle, thus twisting the stitch, and knit into the front of the extra stitch. This increase also does not produce a hole.

Subtracting Stitches: Decreasing

To shape knitted pieces, you will also need to learn how to decrease. For example, when you knit the neckline of a pullover you will need to decrease stitches to create an opening so it fits over your head. Decreases can be worked at any point in a row.

There are various ways to decrease and, just as with increasing, each method results in a different look. However, decreases don't produce decorative holes; rather, they slant either left or right. Using the correct decrease will ensure that your knitting goes right when you want it to go right and left when you want it to go left.

Knit 2 Together (k2tog)

Knit 2 together is the simplest and most common way to decrease stitches. Insert the right needle into the next 2 stitches on the left needle and knit them together. This creates a decrease that leans to the right.

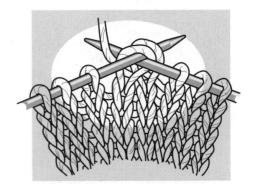

Knitting 2 stitches together.

Knit 2 Together Through Back Loop (k2tog tbl)

You can also knit 2 stitches together through the back loop. This decrease is sometimes used for a decorative effect as it twists the stitches.

Insert the right needle into the back loops (farthest from you) of the next 2 stitches on the left needle and knit them together. This decrease slants to the left.

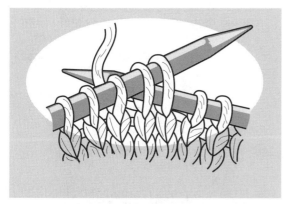

Knitting 2 stitches together through the back loop.

Purl 2 Together (p2tog)

Sometimes you will be asked to purl 2 together, although it's not as common as knit 2 together. Insert the right needle into the next 2 stitches on the left needle and purl them together. This decrease slants to the right.

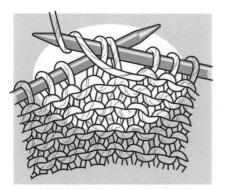

Purling 2 stitches together.

Purl 2 Together Through Back Loop (p2tog tbl)

Purl 2 together through the back loop is not very common but it might be called for on occasion. It's an awkward stitch and difficult to

manipulate so don't be alarmed if you have a problem with it. Insert the right needle into the back loops of the next 2 stitches on the left needle and purl them together. This decrease slants to the left.

Purling 2 stitches together through the back loop.

 Pointers

To make an easy buttonhole, work a yarn over and then knit the next 2 stitches together. Knitting with size 6 U.S. or so needles and worsted weight yarn, this buttonhole accommodates about a ½-inch button.

Slip Slip Knit (ssk)

Slip slip knit is a common and useful decrease. Unfortunately, ssk is often misunderstood because of the way it is worded. It sounds like you slip, you slip, and then you knit. But that's not how to work this decrease. The trick involves how you slip, and what and how you knit.

An accurate way of writing out ssk would be: Slip 1 stitch as if to knit, slip another stitch as if to knit, then knit both those slipped stitches through the back loop. Wordy, huh? Well, that's why we use the term slip slip knit. This stitch causes a decrease that leans to the left. Here's how you do it:

1. At the point you want to decrease, insert the right needle into the next stitch on the left needle as if you were going to knit it. Slip the stitch to the right needle without

working it. Do the same thing with the next stitch on the needle. Be sure to slip these stitches as if you were going to knit them, not as if you were going to purl them. You now have 2 slipped stitches on the right needle.

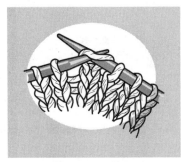

Slipping a stitch.

2. Now insert the left needle through the front loops (closest to you) of the 2 slipped stitches on the right needle.

3. Knit the 2 stitches together.

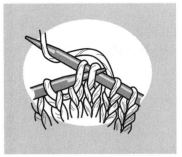

Knitting the 2 slipped stitches together.

Slip, Knit, Pass Slipped Stitch Over (sl 1, k 1, psso)

This decrease appears slightly elongated because you are slipping the stitch without ever working it. It is primarily used for decorative purposes, especially in lace patterns. This decrease slants to the left. You might see this decrease in a pattern written as sl, k, psso, or SKP; they all mean the same thing. Here's how you do it:

1. At the point you want to decrease, insert the right needle into the next stitch on the left needle as if you were going to knit it. Slip the stitch to the right needle without working it. Be sure to slip this stitch as if you were going to knit it, not as if you were going to purl it. You now have 1 slipped stitch on the right needle.

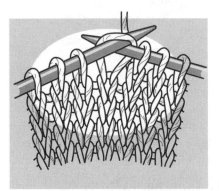

Slipping a stitch.

2. Knit the next stitch.

3. Now insert the left needle into slipped stitch as shown.

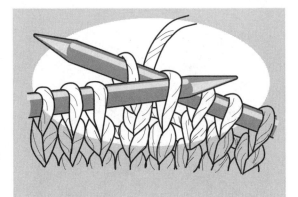

Inserting the needle into the slipped stitch.

4. Using the left needle, bring the slipped stitch over the knitted stitch.

5. Pull the slipped stitch off the right needle.

Passing the slipped stitch over the knitted stitch.

Going Left or Right

You've just learned that some decreases slant right while others slant left as the work faces you. But which do you use? Well-written patterns will tell you but unfortunately, some patterns don't. Details can mean the difference between something that looks handmade and something that looks homemade.

When you are shaping a piece, particularly sweaters, you want to use a decrease that goes in the direction your knitting is moving. Think of a triangle. The right side of the triangle is moving to the left. The left side of the triangle is moving to the right. So at the beginning of a row, use a decrease that slants left; at the end of the row use a decrease that slants right.

Okay, now what? There are so many decreases to choose from! Well, two in particular match very well. They are ssk and k2tog. Ssk slants left and k2tog slants right. When you are decreasing at both ends of a row (which you will often do when knitting sweaters), use ssk at the beginning of the row and k2tog at the end of the row. Your decreases will match and move in the correct direction. Details make the difference!

When Increasing and Decreasing Don't Do Either

If you've tried some of the increases and decreases throughout this chapter, you might have noticed that several not only add or subtract

stitches, they also slightly change the look of the fabric. Suppose you increase and decrease the same number of stitches in a row and place them strategically to create a specific pattern. Do you know what you'd get? Lace.

Take a look at the following illustration. This simple pattern is called *gull-wing lace*. To create the pattern, you increase and decrease the same number of stitches in each row by using techniques you learned in this chapter: yarn over (yo), knit 2 together (k2tog), and slip slip knit (ssk). The number of different patterns you can create using increases and decreases is almost infinite.

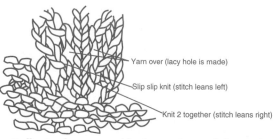

Yarn over (lacy hole is made)

Slip slip knit (stitch leans left)

Knit 2 together (stitch leans right)

Gull-wing lace created by increasing and decreasing stitches.

To try the gull-wing pattern yourself, cast on any number of stitches that is divisible by 7 (such as 14, 21, or 28). The pattern is 7 stitches long, and you repeat this pattern across the row.

Row 1: K1, k2tog, yo, k1, yo, ssk, k1.

Row 2: Purl.

Row 3: K2tog, yo, k3, yo, ssk.

Row 4: Purl.

The Least You Need to Know

◆ With a few simple techniques, you can shape your knitting using increases and decreases.

◆ Different increases and decreases are appropriate for different tasks.

◆ Ssk and k2tog are matching decreases that move in opposite directions.

◆ You can strategically use increases and decreases to create patterns within the fabric rather than to shape it.

In This Chapter

- ◆ Working through the back loop
- ◆ How to slip stitches
- ◆ Working cables
- ◆ Picking up stitches
- ◆ Creating horizontal or vertical buttonholes

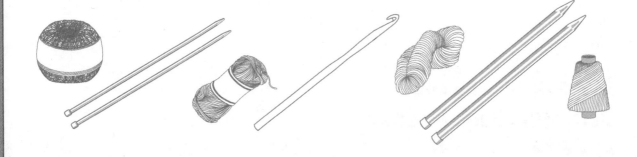

Chapter

9

Beyond the Basics: Adding to Your Knitting Repertoire

With a few small additions to what you've already learned you can change the way stitches look and add to your knitting repertoire. Knitting and purling through the back loop, slipping stitches, and working cables are easy and will open up entirely new possibilities.

You'll also learn how to pick up stitches, which is essential for creating neck bands on sweaters. Finally, you'll learn to make vertical and horizontal buttonholes any size you wish.

Knitting Through the Back Loop (tbl)

When you knit or purl through the back loop, you end up with a twisted stitch. Insert the right needle into the back loop of the next stitch (the loop farthest from you) on the left needle as if to knit (starting from you and moving toward the back as shown). Wrap the yarn around the right needle and knit the stitch; pull the new loop through.

Purling Through the Back Loop (tbl)

Insert the right needle into the back loop of the next stitch (the loop farthest from you) on the left needle as if to purl (from the back toward you as shown). Wrap the yarn around the right needle and purl the stitch; pull the new loop through.

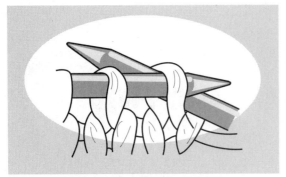

Knitting through the back loop.

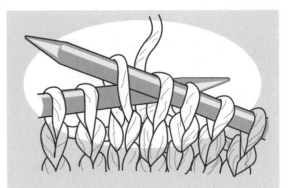

Slipping a stitch as if to purl.

Purling through the back loop.

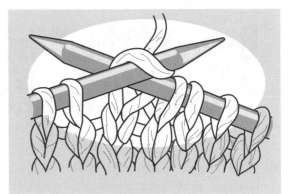

Slipping a stitch as if to knit.

Slip Stitch (sl)

Most stitches are slipped as if to purl. The one exception is decreases, in which stitches are almost always slipped as if to knit. If the directions do not specify, always assume you are to slip as if to purl. Slipped stitches have many uses and you will encounter them often.

To slip as if to purl, insert the right needle from right to left through the front loop of the next stitch on the left needle, as if you were going to purl it. Transfer the stitch to the right needle.

To slip as if to knit, insert the right needle from left to right through the front loop of the next stitch on the left needle, as if you were going to knit it. Transfer the stitch to the right needle.

Pointers

Sometimes instructions will say to slip stitches *purlwise* or *knitwise*. This means the same thing as "slip as if to purl" or "slip as if to knit," respectively.

Stitches can also be slipped through the back loop which, as you would expect, twists them. Insert the right needle through the back loop of the next stitch on the left needle as if to knit or as if to purl in the same way you would knit a stitch or purl a stitch through the back loop. Instead of working the stitch, slip it to the right needle.

Cables

Cables have a reputation for being complex and advanced. Although some very intricate patterns are a challenge even for experienced knitters, the basic cable is easy and rewarding.

Needle Talk _____

Cables use a combination of knit and purl stitches, which are physically re-arranged (crossed over) on the fabric. In the cable's simplest form, the first half of a group of stitches is placed on "hold" while the second half is worked. The stitches on hold are then worked, creating a spiral effect.

Although the strategy you're going to learn here can be applied to knitting any number of stitches out of order and creating eye-popping effects of texture, we'll just make a very simple cable. This type of cable is worked in stockinette stitch, with the knit stitches on the right side of the fabric being cabled. For the cables to stand out, at least 2 purl stitches are worked on both sides of the cable.

To knit a cable, you'll need one piece of specialized equipment: a cable needle. If you don't have a cable needle, you can use a double point needle, a crochet hook, or even a pencil, but the process will be a bit more awkward.

Cable 4 Back (c4b)

The first of the two basic cables is a cable 4 back (c4b). This makes a cable that twists to the right. The following instructions might seem cumbersome, but don't get discouraged as you're reading them. They aren't as difficult as they might seem.

Stitch multiple: 6 plus 2

Row 1 (right side): P2, k4, p2.

Row 2 (wrong side): K2, p4, k2.

Row 3: Repeat Row 1.

Row 4: Repeat Row 2.

Row 5: P2. Now complete the steps shown in the following figures to make your first cable.

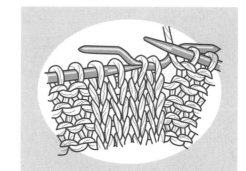

Slip the next 2 stitches onto a cable needle and hold the cable needle in the back of your work—the side that isn't facing you.

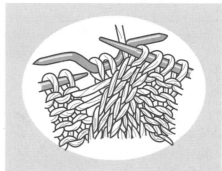

Knit the next 2 stitches from the left needle.

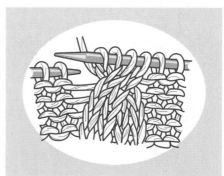

Now knit the 2 stitches from your cable needle.

To finish Row 5, purl 2.

Row 6: Repeat Row 2.

Not too hard, is it? Can you see the variations that are possible? You can make cables on different rows and over a different number of stitches, or even using various combinations of knit and purl stitches.

Yarn Spinning

Legend claims that intricate Aran sweaters were knit using family patterns that could help identify the washed-up bodies of drowned fishermen. In reality, historians now believe that the Aran sweater as we know it was probably a twentieth-century commercial venture, and fishermen most likely wore ganseys, a type of sweater that allows free movement.

Cable 4 Front (c4f)

The cable 4 front (c4f) stitch is almost identical to the cable 4 back, with one exception: You hold the stitches on the cable needle in front of your work. This cable twists to the left.

Stitch multiple: 6 plus 2

Row 1 (right side): P2, k4, p2.

Row 2 (wrong side): K2, p4, k2.

Row 3: Repeat Row 1.

Row 4: Repeat Row 2.

Row 5: Purl 2. Now work as follows to complete the cable.

Slip the next 2 stitches onto a cable needle and hold the cable needle in the front of your work—the side facing you.

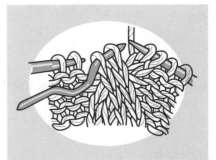

Knit the next 2 stitches from the left needle.

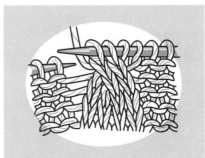

Now knit the 2 stitches from the cable needle.

To finish Row 5, purl 2.

Row 6: Repeat Row 2.

Pointers

When working cables, you have to allow enough rows between your cable twists to see the spiral. The greater the number of stitches in the cable, the more rows you need between twists. Pattern instructions will tell you how often to work the twist.

How to Pick Up Stitches

Although sweaters are constructed in several different ways, usually you'll find that you need to *pick up stitches*, or create new stitches along an edge, to complete the neck band, add ribbing to the armholes of a vest, or work the buttonhole bands of a cardigan. You'll need to know how to pick up stitches to knit socks, and there are many other occasions that call for this simple-to-learn skill as well.

Directions will usually specify to pick up the stitches "with right side facing." This means you should be looking at the right side of the fabric when you begin. A ridge forms on the wrong side when you pick up stitches so unless the pattern specifically states to pick them up from the wrong side, always be sure the right side of the work is facing you.

When you pick up a stitch, a new knit stitch is formed. Sometimes directions will state, "pick up and knit." The directions are actually saying, pick up a stitch as a knit stitch. Don't pick up a stitch and then try to knit it, as the term implies.

You can pick up stitches using either a needle or a crochet hook. Both accomplish the same thing; it's just a matter of personal preference.

We're ready to start. Look closely at the bound off edge. Notice there is a row of stitches directly below this edge. You'll insert your needle or hook directly into the center of each of these stitches. When you finish and complete the next row, each stitch should be lying directly above each other.

To pick up stitches on a horizontal edge with a needle, follow these steps:

1. Hold the piece you're going to pick up the stitches on with the right side facing you.
2. Working from right to left and with the pointed edge of the needle facing left, insert the needle from front to back through the middle of the first stitch.
3. Wrap the yarn around the needle from front to back (away from you) and pull the new stitch through.

If you find the yarn getting away from you, it helps to make a slip knot and begin with the yarn already on the needle, just like when you cast on. Be sure you don't work that stitch later, though; just pull it off the needle when you come to it.

Picking up a stitch along a horizontal edge.

That's it! You've just picked up 1 stitch. Now continue to pick up stitches across the edge.

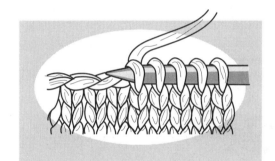

Stitches have been picked up along a horizontal edge and are on the needle.

You pick up stitches along a vertical or diagonal (such as an armhole or neckline) edge exactly the same way. The only difference is where you insert the needle. Stitches are picked up 1 stitch in from the edge.

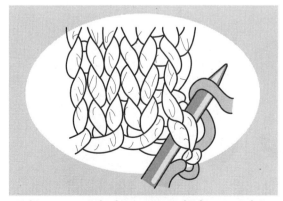

Picking up a stitch along a vertical edge, 1 stitch in from the edge.

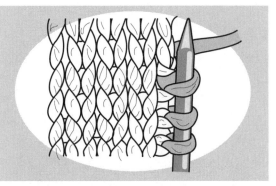

Stitches have been picked up along a vertical edge and are on the needle.

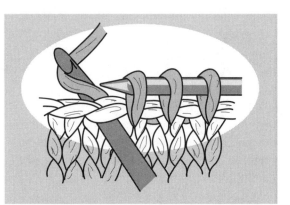

The picked up stitches are placed on the needle. Continue across the row, wrapping the yarn around the hook and pulling each stitch through.

Regardless of whether you're going horizontally, vertically, or diagonally, you pick up stitches with a hook the same way as with a needle. After you pull the new stitch through your work, place it on the needle. The pointed end of the needle should be facing left.

 Tangles _____

Be careful not to twist the stitch when you place the stitch on the needle! It doesn't matter whether you wrap the yarn around the crochet hook toward you or away from you to pull the stitch through. The half of the loop that is on your right as you pull it through should be the front loop on the needle. And don't use a hook larger than the needle, or you'll stretch your knitting.

If you pick up too many stitches in an area, as you continue to work those stitches they'll flare out; if you pick up too few, they'll bunch in. Although patterns will often tell you how many stitches to pick up, it's possible the pattern has an error. Or you might have worked more or fewer rows than the designer had intended (for any number of reasons), which will throw the numbers off.

There is a general rule of thumb for how many stitches to pick up. Along a horizontal edge, where you have bound off stitches, pick up stitch for stitch. Along a vertical or diagonal edge pick up 3 stitches for every 4 rows. If your work doesn't look right, rip it out and try again. You've worked hard to get this far; if the ribbing around your vest armhole has flared enough to fit two arms in there, you won't be happy with it and you likely will never wear it.

You might have to fudge with a stitch or two. Keep in mind that there might be a specific number of stitches you'll need in order to work the pattern stitch that will come next. So if you need an even number of stitches, make sure you don't end up with an odd number.

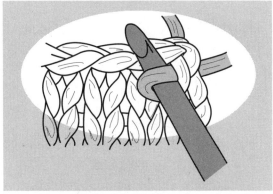

Using a crochet hook, pull a loop through the first stitch.

Buttonholes

There are a number of different ways to work buttonholes. Many patterns will tell you to make a simple buttonhole by working a yarn over and then knitting the next 2 stitches together. It makes a functional buttonhole but this method has a few problems. First, the size of the buttonhole is totally dependent on the yarn you're using and the needle size. The thinner the yarn and the smaller the needle, the tinier buttonhole you'll make. (What if you want a big, funky button instead?) Second, it's not very stable. Third, it can look sloppy, and details count!

Horizontal Buttonhole

This buttonhole can be as big or as small as you like. It requires 1 extra stitch—a 3-stitch buttonhole actually requires 4 stitches—so count your stitches between buttonholes accordingly when determining placement. Here's how to do it:

1. Work to where you want the buttonhole placed.
2. With yarn in front of work (toward you) slip the next stitch from the left to the right needle as if to purl.
3. Place the yarn at the back of your work (away from you) and leave it there.
4. Slip the next stitch from the left to the right needle as if to purl and pass the first slipped stitch over it. Continue to bind off in this way for the required number of stitches.
5. Slip the last bound off stitch back to the left needle.
6. Turn your work.
7. Place the yarn at the back of your work (away from you).

8. Cast on the same number of stitches that you bound off plus 1. The cable cast on method works well.
9. Turn your work.
10. With yarn at the back of your work (away from you) slip the first stitch from the right to the left needle. Knit these 2 stitches together.

Vertical Buttonhole

There are many uses for this type of buttonhole (the felted purse pattern in Chapter 22 uses a vertical buttonhole). Here's how you can make them, any length you wish:

1. Work to where you want the buttonhole.
2. Drop the yarn.
3. Continue across the row with a new, separate ball of yarn.
4. On the next row work across, drop the yarn, pick up the other ball of yarn, and continue across the row.
5. Continue until the buttonhole is the length you want.
6. Work all your stitches across the next row with a single ball of yarn, which will close the gap.

The Least You Need to Know

◆ Working through the back loop twists stitches.

◆ Stitches are usually slipped as if to purl but there are exceptions.

◆ Cables are stitches that are rearranged on your fabric and can twist right or left.

◆ You can pick up stitches using a knitting needle or a crochet hook.

◆ You can work buttonholes horizontally or vertically.

In This Chapter

- ◆ Adding stripes

- ◆ Slip stitch and color

- ◆ Knitting separate blocks of color with intarsia

- ◆ The basics of Fair Isle knitting

- ◆ A little deception through duplicate stitch

Chapter **10**

Making Your Knitting Colorful

Don't let color knitting intimidate you. You can work in multiple colors easily using several different methods. Some methods are as simple as working a row in a single color. Others are more challenging.

This chapter covers five ways to add color: four knitting techniques and an embroidery embellishment. So get ready to add a little color to your knitting!

On Your Mark, Get Set, Stripe

The simplest way to add color is to use stripes. As you might guess, to add stripes you change colors at the end of a row when flat knitting or at the end of a round when knitting in the round (you'll learn about knitting in the round in Chapter 11). You can have one predominant *main color* along with 1, 2, or even 30 *contrasting colors*. The sequences of colors you can use are infinite!

To add a stripe, stop knitting with the first color and begin knitting with the second color, leaving a tail you can weave in later. Do this the same way you add a new ball of yarn when you've run out.

Here are a couple extra pointers about stripes:

- ◆ If you are working stripes of 6 rows or less of one color before changing to the other color, you don't need to cut the yarn. Instead, carry it along the edge and twist the two colors around each other every other row.

- ◆ If you are striping an item such as a scarf or afghan in which both sides will show, do cut the yarn and weave it in on the wrong side near the edge. Loops of yarn between stripes will show and look messy.

Needle Talk

The **main color** (abbreviated MC) is the predominant color in a multicolor piece. The **contrasting color** (abbreviated CC) is an accent color used in a piece. You may have more than one contrasting color.

Slip Stitch and Color

Slip stitch patterns are an easy way to add color because you never knit with more than one color per row. These patterns can look complex, but they're really not. You'll mostly find them done in stockinette, but occasionally you will see a pattern that combines knits and purls, which results in a fabric that is both textured and colorful.

Needle Talk

Slip stitch patterns are worked with one color per row and involve knitting with one color and slipping stitches done in another color from a previous row.

To work a slip stitch pattern, some stitches from a previous row that were worked in a different color are slipped and other stitches are knit or purled with a new color. When you finish a row, you'll have stitches you've worked with the new color along with slipped stitches of a different color on your needle. Those slipped stitches will appear elongated. Don't be alarmed—that's how they're supposed to look!

Usually, no more than 3 stitches are slipped in a row. Be sure you keep the strand that results at the back of your work loose; otherwise your fabric will pucker. Stitches are always slipped as if to purl, unless the instructions tell you otherwise. Slip your stitches with your yarn at the wrong side of the work, whether the wrong side

is facing you or away from you (although an occasional pattern will tell you to have your yarn on the right side, which results in a pattern that looks woven).

Tangles

Slip stitch patterns tend to pull in, and you will find you have fewer stitches to the inch than you would otherwise. Be sure to check your gauge carefully when working these patterns!

Mosaic patterns are a particular type of slip stitch pattern. One color is used every two rows, and the second of these rows is a repeat of the first. They create geometric designs and usually have many stitches and rows per repeat.

Here's an easy slip stitch pattern to try. Use two colors of yarn of the same weight. This pattern is a multiple of 4, so to begin cast on any number of stitches that is divisible by 4 with color A. *With yarn in back* means the side that is facing away from you as you work. *With yarn in front* means the side that is facing you as you work.

Row 1 (right side): With color A, k.

Row 2: With color A, p.

Row 3: With color B, k3, *slip 2 with yarn in back, k2; rep from *, end k1.

Row 4: With color B, p3, *slip 2 with yarn in front, p2; rep from *, end p1.

Rows 5 and 6: With color A, rep rows 1 and 2.

Row 7: With color B, k1, *slip 2 with yarn in back, k2; rep from *, end slip 2, k1.

Row 8: With B, p1, *slip 2 with yarn in front, p2; rep from *, end slip 2, p1.

Repeat Rows 1 through 8.

Intarsia Knitting

In *intarsia* knitting, a separate ball of yarn—or bobbin of yarn—is used for each block of color to avoid the balls getting all tangled. The yarn is not carried across the back of the work.

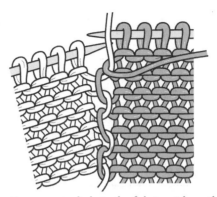

To prevent a hole in the fabric, pick up the new color from under the old color when beginning a new color block.

Needle Talk

Intarsia is a type of color knitting in which each block of color is knit from a separate ball or bobbin of yarn.

Wind yarn around the bobbin if you will be working with bobbins. Use one bobbin for each block of color. The bobbins can hang freely from the back of your work and as you need to use a color, you can unwind the amount that you need. If you need only a small amount of color, you can cut lengths of yarn (usually no longer than 36 inches).

When it's time to change yarn colors, on the wrong side of the piece, twist the new color around the old color by picking up the new color from under the old color. If you skip this step, you'll have a hole where the colors change.

On the wrong side (or purl side) follow these steps:

1. Purl with the first color until you are ready to work with the second color.
2. Let go of the strand of the first color.
3. Pick up the strand of the second color from under the first color.
4. Now purl using the second color.

When knitting in intarsia, you use the same method. The only difference is that you twist the colors at the *back* of your work before continuing knitting in a new color. If you change colors at the same point every row, you will work vertical stripes.

Pointers

Many color patterns are written in charts. To read a color chart, begin at the lower right and read the first row from right to left; the first row is the right side row. On the next row, read row 2 from left to right.

Fair Isle Knitting

Traditional *Fair Isle knitting*, the most complex of color techniques, is worked with two colors per row. At any time, you are using only one of those colors, so the other color is carried, or *stranded*, across the back of the piece. For this reason, if you look on the inside of a traditional Fair Isle piece, you'll see that strands of yarn run horizontally across the fabric on the wrong side.

You should not strand a color for more than 5 stitches. If the pattern calls for more than 5 stitches, you will need to twist or anchor it on the wrong side, to prevent long floats of yarn (which can get caught in fingers). Some people twist the colors every other stitch regardless of whether they are changing colors. Take care to ensure that the stranded yarn isn't pulled so tight that it puckers the front of the piece.

Needle Talk _____

Fair Isle knitting is a form of knitting in which two colors are used per row, and the color not in use is carried or stranded along the wrong side of the piece. Legend has it this form of knitting was brought to Fair Isle, in the North Sea off the coast of Scotland, by the shipwrecked sailors of the Spanish Armada in 1588.

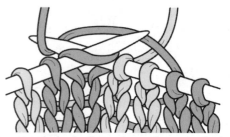

Changing from the first color to the second color.

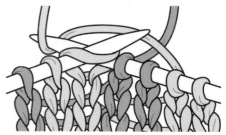

Changing from the second color back to the first color.

Stranding from the Right Side

Fair Isle patterns are worked in stockinette stitch, with the knit side being the right side. You keep the stranded yarn on the purl or wrong side. To work a Fair Isle pattern on the right or knit side of your piece, follow these steps:

1. Knit with the first color until you are ready to work with the second color.

2. Let go of the first color and pick up the second color. Notice in the following illustration the new color you are about to knit with is on top of the old color.

3. Now knit the next stitch with the second color. Be careful not to pull up the stranded yarn so tightly that the front of the piece puckers; let the stranded yarn rest easily in the back of the piece.

4. When you are finished knitting with the second color and are ready to knit again with the first, gently pull the first color across and knit with it. Again, be careful not to pull up the stranded yarn so tightly that the front of the piece puckers.

Stranding from the Wrong Side

Traditional Fair Isle is worked on circulars in stockinette so that you never need to purl. However, a nontraditional pattern might ask you to use this technique on straight needles. You purl in Fair Isle almost the same way that you knit; the only difference is when you're purling you're facing the stranded yarn. Here's what you do:

1. Purl with the first color until you are ready to work with the second color.

2. Let go of the first color and pick up the second color. Notice in the following illustration the new color you are about to purl with is on top of the old color.

3. Now purl the next stitch with the second color. Be careful not to pull up the stranded yarn so tightly that the front of the piece puckers; let the stranded yarn rest easily in the back of the piece.

4. When you are finished purling with the second color and are ready to purl again with
   the first, gently pull the first color across
   and purl with it. Again, be careful not to pull
   up the stranded yarn so tightly that the front
   of the piece puckers.

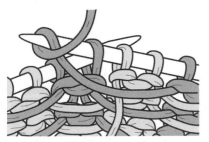

Changing from the first color to the second color.

Changing from the second color back to the first color.

Twisting Stitches

Suppose you need to strand the yarn for more
than 5 stitches. What then? Unless you take a
little extra precaution to catch or anchor the
yarn, you'll end up with cumbersome stranded
loops that can catch and pull. That extra precaution is called *twisting*. This method is similar to stranding; the only difference is that the
yarn is anchored every 2, 3, or 4 stitches by
twisting it around the working yarn.

To twist, you literally twist the color you are
not using around the color you are using. What
you are doing, in essence, is catching the yarn
in the back of the piece. Alternate between twisting clockwise and counterclockwise to prevent
the yarn from getting tangled.

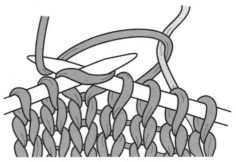

Twisting yarn on the right side.

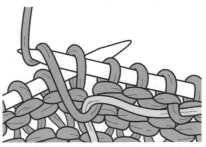

Twisting yarn on the wrong side.

Twisting yarn can create a problem when you
are carrying a dark color behind a light color. In
such cases, the twisted yarn can end up slightly
showing through on the right side at the place the
twist was made. The result is a fabric that doesn't
have completely clean, crisp color changes.

Duplicate Stitch

Duplicate stitch is an easy way to add color to
your knitting. Stockinette works best with
duplicate stitch. Use the same weight of yarn to
work the stitches that you knit with.

Needle Talk

Duplicate stitch is a technique in
which you embroider over knit stitches with
a different color. The result is a color pattern
that appears to be knit in, but is actually
embroidered.

To add duplicate stitch to a finished piece of knitting, follow these steps. If you are working a row of duplicate stitches, you will be working from right to left:

1. Thread a yarn needle with yarn about 20 inches long. Determine where on your knitting you will begin.

2. With the right side of work facing you, insert the needle back to front into the base of the stitch you will be stitching over. Leave a 4-inch yarn tail in the back of your work.

3. Insert the needle through the stitch on the row above, into the right and pulling it out the left.

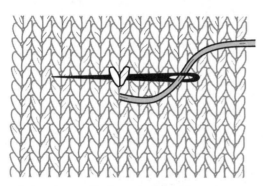

Insert the needle through the stitch on the row above, into the right and pulling it out the left.

4. Now insert the needle, front to back, into the base of the stitch where you began the duplicate stitch. You now have a stitch that appears to have been knit in a different color. If you will be working the stitch to the left of the one you just knit, insert the needle tip back to front into the base of the stitch to the left.

Tangles _____

Duplicate stitch should only be worked over small areas. To cover a large area, you might need to work over each stitch two or even three times; the result will be very bulky.

To work duplicate stitch vertically, you will be working from bottom to top. Begin the first stitch as you did for the horizontal row. However, when you are ready to work the second stitch bring the tip of the needle up through the base of the stitch directly above the stitch that you just worked. Here are the steps:

1. Thread a yarn needle with yarn about 20 inches long. Determine where on your knitting you will begin.

2. With the right side of work facing you, insert the needle, back to front, into the base of the stitch below the stitch you will be working over. Leave a 4-inch yarn tail in the back of your work.

3. Insert the needle through the stitch on the row above, into the right and pulling it out the left. This is the stitch you will be working over.

4. Now insert the needle, front to back, into the base of the stitch where you began the duplicate stitch. Bring it out above the horizontal strand in the middle of the stitch that is now covered.

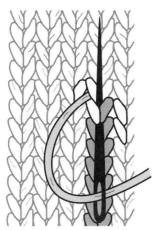

Complete a vertical duplicate stitch by threading the
yarn under the horizontal strand of the stitch.

The Least You Need to Know

◆ Color knitting often seems intimidating
   but is actually easy. One of the simplest
   ways to add color is with stripes.

◆ If you are knitting 6 or fewer rows in a
   stripe, you don't need to cut the yarn;
   carry it along the edge and twist the yarns
   together every other row.

◆ One color per row is used with slip stitch
   patterns.

◆ Intarsia knitting enables you to knit
   blocks of color.

◆ Fair Isle knitting is the most complex
   type of color knitting. Traditionally, two
   colors per row are used.

◆ You can use duplicate stitch to embroider
   color patterns on completed pieces.

In This Chapter

- ◆ The advantages of knitting in the round
- ◆ Twisted stitches
- ◆ Learning to join
- ◆ Knitting with circular needles
- ◆ Using double point needles

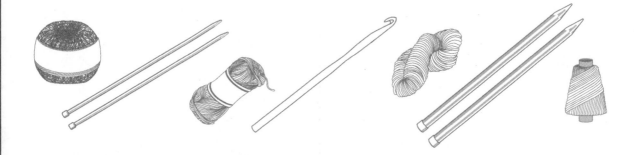

Chapter 11

Knitting in the Round

Knitting flat pieces of fabric by working back and forth on straight needles can limit you. For example, although you can knit a pair of socks back and forth using two needles and then sew up a seam, working the socks in a seamless tube is easier and more comfortable for the wearer ... stepping on a seam can be most annoying!

Knitting in the round allows you to work around in circles, forming seamless tubes. You still increase and decrease using the methods you already learned. Socks, hats, and sweaters are just a few of the things you can knit in the round.

In this chapter, you'll learn the benefits of knitting in the round. You'll also learn how to use circular and double point needles.

Why Go 'Round and 'Round?

Knitting in the round is sometimes called circular knitting. You can knit in the round using circular or double point needles; which you will use depends on the number of stitches and the circumference of the piece.

Knitting in the round has several advantages over flat knitting. Some knitters all but refuse to work pieces flat. Although you can knit many wonderful projects for years to come on straight needles, knitting in the round does have these benefits:

◆ **You get to use the knit stitch more.**
Some people don't like purling or find it
takes just a little longer to purl than it
does to knit. When knitting stockinette
on straight needles, you knit a row and
purl the next. When knitting stockinette
in the round, every round is knit. You'll
still need to purl while working in the
round if the pattern calls for it, though.

Pointers

To work garter stitch in the round,
knit one round and purl the next round. If you
were working back and forth on straight
needles, you would knit every row.

◆ **Finishing is minimal.** Let's say you're
making a sweater. If you knit the pieces
flat, you'll eventually need to sew up at
least six seams: two arm seams, two joining seams of arms and body, and the left
and right body seams. Now look at a
sweater knit in the round. You need to
sew up just two tiny seams; the rest of
your time is spent knitting.

◆ **You can see how a piece will fit.** Unlike
straight needles, circular needles are flexible. As you're working, you can slip into a
pullover sweater knit in the round and see
how it fits.

◆ **Some pieces are simply constructed
better when made in seamless tubes.**
Socks, mittens, and the necks on turtle-
necks are all more ideally made in a
tube without a seam to either irritate the
wearer or break the flow of the knitted
fabric.

So now that you see how circular knitting
might be beneficial, let's work on learning to
knit in the round.

Beware of Twisted Stitches

When knitting back and forth, if your cast on
stitches are twisted around the needle, they'll
right themselves when you knit the first row. In
circular knitting, if you twist the stitches around
the needle, they'll remain twisted and eventually you'll have to rip out and start again.

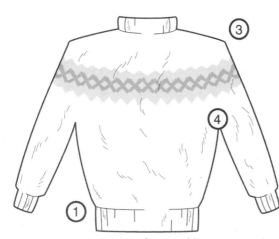

1. Body is knit in a tube.

2. Sleeves are knit in tubes.

3. Sleeves and body are joined on
   one circular needle and yoke is knit.

4. Small seams at underarms joining
   body and sleeves are sewn.

Knitting in the round lets you spend more time knitting than sewing.

Always make sure your stitches aren't twisted when knitting in the round before you begin the first row, whether you are knitting with circulars or double points. All the stitches should be facing inward, toward the middle; if some are facing inward and others aren't, then the stitches are twisted. With your hand, move them so they are all facing the same way. (There's more about twisted stitches in the next chapter, where we discuss common knitting gaffes.)

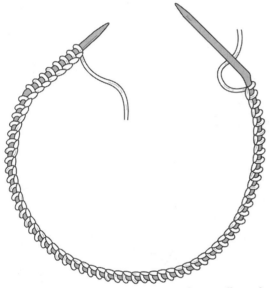

These cast on stitches are on a circular needle and are not twisted.

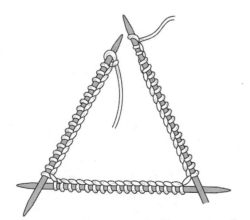

These cast on stitches are on double point needles and are not twisted.

Joining

When working back and forth on straight needles, you work in rows. When knitting in the round, you work in rounds. You don't turn your work around and knit back with the wrong side facing you when knitting in the round. Instead, you form a circle and work with the right side facing you.

After you have cast on the stitches, you *join* them together to form a circle. You will find that patterns often simply instruct you to "join." To join, knit (or purl if that's what the first stitch of the round calls for) the first stitch on the left. Give it a slight tug to be sure it's tight. The last stitch you cast on is now joined with the first stitch of the new round.

Here's another way to join that helps to close the gap or "ladder" that sometimes forms at the point where you've joined:

1. Cast on 1 extra stitch than the pattern calls for.

2. When you're ready to join, slip the stitch on the end of the right side to the left side.

3. Knit the first 2 stitches together. You can also do this on the second round instead after working all the stitches, including the extra one, on round one.

Knitting with a Circular Needle

Some knitters never learn to knit with circular needles because it looks too scary. But it's not any more difficult to knit with circulars in the round than it is to knit with straight needles. There is really only one new skill to learn: how to join the circle.

When knitting in the round with a circular needle, you must use the appropriate needle length. When you knit on straight needles, you can use all or part of the needle you need (such as using 14-inch needles to knit a scarf 7 inches wide). When knitting with circular needles, the needle length must be the same size or slightly shorter than the item you're knitting. If it's too short, you could have trouble keeping stitches on the needle. If it's too long, you'll stretch your fabric. You may need to change to needles of different lengths—or even double point needles—as you increase or decrease.

To knit in the round with a circular needle, follow these steps:

1. Cast on the number of stitches required by the pattern.

2. Lay the circular needle on a flat surface and make sure the stitches are all facing inward (toward the middle of the circle). Check carefully to make sure the cast on row is straight and that none of the stitches are twisted around the needle. The tail of the yarn should be on the left side, and the yarn coming from the skein should be on the right. If you're knitting left handed, reverse these instructions.

3. Pick up the needle and place a stitch marker on the right side. This marks the beginning of the round. You're now ready to begin knitting.

4. Knit the first stitch from the left side of the needle and move it to the right. You've now joined the circle. Give the stitch a tug to make sure it's nice and tight. Knit around the circle.

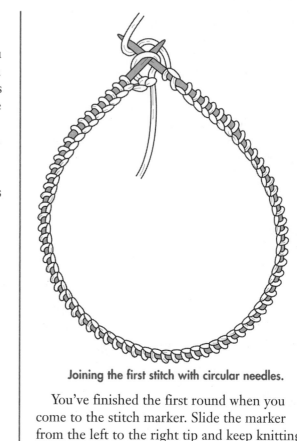

Joining the first stitch with circular needles.

You've finished the first round when you come to the stitch marker. Slide the marker from the left to the right tip and keep knitting. That's it! You're knitting in the round.

You can also use circular needles to knit flat pieces. When you're knitting extremely large pieces, such as afghans, the stitches won't comfortably fit on straight needles; you'll need the extra length that a circular needle provides. You can use any length you choose, as long as it's long enough to hold all the stitches. To knit flat pieces with a circular needle, pretend the two ends of the circular needle are two straight needles. Work a row; then slide the stitches to the other end. Turn your work as you normally would.

Many knitters find the weight of the piece is more balanced when knit with circulars and use them for all their projects, regardless of whether they need the extra needle length circulars provide.

Knitting with Double Point Needles

You may never need to knit on double point needles. If you'd like to knit socks or a hat in the round (where you'll need to use them toward the crown where there aren't enough stitches to continue on circulars), you'll need to learn.

When you begin, you will probably feel like you're all thumbs with needles falling all over the place. Although knitting on double point needles isn't as impossible as it might look, it can be a challenge for new knitters. Be patient as you add this new skill to your knitting repertoire. It gets easier after you've knit the first couple of rounds … really!

Use bamboo double points to begin; they are much less slippery and the yarn will grip the needles. If you use aluminum double points, the stitches are much more likely to slip off the needles and leave you frustrated.

Pointers

Double point needles come in sets of four or five. Always buy a set of five if you can so that you will have four or five needles to use of the same size, depending on what the pattern calls for.

Here's how to knit with double point needles:

1. Cast on all the stitches onto one needle. If you are making a piece small enough so that all the stitches fit onto one double point needle, go ahead and use one. Otherwise, you can cast onto a straight, single point needle of the same size.

2. Determine how many needles you'll be using (your pattern will tell you). You can knit using either a set of four or a set of five needles. If you use a set of four, you'll have stitches on three needles and keep one needle free. If you use a set of five, you'll have stitches on four needles and keep one needle free.

3. A pattern will generally tell you at this point to divide the stitches over three or four needles and figure out the math for you. Let's say you cast on 60 stitches and are using a set of 4 needles in which 3 needles will hold the stitches (you'll be knitting with the fourth needle), you know that you need to have 20 stitches on each needle:

   60 (total stitches) ÷ 3 (number of needles holding stitches) = 20 (stitches on each needle)

4. Evenly divide the stitches by slipping 20 stitches onto each needle.

5. Lay the needles on a flat surface in a triangular shape. If you're using a set of five needles, with four needles holding the stitches, lay the needles in a diamond shape. The top of the triangle or diamond should be the two needles where you began to cast on and where you ended; this is where you'll begin knitting. The tail of the yarn should be on the left side, and the yarn coming from the skein should be on the right. If you're knitting left handed, reverse these instructions.

6. Check carefully to make sure the cast on row is straight and that none of the stitches are twisted around the needle.

7. Using the free needle, knit the first stitch from the left side of the triangle. Pull the yarn fairly tightly; the first stitch joining double point needles is sloppy unless you tug the yarn. You have now joined the circle of knitting.

Knitting the first stitch to join the round.

8. Continue knitting the stitches on the left needle to the spare needle on the right. When you finish knitting all the stitches on that needle, you'll be holding an empty needle in your left hand and you will have completed one round!

9. Transfer the empty needle to your right hand and knit all the stitches from the next needle.

10. Keep on knitting the stitches from each needle onto the spare needle, knitting round and round. The tail coming from where the stitches were first joined shows you where each round starts; you might want to stick a safety pin at this spot so that you can quickly see where the round begins. Keep moving the safety pin up as the knitted fabric grows.

Take special care to knit the first and last stitch of each needle tightly; otherwise, you could end up with a visible ladder of loose stitches running up the fabric where the needles join. To prevent this problem, knit all the stitches on each needle plus one of the stitches on the next needle onto the spare needle. This way you won't have a consistent spot where the needles join, so you won't have a line running up the fabric. If you do this, slip a stitch marker onto the spot where the round begins, just as you would when working on a circular needle.

Pretty neat, isn't it? Now you know how to knit using double points!

The Least You Need to Know

- Knitting in the round lets you create tubes or flat circles of fabric.
- Be sure your cast on stitches aren't twisted before knitting the first row.
- To join, all you do is knit or purl the first stitch.
- You must use the correct needle length when knitting in the round on a circular needle.
- When knitting on double point needles, knit the first and last stitch of each needle tightly to prevent a seam from running up the fabric.

In This Chapter

- ◆ Stopping mistakes before they happen
- ◆ How to turn twisted stitches
- ◆ Catching dropped stitches
- ◆ Correcting sloppy stitches
- ◆ Let 'er rip!

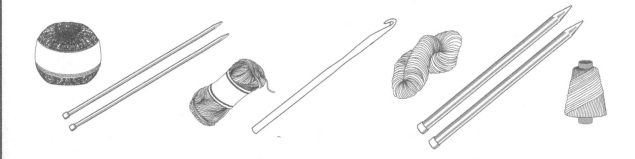

Chapter 12

Correcting Common Knitting Gaffes

We all make mistakes. Even in knitting, one of the most relaxing and enjoyable of pursuits, mistakes occur that can dampen your enthusiasm for the craft.

Fortunately, most knitting *faux pas* are minor and easily correctable. This chapter walks you through the best ways to prevent the most common mistakes, teaches you what to do when mistakes occur, and helps you determine when it's time to forget correcting and just start over. As you learn any new craft, you need to feel comfortable and in control. Don't be afraid to make or to correct mistakes. Mistakes are often how we learn best.

Taking the Bull by the Horns: Preventing Mistakes

Some of the most common knitting errors are due to not watching what you're doing. As you become adept at knitting, you won't even have to look at your knitting. You'll be able to multitask: talk, watch television, listen to music, and more while knitting.

When you're first learning to knit, however, you have to be much more conscious of what your hands are doing. You can usually avoid common mistakes if you pay close attention to the task at hand. Set aside time when you can knit without distractions.

In addition, count your stitches after every completed row. Sure, this exercise seems tedious, but you'll immediately know whether you lost or added a stitch. If you find you've lost or added stitches, look over the row one stitch at a time. Check to see whether a stitch has been dropped from the needle or the needle contains a loop of yarn that isn't a stitch.

Turning Twisted Stitches

Twisted stitches sounds like the name of a 1980s rock band, doesn't it? In knitting, twisted stitches are exactly what the name says: stitches that get twisted on your needle. You generally get twisted stitches one of two ways: by knitting or purling into the back loop of a stitch instead of the front or by incorrectly unraveling stitches (which you'll learn about later in this chapter).

Needle Talk _____

Twisted stitches are stitches that are twisted on your needle. Because the knitted loops are twisted, the stitches are tighter than correctly knit stitches and don't open when stretched.

To correct twisted stitches, use the point of the needle that the stitch isn't on to slide the stitch off the needle. Untwist it and place it back on the needle. Knitting or purling into the back loop of this stitch will also untwist it.

Untwisting a twisted stitch.

Catching Dropped Stitches

Probably the most common mistake in knitting is losing or *dropping* a stitch. You start out with 20 stitches on your needle and after a period of time, you find you have only 19. Being an

optimist, you might shrug and decide to just add back a couple stitches and be on your way. The trouble is, a dropped stitch has a tendency to run. Think of what pantyhose do when they get a small hole; your knitted items will do the same. Now think how wonderful it would be if you could close up the pantyhose hole before it ran. When you're knitting, you can.

Needle Talk _____

Dropped stitches are stitches that accidentally slide off the needle during knitting. If left unfixed, dropped stitches can run down through the knitted fabric.

Picking Up a Dropped Knit Stitch in the Row Below

Let's say you're working in stockinette stitch (knit 1 row, purl 1 row) and notice you have a dropped stitch in the row below. What now? Fortunately, you can use your knitting needles to salvage the stitch before it runs farther down the knitted piece. Here's what you do to pick up a dropped knit stitch:

1. Knit across the row to the position of the dropped stitch. The horizontal strand of yarn from the row above the dropped stitch should be behind the stitch.

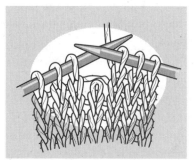

Locate the dropped stitch and knit to that point.

2. Insert the right needle from front to back into the dropped stitch and the horizontal strand of yarn. The strand of yarn should be to the left of the dropped stitch.

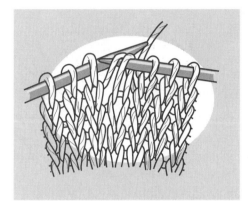

Insert the needle into the dropped stitch and the strand of yarn above the stitch.

3. Insert the left needle from back to front into the dropped stitch. Then lift the stitch over the strand of yarn and off the needle. Now the corrected stitch is on the right needle.

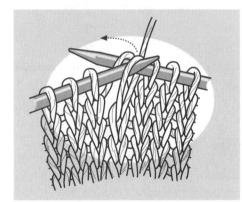

Pass the dropped stitch over the strand of yarn.

4. Slip the corrected stitch from the right needle to the left needle.

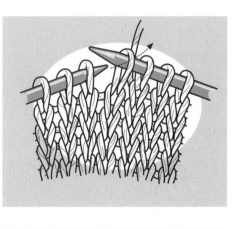

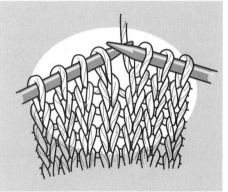

Move the stitch to the left needle and keep knitting.

Knit away. The dropped stitch is now history; let us never speak of it again!

Picking Up a Dropped Purl Stitch in the Row Below

Picking up a dropped purl stitch is a lot like picking up a knit stitch; you just need to reverse a few things. Here's how:

1. Purl across the row to the position of the dropped stitch. The horizontal strand of yarn from the row above the dropped stitch should be in front of the stitch.

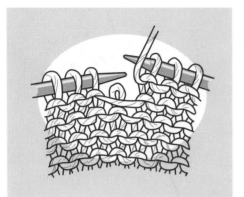

Locate the dropped stitch and purl to that point.

2. Insert the right needle from back to front into the dropped stitch and the horizontal strand of yarn. The strand of yarn should be to the left of the dropped stitch.

Insert the needle into the dropped stitch and the strand of yarn above the stitch.

3. Insert the left needle from front to back into the dropped stitch. Then lift the stitch over the strand of yarn on the needle and off the needle. Now the corrected stitch is on the right needle.

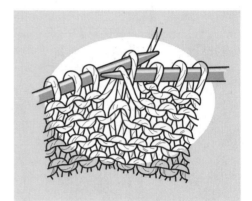

Pass the dropped stitch over the horizontal strand of yarn.

4. Slip the corrected stitch from the right needle to the left needle.

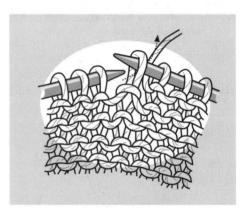

Move the stitch to the left needle and keep purling.

That's all there is to it!

Pointers

Some patterns call for you to drop stitches intentionally. First, you knit an entire piece. On the last row, you drop specific stitches—maybe every tenth stitch. The result is a lacelike pattern running vertically through the piece sometimes called a *condo stitch* or *drop stitch*.

How to Become a Major Pick Up Artist

At times, a dropped stitch goes unnoticed for several rows before you discover that you have a problem. When you notice the mistake, attach a safety pin just under the dropped stitch so you can identify the area.

Although you can use a knitting needle and laboriously follow the stitch-saving steps in the previous sections, you'll find the work goes much faster and easier with a crochet hook. To pick up knit stitches, insert a crochet hook, front to back, into the dropped stitch. The horizontal strands of yarn should be behind the stitch. Now use the hook to catch the horizontal line of yarn above the dropped stitch, and pull this yarn through the stitch. Continue working the stitch up the ladder of yarn until you get to the end.

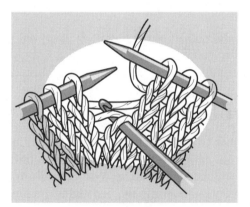

Using a crochet hook to correct dropped knit stitches.

To pick up stitches when purling, follow the same steps as for knitting, but insert the hook from back to front. The horizontal strands of yarn should be in front of the stitch.

To pick up a dropped stitch when working garter stitch (knit every row), alternate the knitting and purling instructions. Make sure you use the knitting technique when the row is smooth and the purling technique when the row is bumpy.

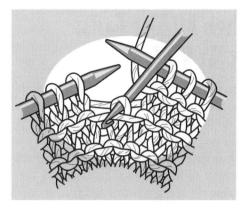

Using a crochet hook to fix a dropped stitch on a garter stitch piece.

Pointers

Stitches can be uneven if you have to pick up a dropped stitch over a large number of rows. Sometimes it helps to gently pull the knitting horizontally and vertically.

Fixing Sloppy Stitches

At some point you're going to stop knitting, hold up your piece to admire it, and notice a hole in the middle. You've checked; it's not a dropped stitch. It's just a much larger (dare we say *sloppier?*) stitch than the others in the piece. What to do?

Simple: Grab your spare knitting needle and gently poke into the stitches surrounding the larger stitch. You're trying to slightly stretch those stitches to take up yarn and even out all the stitches. After a minute or so of adjusting surrounding stitches, you'll never know the larger stitch was there.

When All Else Fails: Let 'Er Rip!

Some mistakes are just too time consuming—or impossible—to fix. For example, suppose you're working a cable and find one row in which you forgot to work the pattern. If you can live with it, do. If you determine that you can't bear to look at your knitting and see that mistake, get ready to learn the fine art of unraveling.

Taking Out Just a Few Stitches

If the area you need to unravel is on the same row or one row below, you'll want to pull the stitches out one stitch at a time. But be careful: If you don't insert the needle into a stitch you want to unravel correctly, you'll wind up with a twisted stitch. To unravel either knit or purl stitches one at a time, follow these steps:

1. Insert the left needle into the last stitch worked on the right needle from front to back.
2. Pull out the right needle.
3. Gently tug the yarn to unravel the stitch.
4. The unraveled stitch will now be on the left needle. Continue to unravel as many stitches as necessary.

Going Wild!

Let's say the mistake isn't 3 stitches down the needle but 3 inches down the knitted fabric. Heartbreaking as undoing all this hard work can be, you're about to be introduced to the most cathartic move in knitting: ripping out rows. *Ripping out* means unraveling or pulling out stitches. You rip out when you find a mistake you need to undo or when you don't like the look of the knitted fabric.

To unravel several rows of stitches, first use a safety pin to mark the offending row. Then slide the knitting off the needles and pull the yarn with wild abandon. (Feels good, doesn't it?) When you've unraveled to the row above the problem row, slow down. Use the procedure in the preceding section to unravel the stitches one by one and place them back on the needle. Wind the unraveled yarn back on your ball, take a deep breath, and proceed.

Yarn Spinning

Knitters on the Internet have their own lingo for ripping out stitches. *Tink* (*knit* spelled backward) refers to taking out stitches one at a time. *Frogging* refers to ripping out large batches of knitting ("rip it! rip it!" sounds like "ribbit! ribbit!").

Extra, Extra!

Another common knitting gaffe is to end up with too many stitches on a row. If you find that one row is a bit hefty, look carefully at your work to identify the problem. Then mark the trouble spot with a safety pin. Chances are you grabbed an extra loop of yarn and didn't notice the problem until you had knit several rows.

To correct the mistake, you'll need to unravel your work back to the problem stitch. Remove that extra stitch. Count the stitches to make sure the number is correct. Wind the yarn back onto the ball and start knitting again.

The Least You Need to Know

◆ Many knitting mistakes are either avoidable or easily fixable.

◆ Use a crochet hook to catch stitches you dropped several rows back.

◆ You can disguise a stitch that is too loose and big by evening out the stitches around it.

◆ Although it can be frustrating to lose your hard work, unraveling several rows of knitting can be wonderfully cathartic!

In This Part

13 Getting Started: Basic Crochet Stitches

14 Shaping Your Work

15 Beyond the Basics: Adding to Your Crochet Repertoire

16 Crocheting Around

17 Colorful Crochet

Part **3**

Learning to Crochet

Welcome to the world of crocheting! In this part, you'll learn all the basic stitches that can be used alone or combined to give your projects a unique look. We'll also take a look at turning chains and their importance.

Once you have the basics down, you'll become skilled at how to work in rounds, crochet with different colors, change the look of your stitches by inserting the hook various ways, and increase and decrease.

And if you want to add to your basic crochet repertoire, you'll find lessons on Afghan crochet and filet crochet.

In This Chapter

- ◆ First things first: holding the crochet hook
- ◆ Making a foundation chain
- ◆ The basic crochet stitches
- ◆ Working the next row
- ◆ Keep practicing!
- ◆ Left-handed crochet principles

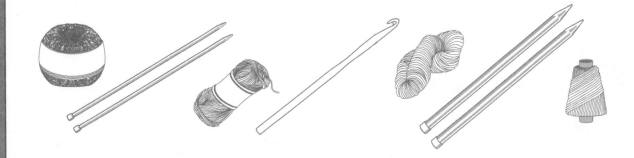

Getting Started: Basic Crochet Stitches

In this chapter, you'll learn the skills that are the foundation of all basic crochet. Following step-by-step illustrations and instructions, you'll learn how to make a slip knot, a chain, and different crochet stitches. And if you're a southpaw, you won't be left out; there's a left-handed section for you.

So get out the yarn. Pick up your crochet hook. Sit down, and let's get going!

Holding the Hook

Crochet is a French word meaning "hook," and like all needlecrafts, it begins with getting a proper grip on your tools. There are two easy ways to hold a crochet hook. Try them and decide which feels best for you.

Practice each of these simple grips shown in the following illustrations. You'll find one of the positions to be the more comfortable. Be prepared to switch positions, though. You won't know how they really feel until you actually start to crochet.

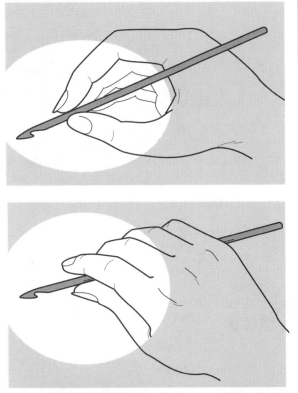

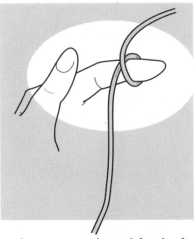

Loop the yarn around your left index finger.

You can hold the hook one of two ways. Either position and lightly grip your hook in your hand as you would hold a pencil, or hold the hook as you would grip a spoon if you were stirring something thick.

Making a Slip Knot

With the crochet hook comfortably in your hand, you're ready to begin working with the yarn. First, make a *slip knot* to attach the yarn to your hook. Here's a simple way to make a slip knot.

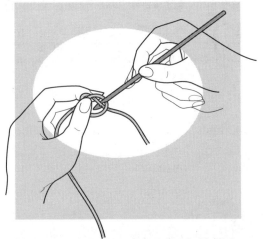

Slip the yarn from your finger and hold the loop between your thumb and index finger.

 **Needle Talk**

A **slip knot** is a knot that slips easily along the cord on which it's tied.

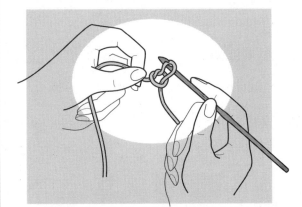

Use the crochet hook, held in your right hand, to draw the loop up and around the hook.

Finally, gently pull each of the ends in opposite directions. This tightens the knot and makes it smaller. It's that simple!

> **Pointers** _____
>
> The slip knot never counts as a stitch. It is simply a way to attach the yarn securely to the hook.

Feeding the Yarn

Now that you've made a slip knot and secured the yarn to the hook, you'll want to practice holding the yarn. It's important that you control how the yarn is fed into your work.

How you hold the yarn is an individual choice. However, it's important not only that you're comfortable, but that you have control over it. Hold the yarn taut enough to be able to *hook* (catch) the yarn with the barb of the crochet hook, but not so tightly that you can't get the hook through your stitches. With practice, you'll get a feel for tension.

For practice, select wool yarn that crochets to 4 or 4.5 stitches to the inch (commonly called *worsted weight*) and size I-9 (5mm) hook. Wool is very elastic and forgiving; you will find it much easier to work with than something like cotton, which is not elastic at all. Choose a smooth yarn, not a novelty yarn full of loops or eyelashes. Those look pretty and you can crochet with them soon enough but using them will only confuse you as you begin.

Take the yarn with your left hand. With the palm of your left hand facing up, thread the yarn through your fingers. Practice holding the yarn so that it can flow through your fingers. Moving your index finger up and down lets you increase or decrease the tautness of the yarn. You'll begin to find a rhythm as you work, and soon the movement will feel very natural.

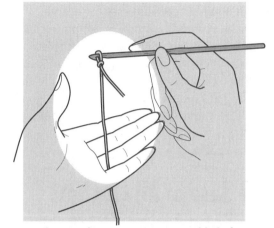

Grasp the yarn between your ring and little fingers, 4 inches or so from the hook.

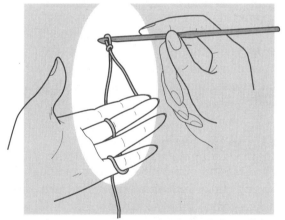

Draw the yarn toward you—from your little and ring fingers—threaded over your middle finger and leading under your index finger.

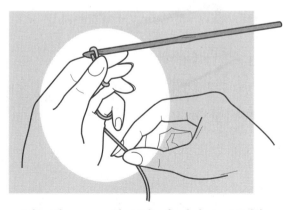

Adjust the yarn so that it lies firmly but not tightly around your fingers.

Not all techniques are easy for everyone. Here's an alternative if you're having trouble wrapping the yarn around all your fingers: Instead of wrapping the yarn, let it flow behind your index finger, in front of your middle and ring fingers, and back behind your little finger. You've now attached the yarn to the hook, and you're holding the yarn in your left hand. It's time to crochet.

The Base of All Crochet: The Foundation Chain

If you were constructing a building, you would need to start with a solid foundation. Crocheting is no different. You start with a *foundation chain*, which is a row of chains that serves as the base of your crocheting—the foundation from which a piece is built. It is this base that holds your stitches and all succeeding rows.

Making the Chain

The following illustrations walk you through the process for making a foundation chain. To make a chain, bring the yarn over the hook and pull it through the slip loop on your hook. Catching your yarn with the hook is called a *yarn over*. Initially, it might feel awkward. With practice it will become natural.

Needle Talk

A **yarn over** (abbreviated yo) is the movement of passing the hook under the yarn and then catching the yarn with the hook. This movement is fundamental to all crochet stitches.

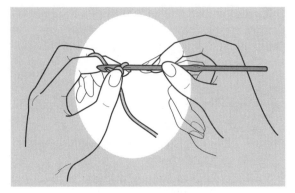

To start a chain, grasp the short end of the yarn, right below the slip knot.

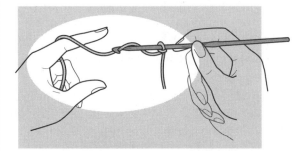

Pass the hook under and over the yarn from back to front. This is called a yarn over.

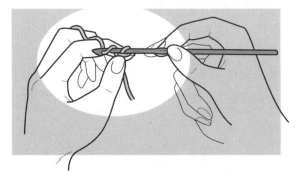

With your crochet hook, catch the yarn. Then pull the hook and yarn through the slip loop on your hook to the shank. The shank determines the size of each chain stitch. You just made your first chain stitch!

Making a row of chain stitches.

Now make another *chain stitch*, and then another, and another. As you work, keep moving your thumb up and hold the yarn right below your hook. It becomes second nature as you practice.

Needle Talk

A **chain stitch** is made each time you catch the yarn with the hook and draw it through the loop on the hook. Think of it as a link in a chain.

Try to make your chains the same size. The chain should be the same size as the shank of your hook. If you make them too tight, you will not be able to insert the hook into the chains to make stitches later. If you have problems with this, use a larger hook to make your foundation chain.

Crochet patterns begin by telling you how many chains to make. It's important to understand how to count the number of chains you are making. Let's say the pattern tells you to chain 20. Begin with a slip knot, yarn over, and pull the yarn through 20 times to make 20 chains. You will have 1 extra loop left on your hook at the end, but that is not a chain. You will use that loop to make the first stitch of the next row.

Heads or Tails?

It's important to distinguish the chain's front from its back. Always count your chain stitches on the front. You will work into the front of the chain stitches as you build on this foundation in the next row.

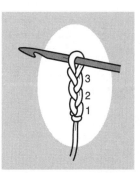

Count chains from the front of the chain. Begin counting with the first complete stitch above the slip knot.

The chain's back has small bumpy loops.

Basic Stitches

The stitches in this section are the basis for almost every crochet technique, no matter how fancy. You will soon learn them by heart and you won't need to refer to instructions. They are all similar—it's just a matter of how many yarn overs are done and how many times yarn is pulled through loops.

You begin by working into a particular chain of the foundation chain, depending on the stitch. This is to accommodate the differing heights of the various kinds of crochet stitches. Always follow the pattern directions; they will tell you where to start your work on the foundation chain.

Whether you're working into the foundation chain to begin or into actual stitches as you will after the first foundation row (more about that later), all these stitches you are about to learn are worked exactly the same way.

Single Crochet (sc)

Single crochet is truly the most basic of all the crochet stitches. It's a short stitch that makes a dense fabric. Make sure that the front side of the chain is facing you.

Count to the 2nd chain from the hook. Insert the hook, front to back, under the 2 top loops of the foundation chain.

Yarn over hook (from the back toward you as shown), and pull through those top loops to draw up a new loop.

You now have 2 loops on your hook.

Yarn over again and pull through both loops on your hook. You now have 1 loop left on your hook and have just made your first single crochet!

Needle Talk

Single crochet (abbreviated sc) is the most basic of crochet stitches. To complete a single crochet, insert the hook through a chain (or stitch); yarn over; pull the loop through the chain (or stitch); yarn over again; and pull through both loops on the hook.

Half Double Crochet (hdc)

Half double crochet is slightly taller than a single crochet. To accommodate the taller stitch, you'll now work your first stitch into the 3rd chain. This stitch is the first of the basic stitches that requires a yarn over before you insert the hook. Again, be sure the front side of the foundation chain is facing you.

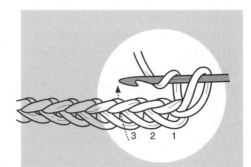

Yarn over and insert the hook, front to back, under the 2 top loops of the 3rd chain from the hook. Yarn over and pull the yarn through to draw up a loop.

There are now 3 loops on your hook. Yarn over
and pull through all 3 loops.

Needle Talk

Half double crochet (abbreviated
hdc) is a cross between a single crochet and
a double crochet. To complete a half double
crochet, begin with a yarn over; insert the
hook into a stitch; yarn over and pull through
the stitch; do another yarn over, and pull
through the 3 loops on your hook.

Double Crochet (dc)

Double crochet is another basic stitch. As with a
half double crochet stitch, you start with a yarn
over before you insert the hook. Because a double crochet has one more yarn over than a half
double crochet, it's taller and creates a somewhat open fabric. Because it's taller, you'll work
your first stitch into the 4th chain from the
hook this time.

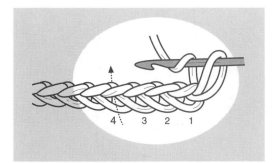

Yarn over and insert the hook, front to back, under
the top 2 loops of the 4th chain from the hook.

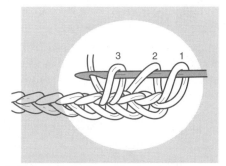

Pull through the loop. You have 3 loops on
your hook. Yarn over again.

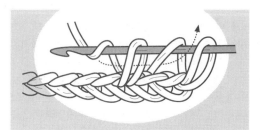

Pull through the 2 loops closest to the hook's
point as shown. Two loops remain on the hook.

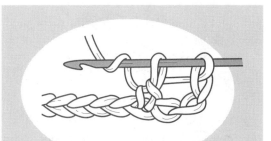

Yarn over once more, and pull through the
2 remaining loops.

You now have a single loop remaining on the hook.

Needle Talk

Double crochet (abbreviated dc) is a common stitch. To make a double crochet, begin with a yarn over; then insert the hook into a stitch; yarn over and pull through the loop; yarn over and pull through 2 loops; yarn over and pull through the remaining loops.

Triple Crochet (trc)

Triple crochet, the last of the basic stitches, is the tallest and creates an open fabric. This stitch starts with 2 yarn overs before you insert the hook. Working this stitch is similar to working double crochet; you just need to work one more yarn over. As the tallest stitch, you'll now work into the 5th chain from the hook.

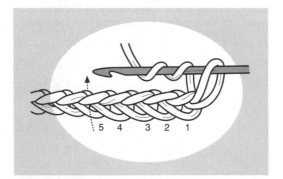

Yarn over and insert the hook, front to back, under the top 2 loops of the 5th chain from the hook. Pull through the loop. You now have 4 loops on the hook.

Needle Talk

Triple crochet (abbreviated trc) is the last of the basic stitches. To make this stitch, yarn over the hook twice; insert the hook into a stitch; yarn over again and pull through the first 2 loops (the 2 closest to the point); yarn over again and pull through the next 2 loops; yarn over one last time and pull through the remaining 2 loops.

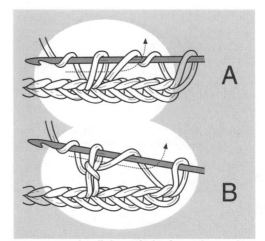

Yarn over and pull through the first 2 loops closest to the point of the hook; then yarn over again and pull through the next 2 loops closest to the point of the hook.

Two loops remain on the hook. Yarn over one last time and pull through both loops.

One loop remains on your hook.

Slip Stitch (sl st)

Slip stitch is the smallest of all the crochet stitches. It is used mainly for joining (such as a ring or seams) and moving across existing stitches without adding stitches or height to them. It's also an ideal stitch to use as a finishing touch because it makes a nice, firm edge.

Because you already know how to do a chain stitch, you know how to make a slip stitch. The only difference is that with a slip stitch, you insert your hook into a foundation chain or stitch.

To make a slip stitch, insert your hook, front to back, under the 2 top loops of a chain or stitch. Yarn over, and in one motion pull through the chain or stitch and the loop on your hook. One loop remains on the hook.

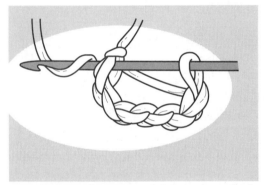

To use a slip stitch to join a ring, insert your hook under the 2 top loops of the first foundation chain, and then yarn over.

 Needle Talk

Slip stitch (abbreviated sl st) is much like a chain stitch except that you insert the hook into a foundation chain or stitch.

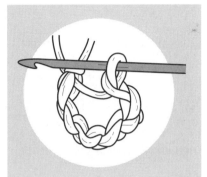

Pull the hook through the chain and the loop on the hook. One loop remains on the hook, and you have now completed a slip stitch and made a ring.

The Next Row

At some point you will have worked into all your foundation chains and you'll be ready to begin the next row (we'll be making some examples later in this chapter). It's not much different from what you've already learned—all the stitches are done exactly the same way. Instead of working into the 2 top loops of a chain, you'll insert your hook into both loops of a stitch you've already made.

Insert your hook into both loops of a stitch.

The fabric you create will have a *right side* and a *wrong side*. The right side is the side that will show on the outside, while the wrong side will not. Think of wearing a shirt or sweater inside out. Your pattern will always specify which is the right side and which is the wrong side (although many times it's obvious). Sometimes the first row you work will be the wrong side and sometimes the right side.

Needle Talk

The **right side** (abbreviated RS) of crocheted fabric is the side that will be showing, such as the outside of a sweater. The **wrong side** (abbreviated WS) is the side that faces inward.

Turning Chains

There are just a few more things to understand. To prepare to begin a new row, you make *turning chains*. When you come to the end of a row, you need to work a certain number of chain stitches to bring your work to the height of the next row. This height is determined by the kind of stitch you will be using on that row: the taller the stitch, the greater the number of extra chains you'll have to make.

Needle Talk

Turning chains are extra chain stitches you make at the end of each row to accommodate the height of the stitch of the next row.

Different stitches are different heights, and turning chains enable you accommodate for the stitch height.

The following table shows the number of turning chains needed to accommodate different crochet stitches.

Stitch Name	Turning Chains Needed
Slip stitch	1
Single crochet	1
Half double crochet	2
Double crochet	3
Triple crochet	4

You've really already learned about turning chains. Remember, you worked a single crochet into the 2nd chain, a half double crochet into the 3rd, a double crochet into the 4th, and a triple crochet into the 5th? This was to accommodate the height of each type of stitch. Turning chains at the end of a row accomplish the same thing.

If you forget to make turning chains at the end of a row, you will find yourself in a real pickle. The ends of your work will squash down because there won't be room for the row of stitches. To fix the problem, carefully unravel your work back to the end of the proceeding row and make the turning chains.

The First or the Second Stitch?

Where you begin the first stitch on the next row depends on how many chains you just made for your turning chain, which in turn depends on what kind of stitch will begin this new row. If the first stitch of this new row is a single crochet (or a slip stitch), you will chain 1 and *turn*. Turn means to literally turn your work around (usually you turn at the end of a row). You'll now be working on the other side. Then work a single crochet into the 2 top loops of the very first stitch. This is the "base" of the turning chain you just worked or the first stitch of the previous row.

Work a single crochet or slip stitch into the first stitch.

If you just chained more than 1 and are about to work any stitch other than a single crochet, skip this first stitch and work into the 2 top loops of the second stitch of the previous row. The longer turning chain you made counts as the first stitch of the new row.

Pointers _____

You might see instructions that state "chain 3 (counts as 1 dc), turn"; sometimes instructions will say "chain 3, turn, skip first stitch." They both mean the same thing.

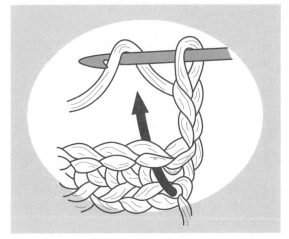

Work any stitch other than a single crochet or slip stitch into the second stitch.

If you worked a half double crochet, double crochet, or triple crochet, the turning chain counted as the first stitch. To end up with the same number of stitches you started with, you will need to work into the turning chain for the last stitch of the row. It sometimes looks as if you've finished the row when you really haven't—so be sure to work the last stitch!

Instructions sometimes state to work a stitch into the "top of the turning chain." This means to work your stitch into the last chain made on the previous row. If you have trouble, try putting a safety pin through that very last chain (not the loop on your hook but the last complete chain) to remind you which is the last chain.

Practice Makes Perfect

Now let's make some samples so you can put everything you just learned into action. Don't worry if your stitches are uneven; that will come with practice. Each sample you're going to make has 15 stitches. If you find your work is getting wider or narrower, count your stitches and see if you have added or subtracted stitches by mistake. When you feel comfortable doing each stitch, you can unravel the yarn and use it again, or cut the yarn and pull it through the last loop to finish.

Single crochet:

1. Make a slip knot and chain 16; you need one more chain than the number of stitches you'll have at the end of the row to accommodate the height of a single crochet. Single crochet into the 2nd chain from the hook and in each of the remaining chains.
2. Chain 1 and turn your work around.
3. Single crochet into the first stitch and each of the remaining single crochets of the row.

Repeat steps 2 and 3.

Half double crochet:

1. Make a slip knot and chain 17; you need two more chains than the number of stitches you'll have at the end of the row to accommodate the height of a half double crochet. Half double crochet into the 3rd chain from the hook and in each of the remaining chains.
2. Chain 2 and turn your work around. This chain counts as the first half double crochet of the next row.
3. Skip the first stitch (the first stitch of the row below) and half double crochet into the next and remaining half double crochets of the row.

Repeat steps 2 and 3. Remember to work into the last stitch of the turning chain when you come to it!

Double crochet:

1. Make a slip knot and chain 18; you need three more chains than the number of stitches you'll have at the end of the row to accommodate the height of a double crochet. Double crochet into the 4th chain from the hook and in each of the remaining chains.
2. Chain 3 and turn your work around. This chain counts as the first double crochet of the next row.
3. Skip the first stitch (the first stitch of the row below) and double crochet into the next and remaining double crochets of the row.

Repeat steps 2 and 3. Remember to work into the last stitch of the turning chain when you come to it!

Triple crochet:

1. Make a slip knot and chain 19; you need four more chains than the number of stitches you'll have at the end of the row to accommodate the height of a triple crochet. Triple crochet into the 5th chain from the hook and in each of the remaining chains.
2. Chain 4 and turn your work around. This chain counts as the first triple crochet of the next row.
3. Skip the first stitch (the first stitch of the row below) and triple crochet into the next and remaining triple crochets of the row.

Repeat steps 2 and 3. Remember to work into the last stitch of the turning chain when you come to it!

Left-Handed Crochet

Can lefties crochet? Absolutely! You just need to adjust some of the basic directions. The following sections illustrate a couple techniques specifically for left handers: how to hold the yarn, how to make a chain stitch, and how to single crochet.

Tangles

Before you begin this section, be sure to read the first part of this chapter. All the information is identical whether you're crocheting with your right or left hand. Because this section details only those concepts that are different for southpaws, you could get very confused reading only the left-handed information and skipping over the remainder of the chapter.

Left-Handed Basics

The beginning procedures in crochet, such as how to hold the hook and yarn, are the same for left-handed people as they are for right-handed people. Of course, you'll be doing the major work with your left hand. So get out your hook and yarn, get comfortable, and let's begin.

The first thing you need to know is how to hold your hook.

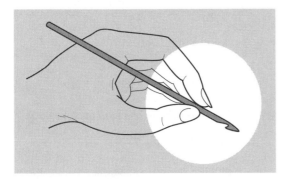

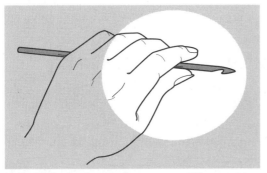

You hold the hook one of two ways. Either position and lightly grip your hook in your hand, as you would hold a pencil, or hold the hook as you would grip a spoon when stirring something thick.

Next, you need to get the yarn onto the hook. The instructions for making a slip knot don't differ whether you're right or left handed. Now you're ready to get down to the business of holding your yarn. Follow these steps:

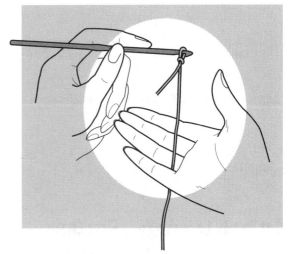

With your right palm facing up, approximately 4 inches or so from your hook, grasp the yarn between your third and little fingers.

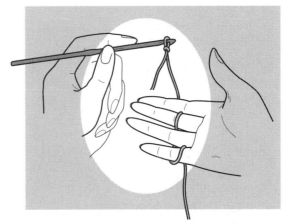

Draw the yarn toward you; thread the yarn over your middle finger, leading under your index finger.

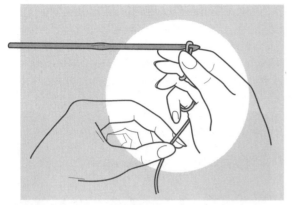

Adjust the yarn so it lies firmly but not tightly around your fingers.

Initially, this may feel a little strange. Practice holding a hook and yarn; it will soon become second nature.

Get Ready to Make Your First Chain

As you have already read in this chapter, the foundation chain is the base of all crochet. The following illustrations show you how to make a chain.

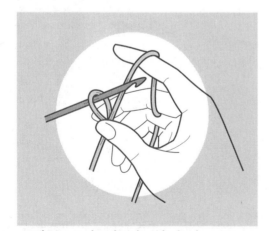

With yarn in hand and on the hook, use your thumb and middle finger to grab the slip knot right below the hook.

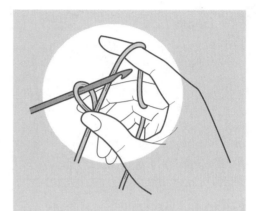

Now use the crochet hook to catch the yarn between your thumb and finger.

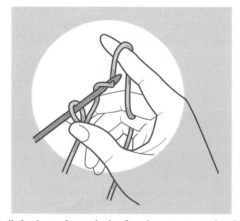

Pull the loop through the first loop on your hook.

Congratulations! You have completed your first chain stitch. Make another chain, and another. When the row of chains gets too long, pull back on your yarn (down to the first loop) and start again.

Left-Handed Single Crochet (sc)

You've reached a moment of truth. Get ready to crochet! To make a single crochet, begin with a foundation chain. Make sure that the front side of the chain is facing you, and then follow these steps:

Count to the 2nd chain from the hook.
Insert the hook, front to back, under the
top 2 loops of the foundation chain.

Yarn over and pull the loop through the
foundation chain.

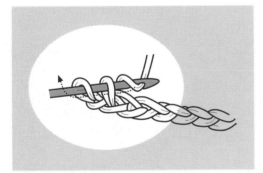

You now have 2 loops on your hook. Yarn over
again and pull through both loops on the hook.
One loop remains.

Kudos to you! You just completed your first
single crochet.

Other Basic Stitches

There are three additional basic crochet
stitches: half double, double, and triple crochet. Knowing how to do a single crochet gives
you the skills necessary to do all these other
stitches on your own. Refer once again to the
remainder of this chapter to see how each
stitch is formed and to learn about turning
chains and their importance.

If you need additional clarification on each
of the remaining stitches, hold a mirror next to
the illustration. You will see the image reversed,
showing the way you would be working it with
your left hand.

The Least You Need to Know

◆ Your way is the right way. Hold your hook
   and yarn so that it's comfortable for you.

◆ Foundation chains are the basis on which
   you build your crochet fabric.

◆ A yarn over is fundamental to all crochet
   stitches.

◆ Each stitch is abbreviated a specific way;
   once you know those abbreviations, you
   can read crochet patterns.

◆ Understanding turning chains and which
   stitch to work into are important in order
   to maintain the same number of stitches
   on each row.

◆ Left-handed crochet is a mirror of right-
   handed crochet.

In This Chapter

◆ Common increase and decrease abbreviations

◆ Adding stitches by increasing

◆ Subtracting stitches by decreasing

◆ Decreasing stitches in single, double, and triple crochet

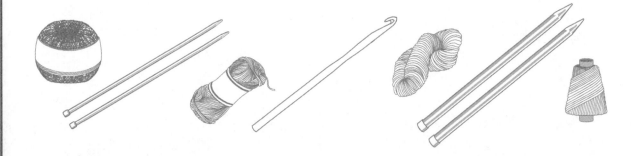

Chapter **14**

Shaping Your Work

By now you've learned how to make a foundation chain, as well as how to single, half double, double, and triple crochet. You can make many types of projects with straight edges just with these skills!

Now you're ready to learn how to shape your crocheted pieces by adding (increasing) and subtracting (decreasing) stitches. With these added capabilities you'll be able to make sweaters, mittens, socks, and other types of projects. You'll also need them to crochet straight-edged projects that use increases and decreases to create pretty stitch patterns. Are you intrigued? Read on!

Common Abbreviations

The following abbreviations are commonly used to indicate increasing and decreasing stitches. (You'll find a full list of common abbreviations in Appendix B.)

Abbreviation	What It Means
dc2tog or 1 dc dec	Double crochet decrease
dec	Decrease
inc	Increase
sc2tog or 1 sc dec	Single crochet decrease

Upping the Ante: Increasing

All is not even in crochet. *Increases* are often used to create exciting stitch patterns (combinations of stitches and techniques in the same row, such as in the scarf pattern you'll find in Chapter 23) and to shape garments. To increase, no matter what the stitch, you work 2 (or sometimes more depending upon the instructions) stitches in the same spot.

To try increasing in single crochet, begin with a foundation chain (see Chapter 13). Make sure the front side of the chain is facing you. Work a row of single crochet, chain 1, and turn.

At the beginning of the next row, increase 1 single crochet by working 2 single crochets into the first stitch. At the end of the row also work an increase. You now have 2 more single crochets at the end of the row than you started with.

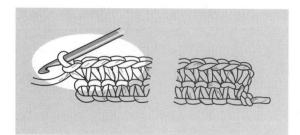

Increasing 2 stitches: one at the beginning and one at the end of the row.

Subtracting Stitches: Decreasing

The buddy of increasing stitches is—you guessed it—*decreasing* stitches. Like increasing, decreasing enables you to shape what you're crocheting. Decreases are also sometimes used in stitch patterns. To complete a decrease, you have to start with 2 partially worked stitches. Sound complicated? It isn't!

Singles, Anyone? Decreasing in Single Crochet

To decrease in single crochet, you partially complete 2 stitches and then merge them. Here's how:

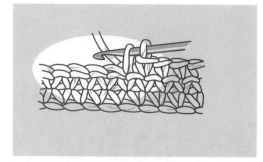

At the point you want to decrease, insert the hook into the top 2 loops of the next stitch, yarn over, and pull through a loop. Don't finish the stitch!

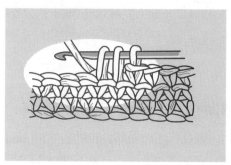

Insert the hook into the next stitch, yarn over, and pull through a loop. You now have 3 loops on your hook.

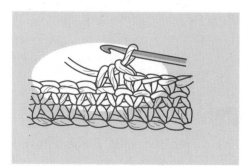

Yarn over one more time. This time, pull through all 3 loops on your hook.

You've just completed a *single crochet decrease!* Follow along making a swatch and continue practicing your decreases. Don't worry about your swatch becoming misshapen; you're learning a valuable new skill.

Needle Talk _____

A single crochet decrease (abbreviated sc2tog or 1 sc dec) subtracts 1 stitch by combining 2 single crochets.

Decreasing in Double Crochet

Decreasing in double crochet is very much like decreasing in single crochet. Here's what you do:

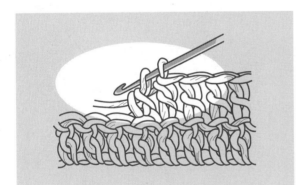

At the point you want to decrease, work a double crochet down to 2 loops on your hook.

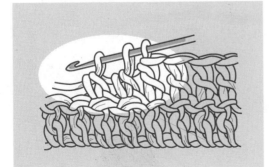

Yarn over, insert the hook into the top 2 loops of the next stitch, and work that stitch down until you have 3 loops on the hook.

Yarn over one more time and pull through all 3 loops.

You have just completed your first *double crochet decrease!* Practice by making a swatch of double crochet: Make your foundation chain, double crochet in each chain, and chain 2 at the end of the row. On the next row, practice your new decrease skill anywhere along the row.

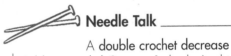

Needle Talk _____

A double crochet decrease (abbreviated dc2tog or 1 dc dec) subtracts 1 stitch by combining 2 double crochets.

Decreasing in Triple Crochet

You work a triple crochet decrease the same way you work the double crochet decrease. The only difference is that you begin each triple crochet with 2 yarn overs; consequently, you have to complete one more step to get down to 2 loops.

As with a double crochet decrease, when you have 3 loops on the hook, work a final yarn over and pull the yarn through all 3 loops.

The Least You Need to Know

- Increases and decreases are used to shape your work and to create exciting stitch patterns.
- Increases can be worked using any stitch anywhere in the row, one or more times.
- Increasing is as easy as working 2 stitches in the same stitch.
- When you decrease, you work 2 stitches together as one.

In This Chapter

- ◆ Changing the look: variations of basic crochet stitches

- ◆ More variations with clusters and shells

- ◆ Filet crochet designs

- ◆ Learning Afghan or Tunisian crochet

Chapter 15

Beyond the Basics: Adding to Your Crochet Repertoire

By making slight changes to the basic crochet stitches you've already learned, you'll change the way these stitches look and add to your crochet repertoire. In this chapter, you'll learn how these stitches are created.

You'll also learn how to create intricate designs with a method called filet crochet. Finally, we'll introduce you to an entirely new concept called Afghan or Tunisian crochet.

Working Under One Loop

To complete any crochet stitch, you normally insert your hook under the 2 top loops of a stitch. It's also possible to insert your hook under only 1 loop of a stitch—either the front or the back. This forms a ridge that gives your finished fabric a different appearance than when you work into both loops. You can work into the *front* or *back loops* using any crochet stitch.

To work under the **front loop** (abbreviated fl or flo meaning front loop only), insert your hook into the front loop only of a stitch. This forms a ridge on the back of your work. To work under the **back loop** (abbreviated bl or blo meaning back loop only), insert your hook into the back loop only of a stitch. This forms a ridge on the front of your work.

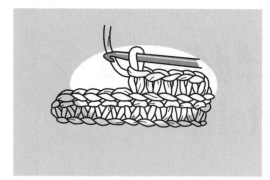

Working into 1 loop creates a ridge.

To try working into the back loop of a stitch, start with a small swatch of single crochet. Work across the row and insert the hook into the back loop only of each stitch (the back loop is the loop farthest from you).

Insert your hook in the back loop only.

Use the same concept to work into only the front loop of each stitch (this is the loop that is closest to you). Try it and see!

Insert your hook in the front loop only.

Working Around the Post of a Stitch

Another interesting technique also involves how you insert the hook. You have gone from working under both loops to working under only the front or the back loop. Now you won't work through any loops. Instead, you'll work using a stitch in the row below. This is called *working around the post of a stitch.*

You can work around the post of a previous stitch in one of two ways: around the front of a post or around the back of a post. This works best with double crochet or triple crochet stitches.

Front Post Double Crochet (fdpc)

A *front post double crochet* involves working into the front of the post of a crochet stitch on the row below. If you want to try this new stitch, make a small swatch of about 20 stitches of double crochet.

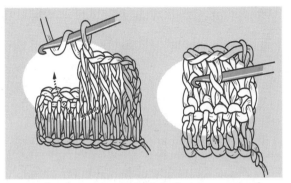

To work a front post double crochet, yarn over. Then insert the hook by going *behind* the post of the stitch in the row below.

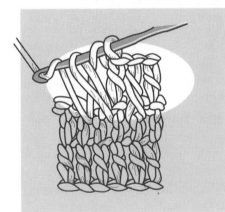

Complete the double crochet as you normally would.

> **Needle Talk**
>
> A **front post double crochet** (abbreviated fdpc) is a special stitch that involves working into the front of the post of a crochet stitch on the row below.

A front post double crochet is three dimensional. If you're working on a swatch, work across the row by alternating 1 stitch of regular double crochet with 1 stitch of front post double crochet. You'll see the difference in these stitches.

Back Post Double Crochet (bpdc)

The *back post double crochet* stitch is similar to the front post double crochet. The only difference is that you're inserting your hook into the back of the post of the row below.

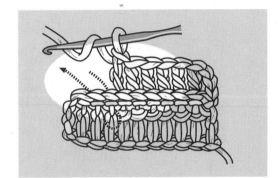

To work a back post double crochet, yarn over. Then insert the hook by going *in front of* the post of the stitch in the row below.

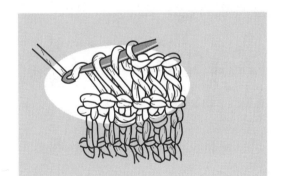

Complete the double crochet as you normally would.

> **Needle Talk**
>
> A **back post double crochet** (abbreviated bpdc) is a special stitch that involves working into the back of the post of a crochet stitch on the row below.

Working in a Space (sp)

When you work into a *space* (abbreviated sp), you are working into the space created by chains in the previous row instead of an actual stitch. The chains can be any length and you can work any type of stitch into these spaces.

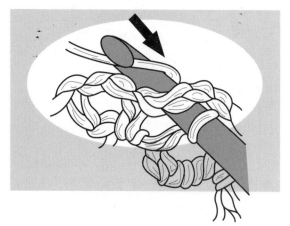

Working in a space.

Reverse Single Crochet (reverse sc)

Reverse single crochet can seem a little difficult at first but keep practicing! It looks somewhat like a braid and it's sometimes used as an edging so it's useful to learn.

Needle Talk

Reverse single crochet (abbreviated reverse sc) is worked exactly like a regular single crochet but worked from left to right instead of right to left.

Here's all you do to work reverse single crochet:

1. With your yarn on the left side of your work, pull up a loop.
2. Moving from left to right, insert your hook into the next stitch and again pull up a loop. Yarn over the hook to complete the single crochet.
3. Continue steps 1 and 2 to complete the row.

Cluster Stitches

Cluster stitches are groups of stitches worked in the same stitch, then finished off as a single stitch. There are three distinct ways to form these stitches, even though the results appear quite similar. The number of stitches involved varies from pattern to pattern.

You can practice these stitches by making a foundation chain of about 20 stitches and then following along. They're worked the same way, regardless of whether you're working into a stitch or into your foundation row.

Needle Talk

Cluster stitches are groups of stitches worked into the same stitch. They are closed in different ways and leave you with a single stitch.

Popcorn Stitch (pc st)

Popcorn stitch (abbreviated pc st) is a group of double crochets worked in the same stitch and then closed together with a slip stitch.

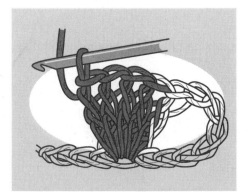

In the 8th chain from the hook, work 5 double crochet stitches. When they are completed, drop the last loop by sliding the hook out from the loop.

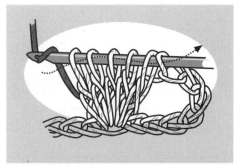

Yarn over, insert hook in the 8th chain from the hook, pull up a loop, yarn over, draw through 2 loops on hook, (yarn over, insert hook in same stitch, pull up a loop, yarn over, draw through 2 loops) 4 times.

Insert the hook into the top of the first double crochet from front to back, then into the dropped loop. Pull the dropped loop through.

To complete the popcorn stitch, chain 1.

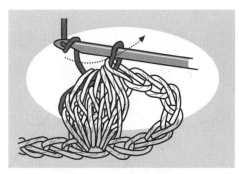

Yarn over and draw through all 6 loops on the hook.

Complete the bobble with a single chain stitch.

Bobble Stitch

Bobble stitch differs from popcorn stitch in that it is made of double crochets that are not fully completed. These stitches are then closed to leave you with a single stitch. Sometimes a pattern will refer to a bobble stitch as a "cluster stitch." Be sure you follow the directions included with the pattern.

Puff Stitch

Puff stitch is similar to a bobble stitch in that it's made up of incomplete stitches that are then closed to leave you with a single stitch. However, the puff stitch is made with half double crochets, so it's shorter than the bobble stitch.

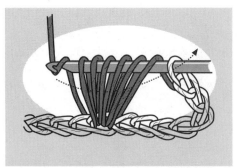

In the 8th chain from the hook, work a half double crochet, yarn over, insert the hook in the same stitch and pull up a loop, yarn over again, and pull up another loop. There are now 7 loops on the hook. Yarn over and draw through all the loops on the hook.

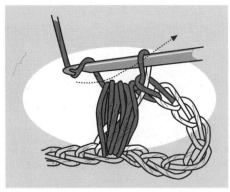

Close the puff stitch with a chain 1.

Shell and V-Stitches

Shell and *V-stitches* also involve working more than one stitch within the same stitch. However, when they're completed, you are left with more than a single stitch and they fan out. Usually, you compensate for these extra stitches by skipping chains or stitches on each side.

There are many variations of shells. They can be worked with any number of half double, double, or triple crochets. In this example we're going to make a 5 double crochet shell. To begin, make a foundation chain of 20 stitches.

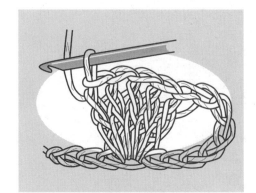

In the 8th chain from the hook, work 5 complete double crochets.

A V-stitch is similar and looks like a V when completed. The most common way to do a V-stitch is to double crochet, chain 1, and then double crochet again into the same stitch.

Filet Crochet: Spaces and Blocks

One of the most popular uses for crochet over the years has been *filet crochet*. Designs are created by forming spaces (called *mesh*) and squares (called *blocks*). Filet crochet is basic, fast, and enjoyable.

> **Needle Talk**
>
> **Filet crochet** is a type of crochet in which a pattern is created by arranging spaces and blocks. Filet crochet is made up of two elements: *background mesh* and *filled blocks*.

Mesh can be put together in a number of different ways. Think of mesh as double or triple crochet stitches separated by chains to form little squares or spaces. These spaces are the background on which blocks of crochet are worked to form patterns. You can work two spaces together as one, thus creating a double space. You can also work what's called a *lacet* over a double space to form a lacier look (more about that later in the chapter).

The following table defines the different stitches and terms used in filet crochet. You might want to refer to it as you work through the following sections.

Term	Definition
Mesh	The filet background
Space	The element formed by chains separating double crochet stitches in the mesh
Double space	Two spaces worked as one
Block	A space filled in with double crochet stitches
Double block	Two spaces filled in with double crochet stitches
Lacet	Two chains, 1 single crochet and 2 chains worked over a double space

Creating Your First Mesh Piece

Are you eager to make a sample of filet crochet? This section shows you how to create mesh by combining double crochet with chains. You can apply the concepts you learn in this section to any other filet crochet project.

Many filet crochet pieces are done with thread and small hooks, but you can use any yarn weight and hook size you choose to follow along. Repeat the directions following the asterisk (*) as many times as indicated; if you need more help, refer to Chapter 21 on how to follow a pattern.

Follow these steps to make your first mesh piece:

1. Make a foundation chain of 23 stitches.
2. Work a double crochet in the 8th chain from the hook to make the first space. Do you know why you left the first 7 chains alone and double crocheted in the 8th chain from the hook? Look at this math:

   2 chains form the bottom of the first space

   + 3 chains count as the first double crochet on row 1 (the right side of the first space)

   + 2 chains form the top of the first space

   = 7 chains total

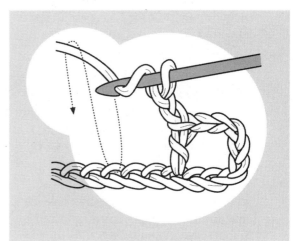

Double crochet in the 8th chain from the hook to create the first space.

3. To continue the row, follow this pattern:

   *Chain 2, skip the next 2 chains, double crochet in the next chain (1 space made), repeat from * 4 more times (total of 6 spaces have been made). Chain 5, turn.

   On the second row, the chain 5 will count as the first double crochet plus the chain 2 space.

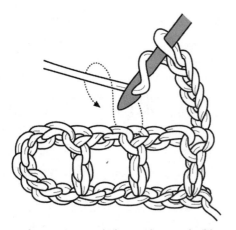

A row of spaces is made by working a double crochet, chain 2 pattern across the row.

4. Double crochet into the second double crochet on the row. You've now made a second space over the first space in the row.

5. To complete the row, follow this pattern:

    *Chain 2, 1 double crochet in next double crochet (space over space made), repeat from * 3 more times. Work last double crochet in 5th chain of initial chain 7 (final space made). Chain 5.

6. Repeat steps 4 and 5 two more times, working the last double crochet on each row in the 3rd chain of turning chain 5. You now have completed 6 rows of mesh.

7. On the next row, work a beginning space over space, as you have done on the last 5 rows. Then make a double space as follows:

    Chain 5, skip the next double crochet, double crochet in the next double crochet. You've now made a double space: The chain 5 counts as 2 chains, 1 double crochet and 2 chains.

8. Chain 5 again, and work another double space. End the row by working a single space over the last space. Chain 5.

9. Start the next row by working a space over a space: Double crochet into the second double crochet, as you have done on the other rows.

10. Now chain 2, skip 2 chains, double crochet into the next chain, chain 2, skip next 2 chains, and double crochet into next chain. You have now completed 2 spaces over a double space.

11. Repeat this procedure over the next double space. End the row working a space over a space.

Are you still with me? Do you like your swatch? It's exciting to see how you can combine the basic steps you learned earlier—chaining and double crocheting—to create a new type of piece.

Yarn Spinning

Over the years numerous subjects have been depicted in filet crochet, from simple botanicals to highly religious themes. During World War II, filet crochet contests awarded prizes to contestants who executed the most beautiful patriotic designs.

Filling in the Dots

To form a pattern on a mesh background, just create blocks of double crochet rather than spaces. In other words, rather than following this pattern to form a space:

    Chain 2, 1 double crochet in next double crochet

You would follow this pattern:

    3 double crochet

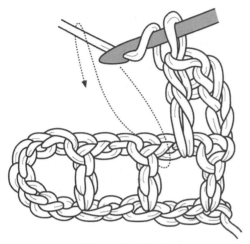

Filling in the blocks.

I told you this was easy!

Forming a Lacet

Up to this point, you've worked only single and double square blocks. As mentioned earlier, you can also form a lacet—a fancy mesh that has a lacier look—by following these steps:

1. At the end of the last double crochet, chain 3, skip the next 2 double crochets, single crochet into the next double crochet, chain 3, skip 2 double crochets, and double crochet in the next double crochet.

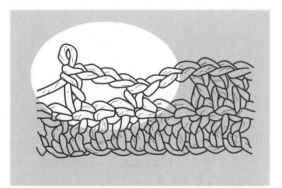

Forming a lacet by single crocheting rather than double crocheting.

2. On the next row, work a double space over the lacet.

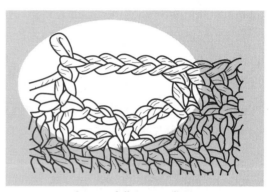

The row following a lacet.

Increasing and Decreasing in Filet Crochet

When you increase and decrease in filet crochet, you can do so a block or a space at a time either at the beginning or the end of a row. The pattern will always tell you when and how to increase or decrease.

To *increase a block at the beginning of a row*, chain 5 at the end of your last row. On the next row, double crochet into the 4th chain from the hook and each of the next 2 chains. Double crochet into the next double crochet. You've now made a block increase.

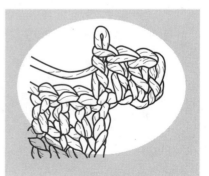

A block increase at the beginning of a row.

To *increase a space at the beginning of a row*, chain 5 at the end of your last row. On the next row, double crochet into the first double crochet. You've now made a space increase.

A space increase at the beginning of a row.

To *increase a block at the end of a row*, you have to follow a specific procedure. In essence, you are making a chain and a double crochet stitch at the same time. It sounds tricky, but it's really not so bad. Give it a try:

1. Work across the row to the last double crochet.

2. Working in the base of the last double crochet, work another double crochet as follows: Yarn over, pull through 1 loop (this step forms the base chain), and complete the double crochet stitch.

3. When you have completed the stitch, repeat this process in the base of this stitch 2 more times. You have now completed a block increase.

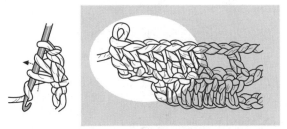

A block increase at the beginning of a row.

To *increase a space at the end of a row*, chain 2, yarn over 3 times, insert hook in the turning chain where the last double crochet was worked, yarn over, and pull up a loop. Yarn over and draw through 2 loops on hook 4 times.

To decrease in filet crochet, just leave your blocks and spaces unworked either at the beginning or end of a row. Let's take a look.

To *decrease at the beginning of a row*, slip stitch over the required double crochets or chains. Then chain the number required to complete the block or space.

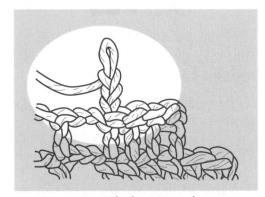

Decreasing at the beginning of a row.

To *decrease at the end of the row*, stop working on the row at the point you want to decrease. Chain the appropriate number of stitches, turn, and start working on the next row.

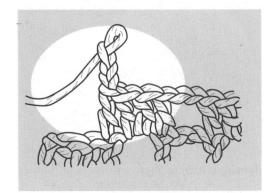

Decreasing at the end of a row.

Reading a Filet Crochet Chart

Filet crochet patterns are written as charts. Often a pattern begins with instructions in words, but after a certain point refers you to the chart for the remaining instructions. A chart is actually easier than written words because you can keep your place more readily and it gives you a visual depiction. As you might expect, the dark areas indicate blocks and the white areas indicate spaces.

To read the chart, begin on row 1 in the lower right corner and read from right to left. Row 2 and all even rows are read from left to right. All odd number rows are read from right to left. To find your place easily while you're reading the chart, stick a Post-it note under the row you're currently working on, and move it up one row as you complete each row.

Afghan (Tunisian) Crochet

When you hear "Afghan crochet," you might think of a blanket or afghan. Actually, *Afghan (Tunisian) crochet* is a specific method that is very different from what you have learned so far. It produces a thick, dense fabric.

Needle Talk _____

Afghan (Tunisian) crochet is a specific method of crochet in which the stitches are held on the crochet hook. Special hooks are used for this type of crochet.

A filet crochet chart shows you how to work the pattern.

Several things separate Afghan crochet from the other types of crochet you've learned so far. Afghan crochet requires a unique afghan hook (named after the stitch, of course). The hook is much longer than a regular crochet hook and resembles a cross between a knitting needle and a crochet hook. This special hook is necessary because, unlike the crochet stitches you've learned so far, you keep all your stitches on the hook half of the time.

To complete one row you work the same row twice: part A, sometimes called *forward*, and part B, sometimes called *return*. The right side is always facing you because you don't turn your work. For part A, you work right to left and for part B, you work left to right without turning.

This section walks you through Afghan crochet. If you want to follow along by creating your own swatch, you can use a straight or a flexible hook. The flexible afghan hook is initially a little harder to handle than the straight hook.

Hooked on Afghans

To start a piece in Afghan crochet, you begin with a foundation chain as you would in any other type of crochet. Make a foundation of 20 chains. Now, we'll work the first row:

1. To begin part A or the forward row, in the 2nd chain from the hook, insert the hook, front to back, under the 2 top loops.

2. Yarn over and draw up a loop, leave the loop on your hook, and draw up another loop in the next chain (the 3rd chain from the hook).

Drawing up loops to begin Afghan crochet.

3. Continue across the row, drawing up a loop in each chain and leaving them all on your hook.

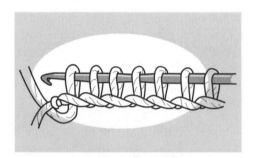

Completing a row of loops.

4. When you get to the end, count your loops. You should have the same number of loops as you had chains. Unlike what you learned before, the first loop on your hook counts as the first stitch.

5. Now you're going to complete the first row by working part B or the return row. Yarn over and draw through 1 loop.

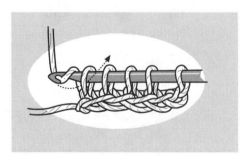

Beginning to work back across the first row.

6. Yarn over and draw through 2 loops. You'll notice the number of stitches on the hook is decreasing.

7. Work across the row as in step 6 until 1 stitch remains on the hook. The last loop left on your hook always counts as your first stitch of the next row. You've completed Row 1.

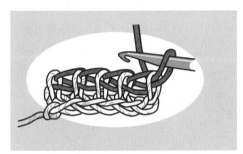

A completed row in Afghan crochet.

Now get ready for Row 2. Remember, to complete one row you work the same row twice:

1. Insert the hook in the second stitch, from right to left through the front vertical bar (formed from the previous row), yarn over, and draw up a loop.

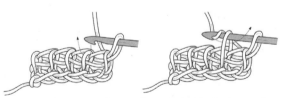

Beginning Row 2 by working through the vertical bars formed from the previous row.

2. Repeat this across in each vertical bar until you reach the last vertical bar.

3. Go through the last vertical bar to the back (through both vertical loops). This gives the piece a firm edge.

4. When you get to the end, count your loops. You should have the same number of loops as you had chains in your foundation chain.

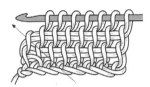

Finishing the first half of Row 2.

5. The second half of this row is worked the same way as the second half of the first row. To complete this row, follow steps 5 through 7 as you did when you worked the first row.

Repeat the second row (both halves) to form the pattern. You can create many lovely stitch patterns using this technique. The one you've just learned is generally called the *Basic Afghan Stitch*.

Increases are always done on the first half of the row. Insert your hook into the horizontal chain stitch between 2 vertical bars, yarn over, and pull up a loop. To decrease, insert the hook through 2 front vertical bars at the same time, yarn over, and then draw up 1 loop. If you're working a decrease on the right side, decrease on the first half. If you're decreasing on the left side, you can decrease on the second half of the row.

The Least You Need to Know

- By varying where you insert the hook, you create an entirely different look.
- Cluster stitches are groups of stitches worked into the same stitch and closed off, leaving you with a single stitch.
- Shell and V-stitches are also groups of stitches worked into the same stitch. However, when they're completed, you are left with more than a single stitch and they fan out.
- Filet crochet is as easy as putting spaces and blocks together.
- Each row of Afghan crochet is worked in two steps and requires an Afghan hook.

In This Chapter

- ◆ Crocheting around rather than back and forth
- ◆ Making a ring
- ◆ Crocheting circles and tubes
- ◆ Granny Squares make a comeback

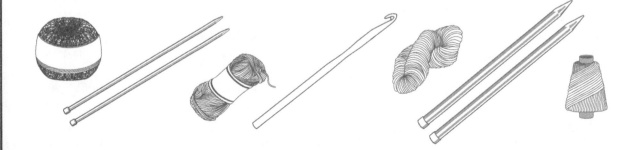

Crocheting Around

Up to this point, you've crocheted back and forth, turning your work when you hit the end of a row. Now it's time to break a few rules and give your work a different look by crocheting in rounds instead of rows.

You'll learn to make circles, tubes, and squares by crocheting around. Once you understand the principle, you'll be able to make hats, fabulous Granny Square afghans, and much more.

Crocheting Around in Circles and Squares

All is not straight in crochet. Working in circles and squares is one of the most interesting concepts you can learn. For example, the pattern for the hat in this book (see Chapter 23) requires you to crochet around in circles.

When working back and forth, you work in rows. When crocheting a circle or square, you work in rounds. You don't turn your work around and crochet back with the wrong side facing you.

You can make endless types of projects by working squares and circles around a central point. To create this "central point," you use a slip stitch to join a small chain; the result is a *ring*.

How to Make a Ring

To begin working around, regardless of whether you are making a circle or a square, you start with a ring. Follow these steps:

1. Make a foundation chain of 4 stitches. This number will vary based on the project you're making.

2. With the right side of the chain facing you, insert your hook into the first chain, going under the 2 top loops. You're going to slip stitch the 2 ends of the loop together.

3. Yarn over the hook, and draw through both the first chain and the loop on your hook. You've just completed the closing slip stitch.

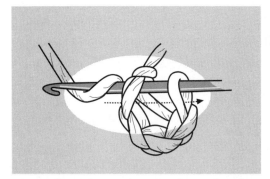

Using a slip stitch to make a ring from a foundation chain.

Working into the Ring

After you make the ring, you work stitches into the center of the ring. The stitches are worked exactly as if you were working into a straight foundation chain; the only difference is you'll be working into the middle of the ring instead of into the chain loops. You'll need to work into the ring to make a circle or a square, although there's an additional step to making a square, which you'll learn later.

Want to see this in action? Here's how to work single crochet stitches into the center of the ring:

1. Insert your crochet hook, front to back, into the center of the ring.

2. Work a single crochet stitch into the ring over the chain loops.

3. Add 7 more single crochet stitches into the ring, working around the ring as you go. The ring now holds a total of 8 single crochet stitches.

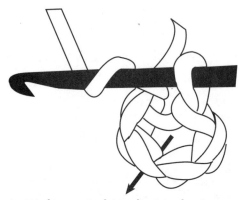

Working a single crochet into the ring.

4. Now close your round with a slip stitch. Insert the hook under the top 2 loops of the first single crochet stitch. Yarn over; draw through both loops on your hook. You have just completed Round 1 of a circle or tube.

When working in rounds, mark the last stitch in each round with a small safety pin. Move the pin up on each round so you will know when you have come to the end of that round.

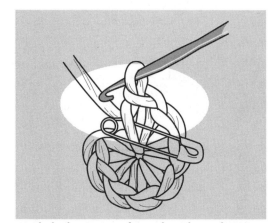

Mark the beginning of rounds with a safety pin.

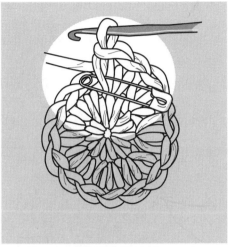

Move up the pin with each round.

Pointers _____

Here's another way to keep track of rounds. Cut a different-colored piece of yarn about 12 inches long. Place this yarn over the space between the last stitch of the round you just finished and the new round you're about to begin. As you complete each round, keep flipping the yarn over that space. When you're done, you can easily pull it out.

Making a Circle or a Tube

As you might guess, if the number of stitches in each round remains constant, you'll make a tube. If you increase stitches every round, you'll make a circle. Sometimes, you work the same number of stitches on some rounds and increase on other rounds; this is how a hat is made.

For Round 2 and subsequent rounds, you'll go back to working your stitches under the two top loops of the stitches just like you did when you were working back and forth. This is true whether you're making a tube, a circle, or a square (although with a square you'll work into both stitches and spaces).

Let's practice making Round 2 of a circle. You have 8 single crochets in your ring. You're going to double the number of stitches from 8 to 16. Remember, you're working into the 2 top loops of the stitches again. Beginning with the first single crochet, work 2 single crochets into each stitch of the round. You now have 16 single crochets. Mark the end of your row.

We're not going to double the number of stitches for Round 3. Work 1 single crochet into the first stitch, then work 2 single crochets into the next stitch. Continue by working 1 single crochet into the next stitch, then 2 single crochets into the following stitch for the round. You should have increased 8 times for a total of 24 single crochets.

Single crochet patterns will sometimes ask you to chain 1 and join the rounds with a slip stitch. This means when you work the last stitch, you'll join it with a slip stitch to the first stitch of the same round. Other times, you won't see those directions or the pattern may say, "Do not join." In this case, just mark the end of your round and continue on with the next round as directed.

Yarn Spinning _____

Colorado State University's Gustafson Gallery contains two fabric books, the linen pages of which hold crochet samples dating back to the early 1900s. As testament to their makers' skill and desire to document the work, each book holds more than 100 samples of beautiful stitchery. These stitching books and others like them have been the basis for preserving some long-forgotten crochet techniques.

Working Rounds in Double and Triple Crochet

When you work in rounds with double or triple crochet stitches, you have to bring your work up to the height of the stitch you will be creating.

To do so, make the number of chains equal to the height of the stitch; your pattern will tell you how many to make. These chains always count as the first stitch of the round. Close the round after working your stitches by slip stitching in the top chain, going under the 2 top loops.

Grannies Have More Fun

The Granny Square is a famous technique. Who hasn't seen a Granny Square afghan? Granny Squares got somewhat of a bad rap from patterns created in the 1960s and 1970s, with afghans made from 50 colors that didn't coordinate. Instead of clashing fuchsia and orange, picture instead a rich blue against a black background or a luscious green with cream. The old Granny Square has gone the way of shag rugs and avocado-colored kitchens. Say hello to today's Granny Square!

You begin a square by making a ring and working stitches into the center of the ring, just as you did with a circle. In fact, there are only two differences between crocheting a circle and a square. The first is the addition of chain stitches to form corner spaces. Second, sometimes you'll work into stitches and sometimes into spaces. Sound complex? It's easy!

Here's how to make a fabulous Granny Square—the foundation for many various creative projects. This Granny Square is made of double crochet stitches. Don't let the number of steps concern you; there are no new stitches or techniques to learn.

1. Make a center ring by making a foundation chain of 6 stitches and joining the stitches with a slip stitch.
2. Bring your work up to double crochet stitch height by chaining 3 stitches. These stitches are the first stitch of the next round.
3. Insert your hook into the center of the ring and work 2 double crochets.
4. Chain 3 stitches; these stitches make up your first corner space.

5. Work 3 more double crochet stitches into the ring and chain 3 stitches for the next corner space.
6. Repeat step 5 two more times.
7. Close the square by slip stitching into the top of the first chain 3 you made at the beginning of the row.

Closing the first round of a Granny Square.

8. Slip stitch into the top of the next 2 double crochet stitches; slip stitch into the corner space. Chain 3.
9. In the same corner space, work 2 double crochets; then chain 3 for a new corner.
10. Complete 3 double crochets in the same corner space. You just made the first corner of Round 2. Chain 1.
11. In the next corner space, work 3 double crochets, chain 3, and work 3 double crochets. You've now completed the next corner. Chain 1.
12. Continue in this manner for the next two corner spaces.
13. To close the round, slip stitch into the top of the first chain 3 as you did in Round 1. This completes Round 2. Round 3 starts out the same as Round 2.

Working around the corners of a Granny Square.

14. Slip stitch into the top of the next 2 double crochets; slip stitch into the corner space.

15. Chain 3; in the same corner space make 2 double crochets, chain 3 for a new corner, and make 3 double crochets all in the same space. This is the first corner of Round 3.

Completing the first corner of Round 3.

16. Chain 1. Skip the next 3 double crochets, and complete 3 double crochets in the next space from the previous row; this space appears between 2 clusters of double crochet stitches.

17. In the next corner, complete 3 double crochets, chain 3, and complete 3 double crochets.

18. Continue working corners, working double crochet stitches into spaces between corners, and using slip stitches to close up rounds.

Once you get the hang of Granny Squares, they're easy, aren't they? You can make them any size you want, use fine or bulky yarn, and change color between rows. (You'll learn all about changing color in Chapter 17.)

Pointers _____

You might get so charged up about Granny Squares that you decide to tackle an afghan. If so, as you finish each square, stack that square on top of the other completed squares. Each square in the stack should be the same size as the others. Uniform square size is very important: When it's time to put the squares together, if the squares aren't the same size and shape, you're going to end up with one funky afghan.

The Least You Need to Know

- Working circles or squares is simply a matter of working around, rather than back and forth.
- To begin to work around, make a circle by joining the ends of a foundation chain with a slip stitch.
- If you work the same number of stitches in each round, you'll make a tube; if you increase stitches every round, you'll make a circle.
- The difference between circles and squares is the addition of corners.

In This Chapter

- ◆ Adding festive stripes
- ◆ Closing a stitch
- ◆ Changing colors in the same row
- ◆ Crocheting with more colors and bobbins

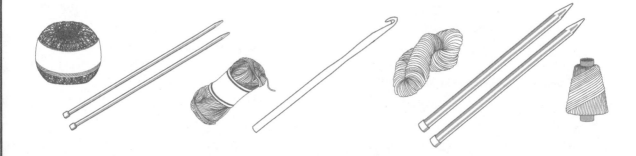

Colorful Crochet

Up to this point you've worked in one color. There's nothing wrong with monochromatic crocheting. Some of the most beautiful pieces are made with only one color. But what if you decide you're ready for a little more pizzazz? An extra challenge? A more eye-popping combination?

Changing colors is easy! With a few simple, basic steps you can introduce new colors by working in stripes or color groups.

Scintillating Stripes

To add stripes, you need nothing more than a crochet hook, two colors of yarn, and your creativity. All you do is change colors at the end of a row. Here's how to stripe:

1. Make a foundation chain and work one row in single crochet. Work across the second row but stop right before the last stitch on the row.
2. Insert your hook into the stitch, yarn over, and pull up a loop. You have 2 loops on your hook.
3. With the new yarn color, leaving a tail of about 4 inches, pull a loop through your stitch to *close* the single crochet. A single loop of the second color remains on your hook.

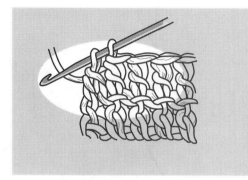

Preparing to change colors.

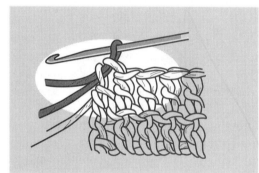

Starting to crochet with a second color.

4. Work the necessary number of turning chains and turn your work. You are now starting the row with your new color.

5. Cut the first color yarn, leaving about a 4-inch tail. You'll have to use a tapestry needle to weave in these ends later. In the meantime, keep striping!

Pointers _____

When you run out of yarn while you are working, it's best—although not mandatory—to add another skein at the end of a row. Add the new skein the same way you just learned to add a new color.

Changing Colors in the Same Row

To change to a new color within the same row, yarn over with the new color and *close your stitch*, just as you learned to do when changing colors at the end of the row. If you're changing colors back within 1 or 2 stitches, carry the yarn not in use loosely along the wrong side of your work. If the yarn is drawn up too tightly, the piece will pucker. Yarn over with the first color you used, and close the stitch.

Needle Talk _____

Closing a stitch refers to the step in which a stitch is finished and only one loop remains on the crochet hook. When changing colors, you always close the last stitch of the current color with the new color, regardless of the stitch you're working.

If you're changing back to the first color after more than 3 stitches, you'll have long strands on the wrong side of your work. These strands will get caught on everything, including fingers. You can still carry the unused color along the wrong side, though, by using a technique called *crocheting over the unused color.*

If you start the procedure 3 stitches before the place you want the actual color change to occur, there will be the bonus of no ends to weave in later! Why don't you try making a swatch along with the instructions? Here's how to do it:

1. Make a foundation chain of 20 stitches and single crochet a couple rows.

2. In the third row, single crochet 5 stitches. You'll make a color change in the 8th stitch.

3. Prepare to add the second color by laying the new color on top of the second row of stitches.

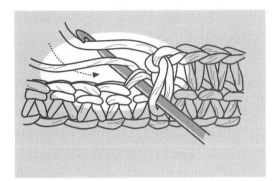

Placing the new color of yarn over the current color.

4. Work 2 single crochet stitches, simultaneously working over the yarn end that is on top of the stitches.

5. Now work 1 more single crochet stitch until you have 2 loops on the hook.

6. Pick up the new color of yarn. With a yarn over, pull the new color through the 2 loops.

7. Close your stitch with the new color.

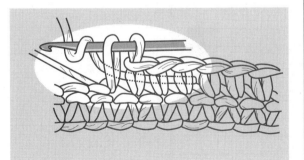

Closing the stitch with the new color.

8. Work 3 single crochets with the new color. Lay the old color on top of the second row of stitches as you did before.

9. Work 3 more single crochets with the new color. Close the last single crochet with the old color and complete the row.

You just completed color changes within the same row!

Tangles _____

If you use a light- and dark-colored yarn, sometimes the dark color that is being crocheted over will show through if you use this technique. You'll need to use bobbins instead, as described in the next section.

Crocheting with Bobbins

Carrying yarn along the wrong side is clever, but the fabric has doubled in weight and colors can show where they're not wanted. If you carry more than one extra color of yarn, your project will become stiff and heavy. Does this mean you're restricted to using two colors only? Absolutely not. You can crochet with as many colors simultaneously as you want; you just have to work with small spools of yarn or bobbins.

Even if you're crocheting with only two colors in the same row, there are times when using separate balls of yarn, wound on bobbins, is the better way to go. Let's say you're working 20 stitches of white in the middle and 5 stitches of black on each side. Carrying the black yarn all across the row will double your fabric and the black might show through to the right side. Instead, use three separate strands of yarn: two bobbins of black and one bobbin of white.

Bobbins help keep all the different strands manageable and easier to untangle as they twist. If you're working only a few stitches in a color, you don't need to use bobbins; just cut a manageable length of yarn (no longer than 36 inches) and crochet with the strand. If you're working one large area of a single color, you can crochet from the ball of yarn instead of using a bobbin.

Needle Talk

The **main color** (abbreviated MC) is the predominant color in a multicolor piece. The **contrasting color** (abbreviated CC) is an accent color used in a piece. You may have more than one contrasting color.

Want to try an example? You'll need three colors of yarn: a *main color*, a second *contrasting* color (color A), and a third contrasting color (color B). Wind colors A and B on separate bobbins; these bobbins will hang from the work and you can unwind more yarn from them as you need it. The main color is worked directly from the ball, although you can wind that color on a bobbin as well. Then follow these steps:

1. Make a foundation row of 20 stitches.

2. With the main color, work 2 rows in single crochet.

3. On the next row, work 2 single crochets with the main color, closing the second stitch with color A.

4. Work 2 single crochets with color A, closing the second stitch with the main color.

5. Now work 2 single crochets with the main color, closing the second stitch with color B.

6. Work 2 single crochets with color B, closing the second stitch with the main color.

7. Repeat steps 3 through 6 one more time.

8. Repeat steps 3 and 4 one more time, closing the last stitch with color A instead of the main color.

You now have an intriguing, colorful row of crochet. If you want to play longer with bobbins, try making the design shown in the following chart. You've already worked the first 3 rows. To read the chart, beginning in the lower right corner, read the odd rows from right to left and the even rows from left to right. Remember, you already worked the first 3 rows!

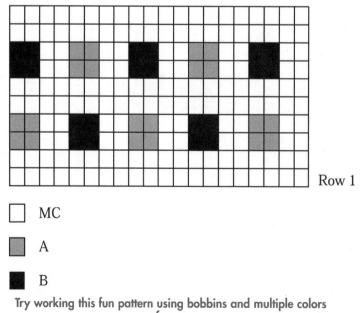

Row 1

☐ MC

▨ A

■ B

Try working this fun pattern using bobbins and multiple colors of yarn.

The Least You Need to Know

◆ To add stripes, change colors at the end of the row.

◆ When changing to a new color, always close the current stitch with the new color.

◆ You can change colors in the same row by carrying the color not in use along the wrong side of your work.

◆ Bobbins let you work with many different colors simultaneously or change colors across a row without doubling the weight of the fabric.

In This Part

18 Finishing Your Work: Seaming and Blocking

19 Edgings

20 Embellishments

Part 4

Finishing Touches for Knitting and Crocheting

Learning how to finish your work correctly can mean the difference between something that looks homemade and something that looks handmade. In this part, you'll learn about different seaming and blocking methods.

You'll also learn how to work knit and crochet edgings to make your projects a little prettier or to help them lie flat. Finally, there are instructions for making tassels, fringe, and pom poms (and a handy little thing for knitters called an I-Cord) that can be used to embellish and add a little pizzazz to your work.

In This Chapter

◆ Weaving in ends

◆ Seaming options

◆ For knitters only: grafting or the Kitchener stitch

◆ Blocking to shape up your pieces

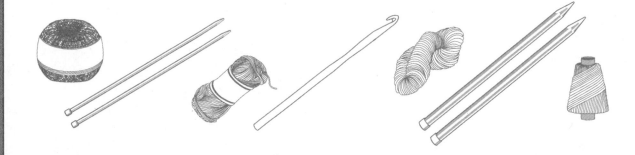

Finishing Your Work: Seaming and Blocking

Nothing can sabotage your hard work like a bad finishing job. You might spend months knitting a complex Fair Isle sweater, but if the seams are sloppy, the results will be mediocre at best.

Many knitters and crocheters skimp on the finishing touches. Don't. The extra time you spend making your pieces look truly professional will be well worth the effort.

Final Call: Weaving in Ends

By the time you finish a piece, you'll find you have yarn tails or ends that need attention. To hide them, you *weave in* the ends on the wrong side of your work.

Begin by threading the tail in a yarn needle. Now use the needle to weave in the ends, going under stitches. Make sure it doesn't show on the right side. You can weave in a horizontal or a vertical direction. Depending on how slippery the yarn is, you may want to weave in one direction, then go back in the opposite direction. If the yarn has more than one ply, you can separate the plies and weave half in one direction and the other half in the other direction. To finish, snip the yarn where you finished weaving with sharp scissors, leaving about ¼ inch of yarn.

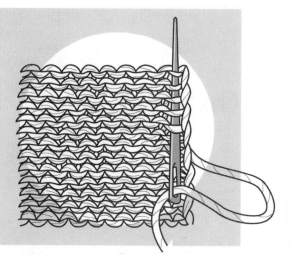

Using a yarn needle to weave in ends on a knitted piece.

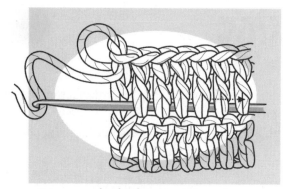

Using a crochet hook to weave in ends on a crocheted piece.

Sewing Up the Seams

Imagine a world-class chef assembling the makings of a wonderful meal: imported truffles, free-range chicken breasts, exotic spices. The chef carefully prepares the meal, and meticulously tastes and re-tastes the sauce. It's prepared with love. And then, moments before this never-before-experienced culinary delight is served, the chef runs out of patience, turns up the heat, and boils every smidgen of flavor from the meal until it's something the worst chain restaurant wouldn't dream of serving.

Have I made my point? All the work, time, and love you put into knitting and crocheting means those pieces deserve your care and attention at the end of the project when it's time to seam them together. If you're feeling impatient or rushed for time, come back to the job later. Don't be afraid to pull out the seams and rework them if they look uneven.

To piece together your work, you'll need a yarn needle and, depending on the method you choose, a crochet hook. You'll also need some straight pins to hold the seams while you're joining them.

Pointers

To assemble pieces, lay them on a flat surface and gently stretch them so they match through the seam. Pin the beginning and end of the seam. Now align the pieces at the center of the seam and pin this area. Continue matching and pinning until the seam is completely pinned, with pins approximately 1 to 2 inches apart. If you are seaming a piece in which the front and back have a matching stitch pattern, match these patterns carefully. Whether you pin the pieces with the right sides together or the wrong sides together depends on the method you're

Mattress Stitch

The *mattress stitch* is sometimes called the "invisible seam." When done correctly, it is truly invisible. It's very flexible and by far the best seam to use for putting together garments. If you learn this seaming method your garments will have the look of professional finishing—and the best thing is it isn't at all difficult!

It has the added advantage of working from the right side so you are always able to see what your seam will look like from the outside. Be careful to match the rows when you put your pieces together and to align your pattern stitch if you've used one.

You don't sew seams together using the mattress stitch. The two pieces to be joined are butted together and woven rather than sewn.

To begin weaving your knit pieces together, thread your tapestry needle, usually with the yarn you used to make the garment. Because this seam is invisible, if you've made a striped sweater you can use any of the colors. If the yarn is very bulky, you might want to use a lighter weight yarn to seam. If your project was made with a fine yarn and you want a little firmer seam, you can use two strands together.

Work 1 stitch in from the edge. Notice there are horizontal strands, or bars, of yarns running between the first stitch and the second stitch.

With the wrong sides together and the right sides facing up, anchor the yarn and the edge of the seam by inserting your needle up between the first and second stitches on the right, and down between the first and second stitches on the left. Bring it back up again where you began. Now run your needle under the first horizontal strand between the first and second stitches on the left. Next, run your needle under the first horizontal strand (or bar) between the first and second stitches on the right.

Every 4 stitches or so, gently stretch the seam to prevent your work from being too tight. If you wish, you can try running the needle under 2 horizontal strands at once; it makes the job go a little faster without any noticeable difference.

To seam crochet pieces, with the wrong sides together and the right sides facing up, anchor the yarn and the edge of the seam by inserting your needle up the first stitch on the right and down through the first stitch on the left. Bring it back up again through the first stitch on the right. Insert the needle through the next stitch on the left side. Now insert the needle through the corresponding stitch on the right side. Continue alternating between left and right all the way up the seam.

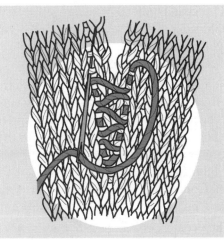

Working the mattress stitch on a knitted piece.

The seam should remain flat. If you notice it puckering, pull out the stitches and rework the seam with a looser hand. This method works best in a smaller stitch such as single crochet.

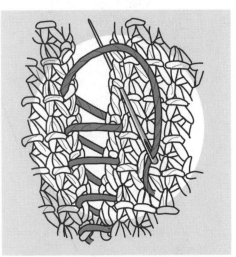

Weaving a seam on a crocheted piece.

Backstitch

Backstitch is a hand sewing technique that provides a sturdy seam. For this reason, it's often used for curved edges and shoulders. However, it's worked from the wrong side, so it's difficult to see how your seam looks on the right side. If you don't pull the stitches too tight, it's fairly flexible.

To backstitch, pin the pieces together with the right sides facing each other. Use the same yarn you used to knit or crochet the piece. You'll seam from right to left.

Insert the needle into the beginning of the seam from front to back, 1 stitch in. Insert it again the same way to anchor the yarn and the edge. Now insert the needle 2 stitches to the left. Count back 1 stitch and reinsert the needle. Count forward 2 stitches and reinsert the needle. Count back 1 stitch and reinsert the needle. Continue all the way down the seam.

When you backstitch, be sure the stitches are close enough together that you don't leave gaping holes. If you can see holes in the seam, you've probably created stitches that are too large. You will need to pull out and redo the seam.

Overcast or Whip Stitch

Overcast or *whip stitch* is often used to join squares or strips together for a decorative effect. It can be stitched from the right or the wrong side, but it's fancier if worked on the right side with the wrong sides pinned together. You can use the same yarn or a contrasting color to enhance the effect. Whether joining knit or crochet pieces, you can work through both loops, the front loop only, or the back loop only.

To whip stitch, you'll work from right to left. Insert your needle from back to front, straight across. Bring the needle over the seam and insert it from back to front again, 1 stitch to the left. Bring the needle out on the front side straight across once again. Repeat this process, being careful not to pull the yarn too tight.

Backstitching a knitted piece.

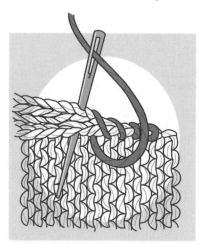

Whip stitching a knitted piece.

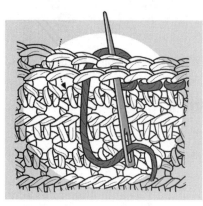

Backstitching a crocheted piece.

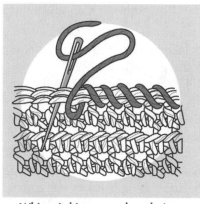

Whip stitching a crocheted piece.

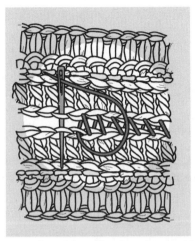

Create a decorative effect by whip stitching through only the 2 front loops.

Slip Stitch

Put down the yarn needle. This next seaming technique requires a crochet hook. A *slip stitch* seam creates a very firm, even seam that works well for straight edges. Because this seaming method produces an inflexible seam, it's not a good choice for garments but it's a fine choice for joining squares and strips.

To slip stitch a seam, place the wrong sides of the pieces together. With the right side facing you, insert your hook, front to back, under the 2 top loops of the stitches of both pieces. Yarn over, and in one motion pull through the stitches and the loop on your hook. (If you need a little extra slip stitch help, turn to Chapter 13.)

 Tangles _____

Check your seam often to be sure it isn't puckering. Don't be afraid to pull out the seam and work more loosely; the seam needs to lie flat. A slip stitch seam can get bulky; if this happens, stitch through one loop of each piece instead of both loops.

Slip stitching a seam on a knitted piece.

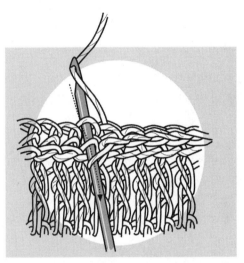

Slip stitching a seam through 1 loop on each crocheted piece.

For Knitters Only: Grafting

Knitters have one final option: *grafting.* Also called the *Kitchener stitch*, active stitches (stitches that have not been bound off) are joined together invisibly by creating a knit row using a yarn needle. You can use grafting to join the toes of socks, shoulders of sweaters, and the tips of mittens. You must have the same number of active stitches to graft them together. When finished, it looks like continuous rows of stockinette.

Yarn Spinning _____

The day he was beheaded in 1649, King Charles (Charles Stuart) wore a shirt made by a master knitter. Today, the shirt is on display at the Museum of London.

Grafting can be a little tricky initially. Just pick a quiet time when you won't be distracted and follow the instructions. As you pull the yarn through each stitch, try not to pull too tightly or too loosely; the aim is to simulate the same gauge as the knit pieces. It's easier to tighten them up a bit than loosen them by pulling the stitches with the end of your yarn needle moving across the row.

To graft stitches together, follow these steps:

1. Cut the active yarn (the yarn currently feeding from the end of your work) with a tail about 1½ inches long for every stitch you'll be grafting. Thread this yarn through a yarn needle.

2. Align the wrong sides of the stitches together. You'll work from right to left. Move the stitches toward the end of the needle.

3. Insert the yarn needle, as if to purl, through the first stitch on the front needle. Leave the stitch on the needle.

4. Insert the yarn needle, as if to knit, through the first stitch on the rear needle. Leave the stitch on the needle.

5. Insert the yarn needle, as if to knit, through the first stitch on the front needle again. Slip the stitch off the needle.

6. Insert the yarn needle, as if to purl, through what is now the first stitch on the front needle. Leave the stitch on the needle.

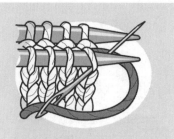

Step 5: Insert the yarn needle, as if to knit, through the first stitch on the front needle again. Slip the stitch off the needle.

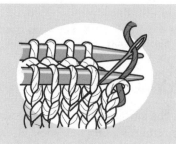

Step 6: Insert the yarn needle, as if to purl, through what is now the first stitch on the front needle. Leave the stitch on the needle.

7. Insert the yarn needle, as if to purl, through the first stitch on the rear needle again. Slip the stitch off the needle.

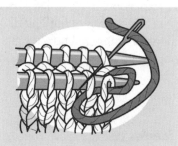

Step 7: Insert the yarn needle, as if to purl, through the first stitch on the rear needle again. Slip the stitch off the needle.

8. Insert the yarn needle, as if to knit, through what is now the first stitch on the rear needle. Leave the stitch on the needle.

Repeat steps 5 through 8 until you have grafted all the stitches. The mantra "knit purl purl knit" makes it easy to remember!

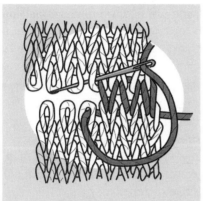

Grafting looks like continuous rows of stockinette.

Blocking

Blocking is a way to even up your work using water or steam. It may or may not be necessary, depending on how your work looks when you're done. If your stitches are uneven, it can do wonders to even them out and make textured patterns "pop out." If the pieces are a little out of shape, you'll need to block them. Lacy patterns almost always need blocking to open up the pattern and make it more visible. It can also make seaming a little easier.

Blocking is not a miracle cure—it won't turn a size 8 sweater into a size 14. But it is your opportunity to even things up a bit.

 Tangles _____

Always check the yarn label for care instructions. Do not attempt to block a project made with yarn labeled "dry clean only." And never, ever apply an iron to your projects in an attempt to block them. The stitches will flatten and the yarn will become limp and lifeless.

Whether you block your project before or after you have seamed it together is entirely up to you. It doesn't hurt anything to block it before you seam and, as mentioned, it can make seaming easier. Sometimes you might think an item doesn't need to be blocked and it's only after you have put it together that you decide it needs a little extra help.

Acrylic yarn, or yarn that has a high acrylic content, does not block well using the methods you're about to learn. Blocking will have little or no effect. The best way to block acrylic is to throw your project in the washer and dryer, following label directions.

Wet Blocking and Washing

Wet blocking involves washing or completely submerging the pieces in water, then shaping them and leaving them to dry. You might want to just go ahead and wash your project, as the yarn has picked up a lot of dirt and oil from your hands.

1. Fill the sink with lukewarm—not hot—water. Use a pH balanced soap or shampoo. Add a little to the water and mix it up.

2. Gently submerge the item into the water. Stir it around gently and let it soak about 20 minutes. Don't agitate it or rub.

3. Empty the water and fill the sink with lukewarm water again to rinse. Keep rinsing until the water is clear.

4. Lay down a couple towels next to the sink, lay the item on these, and roll up the towels. Gently press down on the towels to get rid of excess water. The towels will be soaked. You might need to lay down another set of towels and repeat the rolling and squeezing process. Don't wring or twist all your hard work!

5. Lay out the item on dry towels or a blocking board. Get out your measuring tape and use it to determine how wide and long the piece should be. Gently stretch the piece into this size. Even up the seams. Push any ribbing in with your fingers. Run your hands gently over the piece to smooth it flat; you are essentially ironing the piece with your hands.

6. Replace the towels as necessary. Keep doing this until the piece is dry. It'll be wonderfully shaped, with flat seams, ready to use.

Pinning

If pieces require quite a bit of blocking, try pinning them in place using rust-proof pins while they dry. The pins hold the piece in place and, when dry, it will retain the shape in which it was pinned down.

You'll need to prepare a surface. If the piece is small, you can fold two towels in half and stack them on top of each other (to create a surface four towels thick). If the piece is larger, you can wrap towels over a piece of board such as plywood.

You can begin by wet blocking or washing as you just learned. When the piece has dried until it's damp, pin down the piece on all edges after gently stretching the piece into the correct measurements. Or you can pin the piece in place and then spritz water over it. Leave it alone until it's completely dry.

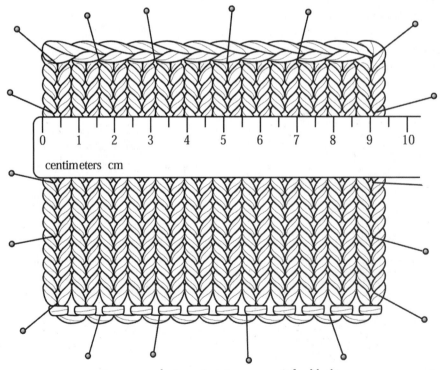

Measure and pin a piece to prepare it for blocking.

Steaming

You can carefully steam a piece in a couple of different ways. But remember, steaming means just that—it doesn't mean ironing! Steaming is not the first choice for blocking, so it's a good idea to test it first on a swatch to see the results you'll obtain.

Lay your piece out and pin in place to the correct measurements as you've already learned. Now hold a steam iron about 10 inches above the piece and let the steam dampen it. You can also lay a wet cloth over the piece and hold the iron over the cloth, but do not touch the iron to the cloth! Leave it in place until completely dry.

Don't steam block ribbing, garter stitch, or cables. It will flatten them instead of helping them to pop out. Avoid steaming acrylic as well.

The Least You Need to Know

◆ Take your time when finishing your piece; a bad finishing job can negate all your hard knitting and crocheting work.

◆ Weave in ends on the wrong side with a yarn needle, being careful they don't show on the right side.

◆ There are a number of options for seaming pieces together; the mattress stitch or invisible seam is usually the best choice.

◆ Blocking can even out stitches and straighten pieces.

In This Chapter

- ◆ Decorative crochet edges
- ◆ Slip stitch, reverse single crochet, and picot edgings
- ◆ Creating knit selvage edges
- ◆ Simple seed stitch edging

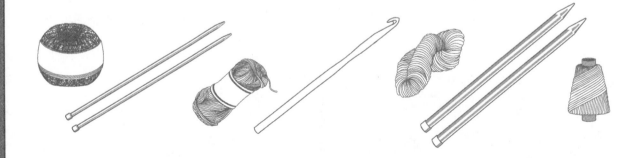

Chapter

19

Edgings

Edgings are often used around square or rectangular pieces such as afghans and scarves. They can be used for decoration or to help the piece lie flat. Consider using them to hide the edges of your work, particularly if you've changed colors. They can be added on later or worked as you go, depending upon the edging.

There are hundreds, if not thousands, of edging patterns for knit and crochet. Some are intricate while others are simple. A fancy edging can dress up an otherwise plain project.

The Finishing Touch: Crocheted Edgings

Crocheted edgings can add a special touch to knitted or crocheted items. Let's play around with a couple; you'll want to keep these little gems in your bag of tricks. You can use these edgings as an accent in a different color from the main piece, or as a finishing edge in the same color.

Slip Stitch Edging

Slip stitch edging is an easy stitch that leaves an attractive, firm edge that resembles a braid. This edging does not add any extra width or height to the finished piece.

To work this edging, follow the same procedure you learned in Chapter 13 for working a slip stitch: Insert your hook, front to back, under the 2 top loops of the stitch (or into the stitch if it's a knitted piece). Yarn over, and in one motion pull through the stitch and the loop on your hook. One loop remains on the hook.

Pointers _____

You don't want your work to pucker or flare when adding an edging. If it's puckering, add more stitches and try keeping your work flat. If it's flaring, you have too many stitches. If you are working around corners, work 3 stitches into each corner so the corners will remain firm squares.

Reverse Single Crochet Edging

Reverse single crochet edging looks similar to slip stitch edging and also resembles a braid. It's a little less firm and adds a row to your work. Follow the same steps you learned in Chapter 15 for reverse single crochet. You'll be working from left to right, instead of right to left.

1. With the right side of your work facing you, attach your yarn to the stitch on the left side of your work and pull up a loop.

2. Moving from left to right, insert your hook into the next stitch and again pull up a loop. Yarn over and pull through both loops on your hook to complete the single crochet.

3. Repeat step 2 to complete the edge.

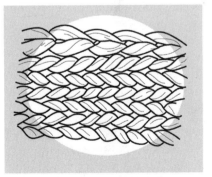

Reverse single crochet adds a braidlike edge to your pieces.

Picot Edging

Picot is a very distinctive edging. It offers a lacy look with points that is wonderful for finishing baby projects and doilies, and it makes a great alternative to fringe on a shawl.

There are many variations of this basic edging. Picots are formed with 3, 4, or 5 chains with different crochet stitches in various combinations.

Here's how to make a 3 chain picot edge formed with single crochet (to work a 4 or 5 chain picot, simply make 4 or 5 chains in the first step):

1. With the right side of the work facing you, attach the yarn, work 1 single crochet in the next 3 stitches, and then chain 3.

2. Repeat step 1 across the edge.

Yarn Spinning _____

When crochet appeared in Middle Europe—Italy, France, Belgium, and England—it was considered a lace-making art. Italy referred to this art as *Orvieto Lace*.

Knit Edgings

Although many knit edgings are worked after your project is completed by picking up stitches and knitting them in an edging pattern, the edgings you're about to learn are knit as you go. They are very simple and, as you'll soon see, quite functional.

Creating Selvage Edges

You can add a finishing touch to your work as you knit by working *selvage* stitches. Selvage really just means edge, so every time you knit you create a selvage because all knitting has an edge. By working the first and last stitches of every row in a certain way, however, you produce a neat edge that will stand alone. Using selvage stitches also provides a clean basis for sewing seams or adding neck ribbing. Even if you're going to seam pieces together, using selvages is a good idea because it makes seaming much easier.

Needle Talk _____

The **selvage** (also spelled *selvedge*) is the edge of the piece, generally the first and last stitches.

A *chain edge selvage* produces a neat chain along the edge, which is perfect for afghans and scarves where you won't work an additional edging. Throughout the piece, work the first and last stitches of the row like this (see Chapter 9 for how to slip stitches):

Row 1: Slip the first stitch knitwise; work across the row; knit the last stitch in the row.

Row 2: Slip the first stitch purlwise; work across the row; purl the last stitch in the row.

Another useful selvage is the *slipped garter edge*. This selvage is also decorative. It's easy to remember because each row is worked the same way: Slip the first stitch knitwise and knit the last stitch.

Seed Stitch Edging

Suppose you want to knit a scarf in a fancy yarn that is just stockinette. You've already learned that, because of the way the fabric is constructed, stockinette will curl. You need an edging to help it lie flat. Selvage stitches alone won't do the trick!

Work the first and last 4 rows in seed stitch (refer to Chapter 7). Then on the first and last 4 stitches of each row, work seed stitch. You can also add in a selvage stitch on each side if you wish. It's really very easy! Here's how:

Row 1 (right side): k1, p1, k1, p1, k across to the last 4 stitches, p1, k1, p1, k1

Row 2 (wrong side): k1, p1, k1, p1, p across to the last 4 stitches, p1, k1, p1, k1

Garter stitch is sometimes used as an edging instead of seed stitch but that doesn't work as well. Although garter stitch does lie flat, it takes more rows to produce an inch of garter stitch than it does stockinette. As a result, your fabric will curve and wander, and you won't end up with a nice, straight scarf.

The Least You Need to Know

◆ You can add decorative crocheted edges to either knitted or crocheted pieces.

◆ If you are crocheting around corners, work 3 stitches into each corner so the corners will remain firm squares.

◆ Selvage stitches add a nice edge and make seaming easier.

◆ Sometimes edgings help the piece lie flat.

In This Chapter

- ◆ Funky fringe
- ◆ No-hassle tassels
- ◆ Big or small pom poms
- ◆ For knitters: how to make I-Cord

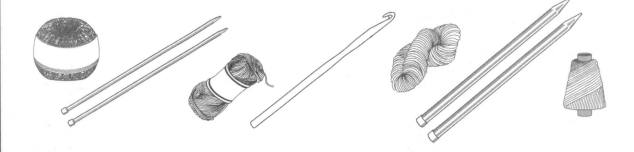

Chapter 20

Embellishments

Embellishments are the little extras that add pizzazz to knit and crochet projects. Use them on hats, slippers, afghans, shawls, and much more. You're only limited by your imagination!

In this chapter, you'll learn how easy it is to make fringe, pom poms, and tassels. Knitters will learn how to make I-Cord, a "tube" of knitting.

Fringe Is Fun

You can add fringe to all sorts of projects. It looks great on afghans, scarves, and shawls. Fringe can be long or short, made with lots of strands or just a few, spaced closed together or far apart—the choice is yours. The strands can be even (as described in the following steps) or you can intentionally make them of various lengths in each fringe section; this is an interesting look when you combine more than one yarn.

Some yarn unravels at the end when it's cut; some people like this look and other folks don't. Again, the choice is yours.

Here's how to add fringe:

1. Cut pieces of yarn 1 inch more than twice the desired length. The number of pieces depends upon how thick you want the fringe, the intervals at which you'll add it, and the width of your project.

2. Pick up the desired number of strands for one section, and line them up evenly.

3. Fold the strands in half.

4. Using a crochet hook, insert the hook from the wrong side to the right side at the place you want the fringe. Grab the folded yarn with the crochet hook and pull it part way through to form a loop. Make sure you pull through all the strands.

5. Pull the ends of the fringe through the loop with your fingers or a hook. Even it out and pull tightly to knot.

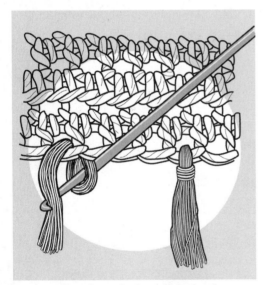

Pulling the ends through the loop.

6. Lay the project on the floor or table and comb the fringe straight with your fingers. Even up straggly ends using a pair of scissors.

Yarn Spinning

As part of the restoration of the eighteenth-century Warner House in Portsmouth, New Hampshire, 47 volunteers knit an elaborate bedspread to mimic one that had been in the house during the nineteenth century. Using tiny needles and miles of cotton thread, the volunteers knit and pieced together 1,024 squares. The project began in January 1996 and was completed in June 1997.

Top It with a Tassel

You can use tassels in place of fringe, or add a tassel to the top of a hat or a bookmark. Or how about making tassels for your curtain tiebacks? They're a little more work than fringe, but not hard at all.

Here's how you do it:

1. Wind yarn around a piece of cardboard. The length of the cardboard determines the length of your tassel. How many times you wind the yarn determines how thick the tassel will be. Cut the yarn.

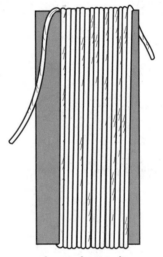

To make a tassel, start by winding yarn around cardboard.

2. Thread another piece of the same yarn about 16 inches long through a tapestry needle. Insert the needle at the top, going under the wound yarn, and knot tightly.

3. Remove the cardboard. With one end of the yarn you used to tie the knot, wind it around your tassel as far down from the top as desired. You can tie and knot a second section with a separate piece of yarn if you'd like.

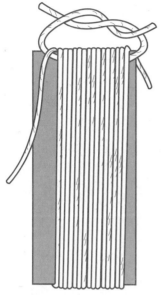

Tie a knot at the top after weaving yarn under the wound yarn with a needle.

4. Weave around the tie several times with the yarn in the tapestry needle to hold it in place. Insert it through the ball of the tassel to anchor it and use it to attach your tassel to the project along with the other end.

5. With scarp scissors, cut at the looped end and trim the ends.

A completed tassel.

Puffy Pom Poms

Pom poms are an easy and fun way to top off hats, slippers, and other projects. These intriguing little "puffs" of yarn are simple to make. You can make them big and fluffy, or smaller and less full.

Here's how to make a pom pom:

1. Wind yarn around cardboard. The more you wind, the fuller the pom pom will be. The longer the cardboard, the bigger the pom pom will be. You can also just wind loops around your fingers.

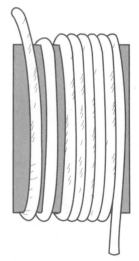

To make a pom pom, start by winding yarn around cardboard.

2. Tie another piece of yarn around the back and front in the middle. Carefully pull out the cardboard, and pull and knot tightly. If you don't knot it tightly, the strands will fall out.

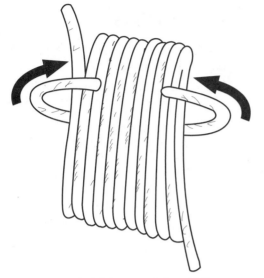

Knot it tightly around the middle.

3. With sharp scissors, cut through the loops you made on each side.

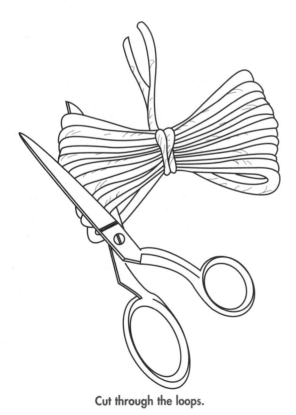

Cut through the loops.

4. Fluff it out with your fingers and trim the ends.

A finished pom pom.

For Knitters: I-Cord

I-Cord is a three-dimensional tube of knitting. It has all sorts of uses. You can make necklaces or use it for purse handles. Make a length of it in a matching or contrasting color and sew it in an abstract swirl design to embellish any project.

You'll need two double pointed needles to make I-Cord. Here's how:

1. Cast on any number of stitches, usually between 3 and 5, on double pointed needles. Use the needle size appropriate to the yarn. The larger the needle, the thicker your I-Cord will be.

2. Knit every stitch.

3. Slide the stitches to the other end of the double pointed needle. Knit every stitch again.

4. Slide the stitches back to the other end again and knit.

5. Continue until the cord is the length you wish. Bind off all stitches.

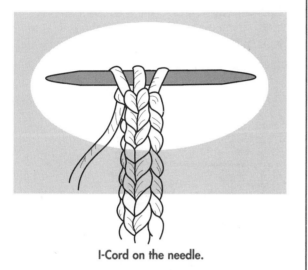

I-Cord on the needle.

The Least You Need to Know

◆ Embellishments add a little pizzazz to almost any project.

◆ Use a crochet hook to attach fringe.

◆ Tassels and pom poms can be made any size or in any thickness.

◆ I-Cord is knit with double pointed needles.

In This Part

21 Talking the Talk: Reading a Knit or Crochet Pattern

22 Knitting Patterns

23 Crochet Patterns

Part **5**

Knitting and Crocheting Patterns

The first chapter in this part will help you understand the language and decipher the "secret code" in which knitting and crochet patterns are written.

You'll also find knitting and crochet patterns for a variety of projects to try out your new skills. They are all easy enough to be worked as first projects, and there is extra help along the way. Give them a try and see how much fun it can be to create something with nothing but yarn and a hook or some needles.

You can see color photos of all the projects at www.knitabit.net.

In This Chapter

- The basic information in patterns
- Cracking the sizing code
- Understanding the language of asterisks and parentheses
- The schematic is a blueprint
- Common terms found in patterns
- Reading charts

Chapter **21**

Talking the Talk: Reading a Knit or Crochet Pattern

Look at any knit or crochet pattern and it seems as if it's written in a secret code. Well, it is written in a kind of code, but it isn't at all a secret. Most patterns are written in a standard format. It not only saves space to write a pattern this way, believe it or not, it actually makes it easier to follow.

Unless you know the code, you can't read the pattern. In this chapter, you'll learn to decipher the hieroglyphics. Knitting and crochet use the same format for patterns; the only difference is the abbreviations that are used for the various stitches.

Understanding the Basics

Aside from instructions, patterns contain basic information you will need to complete the project. This information is found at the beginning of each pattern. Let's take a closer look at what's included.

Common Abbreviations

Common abbreviations and their meanings for both knitting and crochet are listed in Appendix B. Many patterns include a list of abbreviations used within that pattern but if they don't, you can refer to the appendix. Their meanings will soon become second nature and you'll rarely need to reference them.

Yarn

The pattern will you tell you all about the yarn you'll need to complete the project. If it's a garment that can be made in more than one size, it will indicate how many balls or skeins you need for the various sizes, following the same order in which the sizes are given. It will also tell you how much 1 ball or skein weighs and the yardage, along with the fiber content. This is useful if you wish to substitute a different yarn.

Yarn Spinning

Some artists specializing in knitting or crocheting have made their reputations by the unusual "yarn" they choose to manipulate into loops. One example is Maine-based artist Katherine Cobey, who gained fame for knitting a wedding gown from strips of white garbage bags!

Gauge

The gauge you need to obtain to ensure the project ends up the size you want it to will be indicated. Sometimes it will show a row gauge, particularly if it is a color pattern and the designer has worked out a pattern that totally repeats from top to bottom.

Make sure you work your gauge swatch over the pattern stitch you're instructed to. Your gauge will be off if you work up your swatch in stockinette or single crochet and you were supposed to use a lacy, open work stitch pattern.

Suggested Needle or Hook Size

The pattern will also give the estimated needle or hook sizes needed—meaning if the size indicated doesn't give you the proper gauge, by all

means use a different size until you do measure up. The size given is only the size the person who designed the pattern used; it doesn't mean it's the size you should just start knitting or crocheting with without checking your gauge.

Other Materials

The pattern may include information about other materials you'll need, such as buttons. It will explain the number of buttons as well as the size.

Stitch Multiples

A *stitch multiple* is the number of stitches necessary to complete one entire repeat of a pattern stitch. For example, if a pattern stitch is a multiple of 4, any number of stitches that can be evenly divided by 4 will work and ensure your pattern stitch is repeated evenly across the row. Often a stitch multiple includes an extra stitch or two. A stitch multiple of "4 plus 2" means you can use any number of stitches divisible by 4, plus an extra 2 stitches (6, 10, 14, 18, and so on).

Stitch multiples aren't always included, and when they are it's mainly as a courtesy to the reader. It's helpful to know this information if you feel confident in your skills and wish to change the size of the pattern in some way.

Stitch Pattern

Patterns may or may not give you row-by-row instructions for a stitch pattern. It might be that the pattern doesn't call for a special stitch pattern or the actual instructions might contain all the information you need to know. If you're reading along and the instructions suddenly tell you to work 8 inches in stitch pattern (or seed stitch or cable pattern I, etc.), refer to the beginning of the pattern to find out how to do that.

Which Size?

If you're making a garment, the various sizes included with the pattern will be shown, with increasing sizes indicated in parentheses. The pattern will have different instructions for the particular size you are making in parentheses, in the same order in which the sizes are shown. For example, a pattern might read:

> To fit chest size 34" (36", 38", 40", 42")

The entire pattern is written showing slightly different instructions for these sizes in the same order within parentheses. If you are making the 36" size, for example, you will always follow the first number in the parentheses for any shaping instructions:

> Dec 1 st at the beg of the next 4 (5, 6, 6, 7) rows

In this example you would decrease 1 stitch at the beginning of the next 5 rows.

Tangles _____

To avoid accidentally following the wrong sizing instructions, before you start, circle the instructions for the size that you will be making. You then can easily see the numbers you need to follow.

Sweater patterns will also tell you the finished chest measurement of the sweater for each of the sizes. This is not your *chest* size, this is the finished chest size of the sweater. Generally, you don't want your sweaters to fit skin-tight. You want a certain amount of ease or extra fabric. The amount of ease often depends on the style of the sweater. If you're not sure which size to make, measure straight across the chest of a sweater you have that fits you well. This will tell you the final chest measurement of that sweater.

What About Those Asterisks?

Asterisks play a crucial role in patterns. They indicate the start of a section that you will repeat as many times as given. The section to be repeated can be at the beginning of a row or in the middle of a row.

Here's an example:

> *k2tog, yo. Repeat from * to end of row.

These instructions are telling you to knit 2 stitches together and then do a yarn over. You repeat these two procedures all the way across the rest of the row.

Here's an example with an asterisk in the middle of a row:

> k1, *p2, k2; rep from *, end k1

In English, you are being asked to knit 1 stitch, then purl 2 and knit 2 across the entire row until the last stitch, then knit 1 stitch.

Remember, the asterisk is used in the same way in both knitting and crochet patterns.

Here's an example with an asterisk in the middle of a row in crochet instructions:

> sc in first st, *dc in next 3 sc, sc in next sc; rep from *, end sc in last st. Ch 3, turn

Here's the translation: Single crochet in the first stitch, then work 3 double crochets and a single crochet across the entire row until the last stitch, then work a single crochet. Chain 3 stitches and turn your work.

And What About Parentheses?

Parentheses work in much the same way as asterisks in both knitting and crochet patterns. When you see them, it means to *work what is in the parentheses* as many times as given. You will usually find them in a long line of instructions, setting apart a portion of the pattern that is repeated. It makes that long line of instructions shorter and easier to follow.

Here's a knitting example:

> k7, p2, k3, p5, k3, (p2, kl, p1) 3 times, k3, p5, k3

Looking at just the part *within* the parentheses, this means you should purl 2, knit 1, and purl 1 a total of 3 times. Parentheses are also used to indicate to work what is *inside* the parentheses into 1 stitch.

Here's an example you might see in knitting:

> (k1, p1, k1) in next st

This means you would knit 1, purl 1, and knit 1 all in the next stitch. You would be increasing 2 stitches and you might work this to make a bobble.

A crochet pattern might read:

> (dc, sc, dc) in next sc

This means to work a double crochet, then a single crochet, then another double crochet, all in the same single crochet.

Yarn Spinning

During the mid-nineteenth century, the noble ladies of England had time on their hands and an interest in finding a hobby. They turned to crochet. As you might expect, the craft experienced a surge in popularity at this time.

Picture Perfect

People aren't clones of one another; we have many different body types and hence measurements. Some of us are short waisted, some of us have long arms. Sweater patterns often include a *schematic*—a drawing or blueprint of the sweater showing the measurements at various points for all the sizes included with the pattern.

The schematic provides valuable information. It can help you decipher pattern instructions. It can also help you decide if this sweater is right for you. Know your measurements and read the schematic measurements. Once you have mastered the basics of knitting and crochet, take a chance and think about how you can make slight adjustments to the pattern to give you a more personal fit. From there you can springboard to full-fledged designing and never make an ill-fitting sweater.

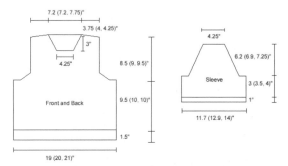

A schematic tells you the measurements of the sweater at various points for all included sizes.

Miscellaneous Considerations

Patterns commonly use some other terminology that can be confusing when you're just starting. The people who write patterns aren't intentionally trying to confuse you; the universal pattern language just expresses certain concepts in a particular way.

Work Even

The term *work even* is commonly seen after working a series of increases or decreases. It means you are to work in the pattern stitch for the given number of inches or rows, without increasing or decreasing.

Ending on WS Row

If you see the term "ending on WS row" or something similar, it means to finish the sequence with a wrong side row completed. It indicates you are going to be doing something on the right side of the work next. You may also see the direction "end on RS row," in which case you would finish with a right side row completed, ready to begin on the wrong side.

Reverse Shaping

Cardigans will almost always give you directions for one side of the cardigan while the instructions for the other side will simply state, "Work as for left front, reversing shaping." When you make a cardigan, you will have two front pieces: a left front and a right front. Each needs to have the armholes and the neck on the appropriate side so when it's all put together, everything is where it's supposed to be.

When you reverse shaping, you'll work the neck and armhole at the opposite ends of where you worked them for the first front. How do you do this? If you created the armhole at the beginning of a right side row for the first piece, create the armhole at the beginning of a wrong side row for the second piece. Do the same thing with the neck opening.

Decreasing or Increasing on Certain Rows

You may be asked to decrease or increase stitches on certain rows; it might be every row, every other row, every 4th row, a different number, or even some combination. It can be downright confusing just which rows they're talking about! Let's take a look at what it all means:

◆ **Every row.** Follow the instructions for as many consecutive rows as you're told.

◆ **Every other row.** The instructions are worked on the given number of alternate rows. For example, "Dec 1 st at each end every other row 3 times" means to decrease 1 stitch at the beginning and end of every alternate row a total of 3 times.

This would be rows 1, 3, and 5; don't confuse these row numbers with the pattern stitch row numbers, if there is one.

◆ **Every 4th row.** There are 3 rows between every 4th row where you wouldn't follow the instructions. "Inc 1 st at each end every 4th row 3 times" means you would increase 1 stitch at the beginning and end of rows 1, 5, and 9. Again, don't confuse these row numbers with the pattern stitch row numbers.

◆ **A combination.** The instructions state, "Dec 1 st at each end every 4th row 3 times, then every 8th row 3 times." In this example, you would decrease 1 stitch at the beginning and end of rows 1, 5, and 9 and then rows 17, 25, and 33.

Pointers _____

Place a Post-it note at the bottom of the row you're currently working. Each time you finish a row, move the paper up one row on the chart. You won't lose your place and you won't accidentally work the wrong row.

Decrease or Increase Evenly

Sometimes you will be asked to decrease or increase a specific number of stitches across a row evenly. The pattern will tell you how many stitches to decrease or increase and you should know at that point how many working stitches you currently have. But what does it mean when you're asked to do it "evenly"?

You don't want your increases or decreases all bunched up at one end of the row. Your work will be lopsided if you do that. You'll need to figure out where to do each increase or decrease so that they're spread out evenly across the row.

Let's suppose you have 100 stitches and the pattern calls for 10 increases evenly across the row. Dividing 100 by 10 equals 10. You might conclude you should increase 1 stitch every

10 stitches. However, this would not quite be even, for the 1st increase would occur on the 10th stitch while the 10th, or last, increase would occur on the 100th stitch. In other words, at the beginning of the row you will have 10 stitches before an increase occurs and at the end of the row there will be no stitches after the last increase. This is not evenly increasing.

Add 1 to the number of stitches you are to increase or decrease, then divide the current number of working stitches by that number. That will tell you how frequently to work each increase or decrease. The numbers don't always come out evenly, however. In this example, 100 divided by 11 equals 9.09. Obviously, you cannot increase 1 stitch every 9.09 stitches. Therefore, you have to cheat a little and increase 1 stitch every 9th stitch 9 times and 1 stitch every 10th stitch 1 time.

> Increase 1 stitch every 9th stitch 9 times = 81
>
> Increase 1 stitch every 10th stitch 1 time = 10
>
> Work the last 9 stitches after the 10th increase = 9
>
> 81 + 10 + 9 = 100

Keeping to Pattern

When you decrease or increase and there is a pattern stitch of some sort (other than just plain single crochet or knit every row for example), you need to determine and keep track of where you're at within the pattern stitch on each row. This is called *keeping to pattern*. You want the piece to look the same throughout, so this is why you need to keep to pattern. There is no magic formula for this and it will continually change as you decrease or increase stitches. Sometimes, you can tell where you're at just by looking at the piece. Otherwise, you'll just have to keep track, using paper and pencil if necessary.

Let's look at an example. You have bound off 3 stitches (in crochet you would have slipped stitch through 3 stitches). Here's the pattern stitch you've been working (knitting terms are used but the same principle applies to crochet):

> Knit 1, *purl 3, knit 2; rep from * across

The first 3 stitches of the row no longer exist. The row begins with knit 1 so you would not work that stitch. The next 2 purl stitches would not be worked either. You would begin the row purl 1, knit 2, then repeat from the *.

At the Same Time

Sometimes you will be directed to do two things at once. When making a sweater, you may have to decrease stitches along the armhole as well as the neck edge. The pattern will give you a set of instructions for the first task, followed by another direction to do something else at the same time.

Knitters Only: Bind Off in Pattern

When you see this, it means you should bind off using whatever stitch you would use to continue the established pattern. Pretend you are going to continue to work the row as you have been. Knit or purl each stitch before it's bound off as appropriate to the pattern. If the next stitch would have been a purl, then purl that stitch and bind off. If the next stitch would have been a knit, then knit that stitch and bind off.

Reading Charts

Knitting and crochet stitch patterns and color motifs are sometimes presented in chart form instead of written out in words. Each square represents a type of stitch to be worked, represented by a symbol, or a color you are to use. Stitch keys are included so that you will know the meaning of each symbol used.

Begin reading charts at the lower right corner. The first row, and all odd rows, is read from right to left. The second row, and all even rows, is read from left to right.

Here's an example of a simple pattern stitch chart for knitting:

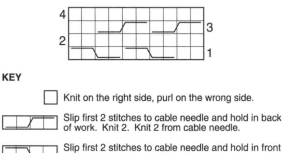

KEY

☐ Knit on the right side, purl on the wrong side.

Slip first 2 stitches to cable needle and hold in back of work. Knit 2. Knit 2 from cable needle.

Slip first 2 stitches to cable needle and hold in front of work. Knit 2. Knit 2 from cable needle.

Charted patterns can make working complex patterns easier.

Here's how the pattern would look if written out:

Row 1: K2, c4f twice.

Row 2: P across.

Row 3: C4b twice, k2.

Row 4: P across.

Charts have several advantages. The visual depiction enables you to easily see where you are in a pattern and helps ensure that you are on the right track. Also, charted patterns generally contain fewer errors. No one's perfect, and patterns can contain typos and other errors. It's much easier to see and correct any errors in a chart than in written instructions.

Don't Skip the Instructions!

Here's a final piece of advice. This may seem obvious, but read the instructions. All of them. Twice, in fact. You might think something is missing but it's probably in the pattern somewhere and you just overlooked it.

Reading through a pattern will also give you a good idea if the project is within your skill level. If you look through it and don't understand half of what it's asking you to do, come back to it when you've got more experience under your belt. This isn't to say that you should never attempt a pattern with a technique you've never used before or one that includes something you

don't quite understand. Your skills will not improve if all you ever make are scarves done in garter stitch or single crochet.

Pointers

Reading pattern speak becomes easier when you really start to work from a pattern. If you're initially confused about what the instructions are saying, write them out in longhand and work through them step by step. This might take a little extra time, but it will help you get used to reading patterns. In addition, it might save you the time and heartbreak of ripping out and redoing your work.

If you come across a particular part of a pattern you don't understand, practice on a swatch. Try following the directions step by step, without thinking ahead. This will often help you make sense of what the pattern is telling you to do.

The Least You Need to Know

- ◆ In addition to instructions, patterns contain other information such as the materials you'll need to complete the project.

- ◆ If a pattern contains instructions for multiple sizes, circle all the instructions you'll work for your size before you begin the project.

- ◆ Asterisks and parentheses indicate repeats in a pattern.

- ◆ A schematic is a drawing or blueprint of a sweater showing the measurements at various points for all the sizes included with the pattern.

- ◆ Charts are easy to read and each square symbolizes a color or stitch.

- ◆ Make sure you read all of the instructions that are included with the pattern.

In This Chapter

◆ An easy dishcloth pattern teaches you to increase and decrease

◆ Knit a simple, pretty scarf

◆ Learn to felt by knitting a two-color purse

◆ Top if off with a hat knit on two needles

◆ Your first sweater: a short sleeved pullover

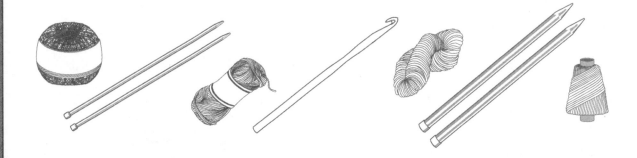

Chapter 22

Knitting Patterns

This chapter has five easy-to-knit patterns to get you started in your knitting adventure. Although they're written in the standard pattern format, extra help is included along the way to ensure success.

Refer to the chapter where each concept was discussed if you find yourself wondering how to work a certain point of the pattern or don't understand something.

Cotton Dishcloth

Dishcloths are simple to make, and you can use just about any stitch pattern. They are fun and quick to create, so making them can also be addictive!

This pattern is knit diagonally and will give you lots of practice with increases and decreases. You start out by casting on a few stitches and then increase until you have a triangle. Then you begin decreasing and end up with a square!

Knitted dishcloth.

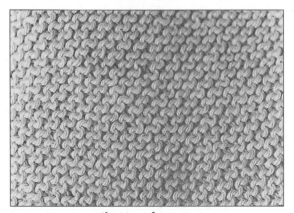

Close-up of pattern.

Size:

8.5 " × 8.5 "

Materials:

- 1 ball Lily Sugar 'N Cream (color of your choice)

  100% cotton

  Solid colors:

  109 meters/120 yards

  70 grams/2.5 ounces

- Needles size 8 U.S. (5mm) or size needed to obtain gauge

- Tapestry needle

Gauge:

17.5 sts = 4" in garter st (knit every row)

Instructions:

CO 4 sts.

Row 1: Knit across.

Row 2: K2. In the next stitch, knit into the front and then the back of the stitch (1 bar increase made). K1.

Row 3: K2. YO (1 increase made). Knit to the end of the row.

Repeat Row 3 until you have 46 stitches on the needle. You have a triangle at this point, and the long edge of the triangle is on your needle.

Next Row: K1, k2tog (1 decrease made), yo (1 increase made), k2tog (1 decrease made), knit to the end of the row.

Repeat this last row until 5 stitches remain on the needle.

Next Row: K2, k2tog (1 decrease made), k1.

Last Row: BO the 4 stitches on the needle.

Finishing:

Weave in ends near edge with tapestry needle.

Abbreviations:

BO	Bind off
CO	Cast on
K	Knit
K2tog	Knit 2 together
YO	Yarn over

Variations:

- You can use any yarn or gauge with this pattern. Make it larger by continuing to increase and then following the decreasing instructions. You've knit a baby afghan! Knit it larger still and you have an adult afghan.

- Continue to make the triangle larger and you have a bandana; just bind off the stitches when it's the size you want. Make it larger still and you have a shawl. Add fringe if you like.

Simple Scarf

Knit scarf.

Close-up of pattern.

This simple scarf uses a reversible pattern; each side looks the same. It's knit on big needles so it goes fast. You can make it any length you like, with or without fringe.

To make this scarf, you will knit with two different yarns held together. How do you do this? It's simple! Hold the yarn from both skeins in your hand and knit with them both, just as you would a single strand of yarn. That's it! The end result is that your scarf looks very different than if you had knit it alone with either yarn. Essentially, you've created a brand new yarn by combining them.

Size:

- 6" × 36" (1 skein Magpie, 1 skein Kidsilk Haze without fringe)
- 6" × 55" (2 skeins Magpie, 1 skein Kidsilk Haze with fringe—shown in photo)
- 6" × 60" (2 skeins Magpie, 1 skein Kidsilk Haze without fringe)

Materials:

- 1 or 2 skeins (depending upon the length desired) Magpie by Rowan (color 002 Natural or color of your choice)

    100% pure new wool

    100 grams/3.5 ounces

    140 meters/153 yards

- 1 skein Kidsilk Haze by Rowan (color 602 Tropic or color of your choice)

    70% super kid mohair/30% silk

    25 grams/.88 ounces

    210 meters/229 yards

- Needles size U.S. 10.5 (6.5mm) or size needed to obtain gauge
- Crochet hook for fringe
- Tapestry needle

Gauge:

12.75 sts = 4" in stockinette with both yarns held together

Instructions:

CO 29 sts.

Row 1: Slip the 1st st knitwise, *k3, p3; rep from *, end k4

Row 2: Slip the 1st st purlwise, *p1, k1; rep from *, end p2

Rep Rows 1 and 2 until scarf is desired length and BO in pattern.

Tip: What does it mean to "bind off in pattern"? Instead of knitting each stitch and binding off or purling each stitch and binding off, knit or purl the stitch as if you were continuing to work the next row of the pattern, then bind it off.

Finishing:

With a tapestry needle, weave in ends near edge.

Fringe:

Cut 30 12" lengths of each yarn used (60 total). Use 3 pieces of each yarn for each section of fringe. Attach 5 sections of fringe on each end of scarf, spacing them evenly. See Chapter 20 for more information on fringe.

Abbreviations:

BO	Bind off
CO	Cast on
K	Knit
P	Purl
Rep	Repeat
St	Stitch

Felted Purse

Have you ever thrown a wool sweater into the wash by accident and ended up with a matted miniature version that would fit a doll? That's called *felting*. Well, ordinarily you don't want to do that! But sometimes we do it on purpose, as is the case with this purse.

Felted purse.

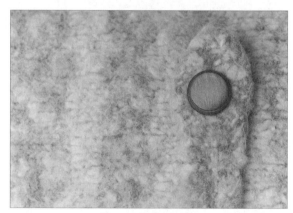
Close-up of pattern.

Only yarn that is spun from animals or is protein based will felt such as wool, alpaca, and mohair. Superwash wool won't felt because, after all, the point is to be able to safely throw it in the washer and dryer. Acrylic won't felt nor will yarn that is spun from plants such as cotton.

Fiber felts because there are microscopic scales all over it. The scales open up when exposed to hot water and detergent; friction or agitation tangles up these scales. The end result—felt—is sturdy, thick, and very stunning!

Size:

◆ 16.5 " × 13" before felting
◆ 11" × 11" after felting as shown

Materials:

◆ 1 skein Labrador by Crystal Palace Yarns in a solid color for CC (color 6885 Oat or color of your choice)
◆ 2 skeins Labrador by Crystal Palace Yarns in a print color for MC (color 7163 Mustard Combo or color of your choice)

    100% wool

    100 grams/3.5 ounces

    82 meters/90 yards

    This is a thick and thin yarn.

◆ Needles size U.S. 13 (9mm) or size needed to obtain gauge
◆ Tapestry needle
◆ One 1" button

Gauge:

10 sts = 4" in stockinette (knit every row)

14 rows = 4" in stockinette

Instructions:

Make 2 identical pieces.

With MC, CO 23 sts.

Row 1 (RS): Knit

Row 2 (WS): Purl

Row 3: K1, k into the front and back of the next st, k to the last 2 sts of the row, k into the front and back of the next st, k1

Tip: Remember, knitting into the front and back of the next stitch is also called a bar increase.

Row 4: Purl

Rep Rows 3 and 4, four additional times (33 sts).

Work Stripes:

Tip: When working the stripes in the middle of this pattern, there is no need to cut your yarn when changing colors. Carry the color not in use along the side, twisting one color around the other every other row.

Change to CC. Work 4 rows of St st.

Change to MC. Work 6 rows of St st.

Change to CC. Work 4 rows of St st.

Change to MC. Work 6 rows of St st.

Change to CC. Work 4 rows of St st.

Change to MC. Work 6 rows of St st.

Change to CC. Work 4 rows of St st.

Change to MC.

Row 1: K1, SSK, k to the last 3 sts, k2tog, k1

Row 2: Purl

Rep Rows 1 and 2 four additional times (23 sts).

Work 2 more rows of St st.

BO all sts.

Buttonhole Flap Closure:

Both pieces are the same so choose either one to work the buttonhole flap closure. Turn the piece so that the stripes are vertical. Along the edge where you did not change colors, with RS facing and MC, pick up 6 sts in the middle. In other words, you will pick up 6 sts along the middle MC stripe.

Knit these 6 sts every row for 5". End with WS completed.

Make Vertical Buttonhole:

K3. Cut the yarn, leaving a 36" tail. K the rem 3 sts with the main ball of yarn you just cut. Just begin knitting and leave a 4" tail you'll weave in later. You are creating a split in the fabric that will serve as the buttonhole.

Next Row: K3, drop the yarn, pick up the other length of yarn and k3 with it.

Next Row: K3, drop the yarn, pick up the other length of yarn and k3 with it.

Next Row: K all 6 sts with the same length of yarn (you should be working with the main ball of yarn at this point).

Knit 2 more rows.

Next Row: K1, SSK, k2tog, k1

Next Row: SSK, k2tog

BO rem 2 sts.

Finishing:

Turn pieces so that stripes are vertical. Starting at the upper left corner and including the slanting edge where you decreased, seam the pieces together with either color. Continue until you have seamed together the slanting edge on the other side. Weave in loose ends on WS.

Handle:

Cut nine strands of yarn 60" in length or desired length. Use any combination you like. Make a slip knot with three strands and attach to a door knob. Braid the strands loosely and tie a knot at the end, leaving a 4" tail to weave in. Make three braids in this manner and then braid them together again. Remove from the door knob and tighten the slip knots; then knot together on both ends. Sew to purse, using one of the tails, at the top of each side seam. Weave in ends on WS.

Felting:

Put the purse in the washer along with a pair of jeans or canvas tennis shoes. The friction will help the felting process. Don't use towels as they can shed and leave bits of fuzz embedded in your new purse. If you throw in jeans, use older ones that are no longer bleeding dye.

Use a small amount of detergent and a low water level with a hot temperature. Wash for three minutes. Stop the cycle and check to see if it is felted as tightly as desired—the longer you wash it, the smaller and more felted it will become. If it's not quite felted enough, wash it again and check every two minutes.

When you're satisfied, rinse it out by hand with cold water. Blot with an old towel that is free of fuzz. Shape it and lay flat to dry out of the sun.

Sew on the button and enjoy your new purse!

Abbreviations:

BO	Bind off
CC	Contrasting color
CO	Cast on
K	Knit
K2tog	Knit 2 together
MC	Main color
P	Purl
Rem	Remaining
Rep	Repeat
RS	Right side
SSK	Slip, slip, knit
St st	Stockinette stitch
WS	Wrong side

Two Needle Hat

This is a very easy hat pattern, knit entirely on two needles with one seam. You could knit this in multiple stripes or no stripes at all. The ribbed brim can be made longer, depending on your preference. Add a pom pom on top if you like (see Chapter 20).

Knit hat.

Close-up of pattern.

Sizes:

Small (large child, small woman), Medium (woman), Large (man)

Materials:

If you knit this hat in one color, you need only 1 skein for all sizes.

- 1 skein Plymouth Encore (MC color 1415 or color of your choice)
- 1 skein Plymouth Encore (CC color 054 or color of your choice)

    75% acrylic/25% wool

    100 grams/3.5 ounces

    183 meters/200 yards

- Needles sizes 8 and 9 U.S. (5 and 5.5mm) or size needed to obtain gauge
- Tapestry needle

Gauge:

4.25 sts and 8 rows = 1" in garter stitch with larger needles

Instructions:

With smaller needles and MC, CO 78 (86, 94) sts. Work in k2, p2 rib for 3.5" (4", 4") as follows:

Row 1: *k2, p2; rep from *, end k2

Row 2: *p2, k2; rep from *, end p2

Change to larger needles and work in garter stitch (knit every row) and stripe pattern (knit 10 rows with MC, then 2 rows with CC) for an additional 3" (3.5", 3.5").

Cont in garter stitch and stripe pattern and beg decreasing:

Row 1: k1 (k1, k2), *k13 (k12, k13), k2tog; rep from *, end k2 (k1, k2)—73 (80, 88 sts)

Row 2 and all even rows: knit across

Row 3: k1 (k1, k2), *k12 (k11, k12), k2tog; rep from *, end k2 (k1, k2)—68 (74, 82 sts)

Row 5: k1 (k1, k2), *k11 (k10, k11), k2tog; rep from *, end k2 (k1, k2)—63 (68, 76 sts)

Row 7: k1 (k1, k2), *k10 (k9, k10), k2tog; rep from *, end k2 (k1, k2)—58 (62, 70 sts)

Row 9: k1 (k1, k2), *k9 (k8, k9), k2tog; rep from *, end k2 (k1, k2)—53 (56, 64 sts)

Row 11: k1 (k1, k2), *k8 (k7, k8), k2tog; rep from *, end k2 (k1, k2)—48 (50, 58 sts)

Row 13: k1 (k1, k2), *k7 (k6, k7), k2tog; rep from *, end k2 (k1, k2)—43 (44, 52 sts)

Row 15: k1 (k1, k2), *k6 (k5, k6), k2tog; rep from *, end k2 (k1, k2)—38 (38, 46 sts)

Row 17: k1 (k1, k2), *k5 (k4, k5), k2tog; rep from *, end k2 (k1, k2)—33 (32, 40 sts)

Row 19: k1 (k1, k2), *k4 (k3, k4), k2tog; rep from *, end k2 (k1, k2)—28 (26, 34 sts)

Row 21: k1 (k1, k2), *k3 (k2, k3), k2tog; rep from *, end k2 (k1, k2)—23 (20, 28 sts)

Row 23: k1 (k1, k2), *k2 (k1, k2), k2tog; rep from *, end k2 (k1, k2)—18 (14, 22 sts)

Row 25: k1 (k1, k2), *k1 (k0, k1), k2tog; rep from *, end k2 (k1, k2)—13 (8, 16 sts)

For sizes:

Small: K1, k2tog across. Knit 1 row. K1, k2tog across (4 sts).

Medium: K2tog across. Knit 1 row. K2tog across (2 sts).

Large: K2tog across. Knit 1 row. K2tog across (4 sts).

Do not BO sts.

Finishing:

Cut yarn, leaving a long tail (about 36") for sewing. Thread through tapestry needle and draw yarn through rem sts on needle and remove needle. Pull. Begin seaming, using the mattress stitch. Fold up brim to desired point and switch your seam at the appropriate point to the other side so the seam will be invisible on both the brim and the hat. Weave in ends on WS.

Abbreviations:

Beg	Begin
BO	Bind off
CC	Contrasting color
CO	Cast on
K	Knit
K2tog	Knit 2 together
MC	Main color
Rem	Remaining
Rep	Repeat
Sts	Stitches
WS	Wrong side

Short Sleeved Pullover

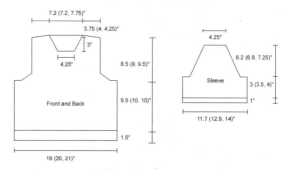

Schematic of sweater.

Short sleeved pullover.

Close-up of pattern.

Size:

Small, Medium, Large

Finished Chest Measurement 38'' (40'', 42'')

Materials:

- 10 (11, 12) balls Deco-Ribbon by Crystal Palace Yarns (color 101 or color of your choice)

    70% acrylic/30% nylon

    50 grams/1.75 ounces

    73/80 yards

    This is a ⅜'' wide ribbon that comes in solid colors or stripes.

- Straight needles size U.S. 10.5 and 11 (6.5 and 8mm) or size needed to obtain gauge

- Circular needle size U.S. 10.5 (6.5mm), 29'' length

- Tapestry needle

Gauge:

14 sts and 22 rows = 4'' over garter st with larger needles

Seed Stitch Pattern:

Row 1: *k1, p1; rep from *, end k1

Rep this row.

Instructions:

Back

With smaller needles, CO 67 (71, 75) sts.

Work seed stitch for 1.5'' for all sizes.

Change to larger needles.

Work in garter stitch (k every row). Mark Row 1 as the WS.

Tip: How do you mark the wrong or right side? On the side you wish to mark, thread a piece of yarn using a tapestry needle, or place a safety pin or slit stitch marker through the fabric.

Work in garter st until piece measures 11'' (11.5'', 11.5'') from the beg. End with WS completed.

Shape Armhole:

BO 4 sts at the beg of next 2 rows for all sizes.

Dec 1 st at each end every other row 5 (6, 6) times as follows: K1, SSK, k to last 3 sts, k2tog, k1—49 (51, 55) sts.

Tip: How do you decrease every other row? Decrease on the row indicated. The next row you will not decrease. The row after you will decrease again as instructed.

Work even until armhole measures 8.5'' (9'', 9.5''). End with WS completed.

Tip: Work even means to continue to work in the pattern stitch—in this case knit every row—without increasing or decreasing.

Tip: Measure the armhole length from the point you bound off stitches in a straight vertical line. Don't try to curve your tape measure around the armhole. Another way to measure the armhole length is to measure from the bottom of the piece where you began to the point you're at, subtracting the number of inches you knit for the body of the sweater.

Shape Shoulders:

BO 4 (5, 5) sts at the beg of the next 2 rows, then BO 4 (4, 5) sts at the beg of the next 2 rows, then BO 4 (4, 4) sts at the beg of the next 2 rows. K across the rem 25 (25, 27 sts). BO these sts for back of neck.

Front:

Work same as back until armhole measures 5.5" (6", 6.5"). End with WS completed. This will include the armhole shaping.

Shape Neck:

K17 (18, 20). With a new ball of yarn, BO the next 15 (15, 15) sts. With this same ball, k17 (18, 20).

Tip: You're going to be knitting with two separate balls of yarn at the same time. With the first ball, knit the first sequence of stitches. You'll add in the second ball that you will use to bind off the neck stitches the same way you would add in a new ball when you run out—knit the first stitch you'll be binding off, leaving a 4" tail you'll weave in later. After you've bound off the stitches, knit the next sequence of stitches with the same ball. Knitting with two balls at the same time ensures both sides will be equal in length. You can only bind off stitches at the beginning of a row and have the yarn be in the correct place to continue.

K17 (18, 20) and drop the ball of yarn you're knitting with. Pick up the yarn from the other ball and k17 (18, 20).

Next Row (RS): Dec 1 st at neck edge every other row 4 (4, 5) times—13 (14, 15) sts.

Tip: Remember, you're working the decreases at the neck edge this time. Work each decrease row above as follows: K across to last 3 sts, k2tog, k1. Drop the yarn you're knitting with and pick up the other ball. K1, SSK, k rem sts.

Work until armhole measures the same as the back (8.5", 9", 9.5").

Shape Shoulders:

At armhole edge, BO 4 (5, 5) sts, then 4 (4, 5) sts, then 4 (4, 4) sts.

Tip: Again, you can only bind off stitches at the beginning of a row so that the yarn will be in the correct place to continue. Here's how to shape the shoulders for the front of the sweater: BO 4 (5, 5) sts, k across rem sts of row. K 1 row.

BO 4 (4, 5) sts, k across rem sts. K 1 row. BO 4 (4, 4) sts.

Sleeves:

With smaller needles, CO 41 (45, 49) sts.

Work seed stitch for 1".

Change to larger needles.

Work in garter st for an additional 4" (4.5", 5"). Mark row 1 as WS. End with WS completed.

BO 4 sts at the beg of the next 2 rows—33 (37, 41) sts.

Shape Sleeve Cap:

Dec 1 st at each end every other row 1 (3, 6) times, then every 4th row 8 (8, 7) times as follows:

K1, SSK, k to last 3 sts, k2tog, k1.

BO rem sts.

Tip: How do you count every 4th row? Let's use the size small as an example. Decrease every other Row 1 time—the first row you decrease on is Row 1. You'll work another row without decreasing (Row 2). You won't decrease on Rows 3 and 4. Row 5 will be the 4th row and you'll decrease again. You will decrease again on the next 4th row, which will be Row 9. So in this example, decreases will occur on Rows 1, 5, 9, 13, 17, 21, 25, 29, and 33.

Make a second sleeve.

Finishing:

Seam right shoulder (the shoulder that will be on the right side when the sweater is on).

With RS facing and circular needle, pick up 25 (25, 27) sts along the back of neck, 16 (16, 16) sts along the right neck edge, 15 (15, 15) sts from the front of the neck, and 16 (16, 16) sts along the left neck edge. Work in seed st for 3 rows, working back and forth just as if you were using straight needles.

BO loosely in pat.

Tip: Be sure to bind off your stitches loosely, otherwise you may have a hard time getting the sweater over your head.

Tip: How do you bind off in pattern? Pretend you are going to continue to work the row as you have been. Knit or purl each stitch before it's bound off as appropriate to the pattern. If the next stitch would have been a purl, purl that stitch and bind off.

Seam other shoulder.

Sew in sleeves.

Seam sleeves.

Seam sides.

Weave in ends on WS.

Abbreviations:

Beg	Beginning
BO	Bind off
CO	Cast on
Dec	Decrease
K	Knit
K2tog	Knit 2 together
P	Purl
Pat	Pattern
Rem	Remaining
Rep	Repeat
RS	Right side
SSK	Slip, slip, knit
St	Stitch
WS	Wrong side

The Least You Need to Know

◆ The diagonal dishcloth pattern can become an afghan, a shawl, or a bandana.

◆ Only yarn that is spun from animals or is protein based (such as wool, alpaca, and mohair) will felt.

◆ Always bind off stitches loosely.

◆ "Work even" means to work in pattern without increasing or decreasing.

In This Chapter

- ◆ Crochet a simple scarf

- ◆ Create an easy, cozy afghan

- ◆ Learn to felt by crocheting a two-color purse

- ◆ Top if off with a hat

Chapter 23

Crochet Patterns

This chapter has four easy-to-crochet patterns to get you started in your crocheting adventure. Although they're written in the standard pattern format, extra help is included along the way to ensure success!

Refer to the chapter where each concept was discussed if you find yourself wondering how to work a certain point of the pattern or don't understand something.

Simple Scarf

Crocheted scarf.

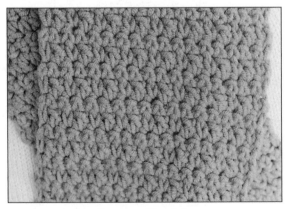

Close-up of pattern.

This scarf uses a simple but interesting pattern stitch. It crochets quickly and the pattern is easy to remember. It's not a reversible pattern (the right side looks different than the wrong side) but both sides are pretty.

Size:

- 7.5" × 37" (3 skeins)
- 7.5" × 50" (4 skeins)
- 7.5" × 63" (5 skeins [shown in photo])

Materials:

- 3, 4, or 5 skeins (depending on the length desired) Kool Wool by Lion Brand Yarn (color 130 Grass or color of your choice)

  50% merino wool/50% acrylic

  50 grams/1.75 ounces

  54 meters/60 yards

- Crochet hook size U.S. K-10.5 (6.5mm) or size needed to obtain gauge
- Tapestry needle

Gauge:

9.4 sc = 4"

Instructions:

Ch 18.

Foundation Row (RS): Sc in 2nd ch from hook, dc in next ch, *sc in next ch, dc in next ch; rep from *, end sc in last ch, ch 1, turn.

Row 1 (WS): Sc in 1st st and in each st across, ch 1, turn.

Row 2 (RS): *Sc in 1st st, dc in next st; rep from *, end sc in last st, ch 1, turn.

Tip: Mark the RS with a safety pin so you'll know where you left off.

Tip: What does it mean to "end sc in last ch or st" in these instructions? There are a total of 17 sts in this pattern. In Row 2 there is an even number of sts that are repeated across (sc in a st, then dc in a st). This leaves you with 1 st left at the end of the row. So you end the row with a sc in the last st.

Rep Rows 1 and 2 until scarf is desired length and fasten off.

Finishing:

With a tapestry needle, weave in ends near edge on WS.

Abbreviations:

Ch	Chain
Dc	Double crochet
Rep	Repeat
RS	Right side
Sc	Single crochet
St	Stitch
WS	Wrong side

Southwestern Stripes Afghan

Crocheted afghan.

Size:

43" × 56" before fringe

Materials:

- Jiffy by Lion Brand Yarns
  100% brushed acrylic:
    7 balls Fisherman (color #099)
    3 balls Country Green (color #181)
    4 balls El Paso (color #325)
  Fisherman and Country Green:
    85 grams/3 ounces
    123 meters/135 yards
  El Paso:
    70 grams/2.5 ounces
    105 meters/115 yards
- Crochet hook size U.S. K-10.5 (6.5mm) or size needed to obtain gauge
- Tapestry needle

Gauge:

12 tc = 4"

Instructions:

With MC, ch 105.

Row 1: Tc in 5th ch from hook and in each ch across (101 triple crochets).

Rows 2–4: Ch 3 (counts as 1 tc), turn. Tc in each stitch across.

Row 5: Ch 3, turn. Tc in each stitch across, close last tc with color A.

Row 6: With color A, ch 2 (counts as 1 dc), turn. Work 1 dc in each stitch across (101 double crochets). Close last dc with color B.

Row 7: With color B, ch 2, turn. Work 1 dc in each stitch across. Close last dc with color A.

Row 8: With color A, ch 2, turn. Work 1 dc in each stitch across. Close last dc with MC.

Rows 9–12: With MC, repeat Rows 2–4.

Row 13: Ch 3, turn. Tc in each stitch across, close last tc with color B.

Row 14: With color B, ch 2, turn. Work 1 dc in each stitch across. Close last dc with color A.

Row 15: With color A, ch 2, turn. Work 1 dc in each stitch across. Close last dc with color B.

Row 16: With color B, ch 2, turn. Work 1 dc in each stitch across. Close last dc with MC.

Repeat Rows 1–16 (work Row 1 in the same way you work Rows 2–4) until afghan is approximately 56" from beginning, ending with Rows 1–5 and MC. Weave in ends near edge with a tapestry needle.

Fringe:

Cut nine 22" lengths of yarn for each section of fringe. Alternate colors A and B for each section, spacing fringe 3 tc apart. Trim ends evenly. See Chapter 20 for more information on fringe.

Abbreviations:

Ch	Chain
Dc	Double crochet
MC	Main color
Tc	Triple crochet

Felted Crochet Purse

Felted purse.

Close-up of pattern.

Have you ever thrown a wool sweater into the wash by accident and ended up with a matted miniature version that would fit a doll? That's called *felting*. Well, ordinarily you don't want to do that! But sometimes we do it on purpose, as is the case with this purse.

Only yarn that is spun from animals or is protein based will felt such as wool, alpaca, and mohair. Superwash wool won't felt because, after all, the point is to be able to safely throw it in the washer and dryer. Acrylic won't felt nor will yarn that is spun from plants such as cotton.

Fiber felts because there are microscopic scales all over it. The scales open up when exposed to hot water and detergent; friction or agitation tangles up these scales. The end result—felt—is sturdy, thick, and very stunning!

Size:

11" × 8" before felting

10" × 6.5" after felting as shown

Materials:

- 1 skein Labrador by Crystal Palace Yarns in a solid color for CC (color 8166 Sienna or color of your choice)
- 1 skein Labrador by Crystal Palace Yarns in a print color for MC (color 7160 Candy Combo or color of your choice)

  100% wool

  100 grams/3.5 ounces

82 meters/90 yards

This is a thick and thin yarn.

◆ Crochet hook size U.S. N-15 (9mm) or size needed to obtain gauge

◆ Tapestry needle

Gauge:

9 dc = 4''

Instructions:

With MC, ch 28.

Row 1 (RS): Dc in 4th ch from hook and each ch across. Ch 3 (counts as 1 dc), turn.

Row 2 (WS): Skip 1st st, Dc in each dc across, closing last st with CC. Ch 2 (counts as 1 hdc), turn.

Tip: You can cut each color as you change them and weave in the ends later, but it's not necessary to do that with this pattern. After you've chained with the new color, wrap the color not in use around the chain to the other side, then turn. There will be lengths of yarn carried up the side that are quite long but they will fuse into the purse after felting and you'll never notice them.

Row 3: With CC, skip 1st st, hdc in each dc across, ending 1 hdc in top (3rd ch) of t-ch. Ch 2 (counts as 1 hdc), turn.

Row 4: With CC, skip 1st st, hdc in each hdc across, ending 1 hdc in top (2nd ch) of t-ch and closing last st with MC. Ch 3 (counts as 1 dc), turn.

Row 5: With MC, skip 1st st, dc in each hdc across, ending 1 dc in top (2nd ch) of t-ch. Ch 3 (counts as 1 dc), turn.

Row 6: With MC, skip 1st st, dc in each dc across, ending 1 dc in top (3rd ch) of t-ch and closing last st with CC. Ch 2 (counts as 1 hdc), turn.

Rep Rows 3–6 three more times or until piece measures approximately 22'' in length and fasten off.

Finishing:

Place piece flat on a table or floor with WS facing you. It should be longer than it is wide. Measure 16'' from bottom (either end can be the bottom). Fold bottom up and pin at the 16'' point at each side. Sew sides together using slip stitch seam with CC yarn. Weave in loose ends on WS.

Handle:

Cut three strands of yarn 48'' in length or desired length. Two lengths of CC and one length of MC were used in this sample but you can use any combination you like. Make a slip knot with the 3 strands and attach to a door knob. Braid the strands loosely and tie a knot at the end, leaving a 4'' tail to weave in. Remove from the door knob and tighten the slip knot. Sew to purse using one of the tails at the top of each side seam. Weave in ends on WS.

Tip: If you'd like a thicker handle, make three braids and then braid them together again.

Felting:

Put the purse in the washer along with a pair of jeans or canvas tennis shoes. The friction will help the felting process. Don't use towels as they can shed and leave bits of fuzz embedded in your new purse. If you throw in jeans, use older ones that are no longer bleeding dye.

Use a small amount of detergent and a low water level with a hot temperature. Wash for three minutes. Stop the cycle and check to see if it is felted as tightly as desired; the longer you wash it, the smaller and more felted it will become. If it's not quite felted enough, wash it again and check every two minutes.

When you're satisfied, rinse it out by hand with cold water. Blot with an old towel that is free of fuzz. Shape it and lay flat to dry out of the sun.

Abbreviations:

Ch	Chain
CC	Contrasting color
Dc	Double crochet
Hdc	Half double crochet
MC	Main color
Rep	Repeat
RS	Right side
St	Stitch
T-ch	Turning chain
WS	Wrong side

Easy Hat

Crocheted hat.

Close-up of pattern.

Size:

Fits average adult woman

Materials:

- 1 skein Polar by Rowan (color 646 Silver Lining or color of your choice)

  60% wool, 30% alpaca, 10% acrylic

  100 grams/3.5 ounces

  100 meters/109 yards

- Crochet hook size U.S. K-10.5 (6.5mm) or size needed to obtain gauge

- Tapestry needle

Gauge:

10 sc = 4"

Note: Do not join rounds. Do not chain to begin rounds.

Instructions:

This hat is worked from the crown down to the band.

Ch 5. Join with sl st in 1st ch to form a ring.

Work 9 sc in ring.

Tip: Here's an easy way to keep track of rounds. Cut a different colored piece of yarn about 12" long. Place this yarn over the space between the last stitch of the round you just finished and the new round you're about to begin. As you complete each round, keep flipping the yarn over that space. When you're done, you can easily pull it out.

Rnd 1: 2 sc in each sc around—18 sc

Rnd 2: *1 sc in next sc, 2 sc in next sc; rep from* to end of rnd—27 sc

Rnd 3: *1 sc in each of the next 2 sc, 2 sc in next sc; rep from * to end of rnd—36 sc

Rnd 4: *1 sc in each of the next 3 sc, 2 sc in next sc; rep from * to end of rnd—45 sc

Rnd 5: *1 sc in each of the next 4 sc, 2 sc in next sc; rep from * to end of rnd—54 sc

Sc in each sc around for 13 rnds. Hat should measure about 7" from top of hat to the last round you worked.

Band:

Sc through the back loop of each sc around for 6 rnds or about 2". End with sl st to back loop of 1st st of row.

Fasten off. Flip band up to RS. Weave in ends on WS.

Abbreviations:

Ch	Chain
Sc	Single crochet
Sl st	Slip stitch
Rnd(s)	Round(s)
RS	Right side
WS	Wrong side

The Least You Need to Know

- Mark the right side of a project with a safety pin so you'll know where you left off.
- Change colors by closing the last stitch of a row with the new color.
- Only yarn that is spun from animals or is protein based, such as wool, alpaca, and mohair, will felt.
- Keep track of rounds by placing a different colored yarn over the space between rounds.

Resources

This appendix lists knitting and crocheting websites, magazines, and suppliers. As you explore knitting and crocheting, these resources can provide answers to questions you might have, patterns, and tell you where to buy yarn and other supplies.

Websites

Knitting

Introduction to Knitting
www.wonderful-things.comnewknit.htm

Knitting.About.com
knitting.about.com

Knitting Basics
www.bhg.combhg/category.jhtml?catref=SC1649

Knitting Techniques
www.dnt-inc.combarhtmls/knittech.html

Learn to Knit
www.knitting.co.nz//pages/knitting/learntoknit.php

StitchGuide.com
www.stitchguide.com/stitches/knitting/index.html

Crocheting

Crochet.About.com
crochet.about.com

Crochet Cabana
www.crochetcabana.com/
learning_to_crochet.htm

Crochet Guild of America Crochet Lessons
www.crochet.com/lessons/lessonr/lessonr.html

Crochet Lessons
www.maryscrochetspot.com/crochetlessons/
index.html

StitchGuide.com
www.stitchguide.com/stitches/crochet/
index.html

Magazines

Knitting

Cast On
The Knitting Guild of America
PO Box 3388
Zanesville, OH 43702-3388
740-452-4541
www.tkga.com

Family Circle Easy Knitting
PO Box 3000
Denville, NJ 07834-3000
866-214-1203
www.fceasyknitting.com

Interweave Knits
201 East Fourth Street
Loveland, CO 80537-5655
970-669-7672
www.interweave.com/knit/knits/

Knit 'N Style
All American Crafts Publishing, Inc.
243 Newton-Sparta Road
Newton, NJ 07860
973-383-8080
www.knitnstyle.com

Knitter's
XRX, Inc.
824 West 10th Street
Sioux Falls, SD 57104-3518
605-338-2450
knittinguniverse.com

Knitting Digest
PO Box 9025
Big Sandy, TX 75755
1-800-449-0440
www.knittingdigest.com

Vogue Knitting
PO Box 1808
Denville, NJ 07834-9449
866-214-1200
www.vogueknitting.com

Crochet

Annie's Favorite Crochet
103 N. Pearl
Big Sandy, TX 75755
1-800-282-6643
www.anniesfavoritecrochet.com

Crochet!
23 Old Pecan Road
Big Sandy, TX 75755
1-800-449-0440
www.crochetmagazine.com

Crochet Fantasy
All American Crafts Publishing, Inc.
243 Newton-Sparta Road
Newton, NJ 07860
973-383-8080
www.crochetfantasy.com

Crochet World
PO Box 9001
Big Sandy, TX 75755
1-800-829-5865
www.crochet-world.com

Fast & Fun Crochet
PO Box 9001
Big Sandy, TX 75755
1-800-829-5865
www.fastandfuncrochet.com

Hooked on Crochet
23 Old Pecan Road
Big Sandy, TX 75755
1-800-449-0440
www.hooked-on-crochet.com

Old-Time Crochet
PO Box 9001
Big Sandy, TX 75755
1-800-829-5865
www.oldtimecrochet.com

Yarn

Baabajoe's Wool Company
PO Box 260604
Lakewood, CO 80215
www.baabajoeswool.com

Bernat
320 Livingstone Avenue South
Listowel, ON N4W 3H3
Canada
www.bernat.com

Berroco
PO Box 367
14 Elmdale Road
Uxbridge, MA 01569-0367
www.berroco.com

Brown Sheep Yarn Company
100662 County Road 16
Mitchell, NE 69357
308-635-2189
www.brownsheep.com

Caron International
PO Box 222
Washington, NC 27889
www.caron.com

Cascade Yarns
1224 Andover Park East
Tukwila, WA 98188
www.cascadeyarns.com

Coats & Clark
PO Box 12229
Greenville, SC 29612-0229
1-800-648-1479
www.coatsandclark.com

Colinette Yarns
Unique Kolours
1428 Oak Lane
Downingtown, PA 19335
610-280-7720
www.colinette.com

Crystal Palace Yarns
2320 Bissell Avenue
Richmond, CA 94804
510-237-9988
www.straw.com

Dale of Norway
N16 W23390 Stoneridge Drive, Suite A
Waukesha, WI 53188
www.dale.no

Harrisville Designs
Center Village
PO Box 806
Harrisville, NH 03450
1-800-338-9415
www.harrisville.com

Knitting Fever, Inc.
35 Debevoise Avenue
Roosevelt, NY 11575
516-546-3600
www.knittingfever.com

Koigu Wool Designs
RR# 1
Williamsford, ON N0H 2V0
Canada
1-888-765-9665
www.koigu.com

Lily Sugar 'N Cream
320 Livingstone Avenue South
Listowel, ON N4W 3H3
Canada
www.sugarncream.com

Lion Brand Yarn Company
34 West 15th Street
New York, NY 10011
1-800-258-9276
www.lionbrand.com

Mission Falls
Unique Kolours
1428 Oak Lane
Downingtown, PA 19335
610-280-7720
www.missionfalls.com

Muench Yarns
285 Bel Marin Keys Boulevard, Unit J
Novato, CA 94949-5763
415-883-6375
www.muenchyarns.com

Needful Yarns
4476 Chesswood Drive
Unit 10-11
Toronto, ON M3J 2B9
Canada
866-800-4700
www.needfulyarnsinc.com

Patons
PO Box 40
Listowel, ON N4W 3H3
Canada
www.patonsyarns.com

Plymouth Yarn Company, Inc.
PO Box 28
Bristol, PA 19007
1-800-523-8932
www.plymouthyarn.com

Rowan Yarns
5 Northern Blvd.
Amherst, NH 03031
www.knitrowan.com/

Skacel
PO Box 88110
Seattle, WA 98138-2110
www.skacelknitting.com

S. R. Kertzer Limited
105a Winges Road
Woodbridge, ON L4L 6C2
Canada
1-800-263-2354
www.kertzer.com

Tahki–Stacy Charles, Inc.
8000 Cooper Avenue, Building 1
Glendale, NY 11385
1-800-338-9276
www.tahkistacycharles.com

List of Abbreviations

Most common terms have a universal abbreviation. You will see abbreviations used in almost every pattern. Although it may seem confusing at first, you will learn them quickly and find this abbreviation system actually makes patterns easier to read and follow.

Knitting

Abbreviation	Full Name
alt	Alternate
approx	Approximately
beg	Begin(ning)
bet	Between
BO	Bind off
CC	Contrasting color
cm	Centimeter
cn	Cable needle
CO	Cast on, Cast off
col	Color
cont	Continue(ing)
dec	Decrease(ing)
dpn	Double pointed needle
eor	Every other row

Abbreviation	Full Name
est	Established
foll	Following
g or gr	Gram(s)
in(s)	Inch(es)
inc	Increase(ing)
k	Knit
k tbl	Knit through back loop
k2tog	Knit 2 together
k2tog tbl	Knit 2 together through back loop
kwise	Knitwise
MC	Main color
mm	Millimeter
m1	Make 1
mult	Multiple
opp	Opposite
oz	Ounces
p	Purl
p tbl	Purl through back loop
p2tog	Purl 2 together
p2tog tbl	Purl 2 together through back loop
pat(s)	Pattern(s)
pm	Place marker
psso	Pass slip stitch over
pwise	Purlwise
rem	Remaining
rep	Repeat
rev st st	Reverse stockinette stitch
rib	Ribbing
rnd(s)	Round(s)
RS	Right side
sc	Single crochet
sl	Slip
sl st	Slip stitch

Abbreviation	Full Name
ssk	Slip slip knit
st(s)	Stitch(es)
St st	Stockinette stitch
tbl	Through back of loop
tog	Together
WS	Wrong side
wyib	With yarn in back
wyif	With yarn in front
yfon	Yarn forward over needle
yfrn	Yarn forward and round needle
yo	Yarn over
yon	Yarn over needle
yrn	Yarn round needle

Crochet

Abbreviation	Full Name
alt	Alternate
approx	Approximately
beg	Begin(ning)
bet	Between
bk lp(s)	Back loop(s)
blo	Back loop only
bp	Back post
bpdc(s)	Back post double crochet(s)
bptr(s)	Back post triple crochet(s)
CC	Contrasting color
ch(s)	Chain(s)
cl(s)	Cluster(s)
cont	Continue(ing)
dc	Double crochet
dec	Decrease(ing)

Abbreviation	Full Name
est	Established
flo	Front loop only
foll	Following
fp	Front post
fpdc	Front post double crochet(s)
fptr	Front post triple crochet(s)
ft lp(s)	Front loop(s)
g or gr	Gram(s)
hdc	Half double crochet
inc	Increase(ing)
lp(s)	Loop(s)
MC	Main color
mm	Millimeter
oz	Ounces
pat(s)	Pattern(s)
pc(s)	Popcorn(s)
rem	Remaining
rep	Repeat
rev sc	Reverse single crochet
rnd(s)	Round(s)
RS	Right side
sc	Single crochet
sk	skip(ped)
sl st	Slip stitch
slip	Slip
sp(s)	Space(s)
st(s)	Stitch(es)
t-ch	Turning chain
tog	Together
trc	Triple crochet
WS	Wrong side
yo	Yarn over

Glossary

Afghan crochet   A special type of crochet that requires the crocheter to hold many stitches on the crochet hook. Special afghan hooks that look like a cross between a crochet hook and a knitting needle are available for this purpose. Also called Tunisian crochet.

back post double crochet (bpdc)   A special crochet stitch that involves working into the back of the post of a crochet stitch on the row.

backstitch   A sewing method of joining seams. It provides a sturdy seam.

binding off (BO)   The process in which you "lock up" all active stitches on the needle so they can't unravel. You bind off stitches when you're finished with a piece or want to shape an area, such as an armhole in a sweater. It's the same thing as casting off.

blocking   Wetting or steaming a piece and working it into its final shape.

bobbins   Plastic tabs that hold small amounts of yarn. Bobbins are invaluable when working on pieces that have many color changes.

cable needles   Small double pointed needles made expressly for creating cables.

cables   Specialized knitting patterns created by physically moving stitches and knitting them out of their original order.

casting on (CO)   The process of creating the foundation row of stitches from which you will knit.

chain (ch)   A group of chain stitches.

chain stitch (ch st)   A crochet stitch made by catching the yarn with the crochet hook and drawing the yarn through the loop on the hook. Multiple chain stitches form a chain. The term chain stitch is often used interchangeably with chain.

circular needles   Knitting needles that allow you to knit fabric in tubes or in the round.

closing a stitch   The step in crochet in which a stitch is finished and only one loop remains on the crochet hook. When changing colors, you always close the last stitch of the current color with the new color.

cluster stitches   Groups of crocheted stitches that, when worked, leave you with a single stitch.

Continental knitting   A style of knitting in which you catch the yarn using the needle. Also called German knitting.

contrasting color (CC)   An accent color used in a piece. You may have more than one contrasting color.

crochet   A French word meaning "hook." The craft of crochet involves using a hook to join loops of yarn into a fabric.

decrease (dec)   Subtracting the number of active stitches in your work.

double crochet (dc)   A versatile, tall crochet stitch. To make a double crochet, begin with a yarn over; insert the hook into a stitch; yarn over and pull through loop; yarn over and pull through 2 loops; yarn over, and pull through the remaining loops.

double crochet decrease (dc 2tog)   A crochet stitch that subtracts 1 stitch by combining 2 double crochets.

double point needles   Knitting needles that have points on both ends used to make things such as socks, collars, and hats.

dropped stitches   Stitches that accidentally came off the needle during knitting. If left unfixed, dropped stitches can run down through the knitted fabric.

duplicate stitch   A technique in which you embroider over knit stitches. The result is a color pattern that appears to be knit in, but is actually embroidered.

dye lot   An indicator of the time the yarn was dyed. Different dye lots have variations in tone.

edging   Used as a decoration or to help a piece lie flat. You can add it on or work it as you go.

English knitting   A style of knitting in which you use your hand to throw the yarn over the needle. Also called American knitting.

Fair Isle knitting   A form of knitting in which two colors are used per row, and the color not in use is carried or stranded along the wrong side of the piece.

filet crochet   A type of crochet in which a pattern is created in the crocheting by arranging blocks and spaces.

foundation chain   A row of chains that is the base of all crocheting.

front post double crochet (fpdc)   A special crochet stitch that involves working into the front of the post of a crochet stitch on the row below.

garter stitch   A pattern created by knitting every row. It creates ridges.

gauge   The number of stitches you need to complete to finish a specified length of knitted or crocheted fabric. Gauge is typically measured by the inch and sometimes by the row as well.

grafting   A means of joining 2 active rows of knitting so the join resembles a row of knitted stitches. Also called Kitchener stitch.

half double crochet (hdc)   A cross between a single crochet stitch and a double crochet stitch. To complete a half double crochet, begin with a yarn over; insert the hook into a stitch; yarn over and pull through the stitch; do another yarn over; and pull through the 3 loops on your hook.

increase (inc)   Adding more stitches to your work.

intarsia   A type of color knitting in which each block of color is knit from a separate ball or bobbin of yarn.

Kitchener stitch   *See* grafting.

knitting (k) Forming rows of interconnecting loops in which the loops face toward you as you work.

lacet A special type of mesh in filet crochet that is made by using a single crochet rather than a double or triple crochet. A lacet creates a soft, slightly rounded space.

main color (MC) The predominant color in a multicolor piece.

mattress stitch A seaming method in which pieces are butted together, a join is worked on the right side of the piece, and no visible seam appears.

mesh The background of filet crochet; mesh is made up of double or triple crochet stitches separated by a chain or chains.

mosaic pattern A particular type of slip stitch pattern in knitting. One color is used every 2 rows, and the second of these rows is a repeat of the first.

motifs In crochet, pieces worked around a central point rather than back and forth. Doilies and granny squares are two examples of motifs. In knitting, motifs are designs that are knit in the fabric, although sometimes they are done in duplicate stitch.

picking up stitches Creating stitches along an edge that you will work later.

picot A decorative stitch that features little points of crochet.

ply In the United States, the term ply simply refers to the number of strands that make up the yarn. It does not indicate how thick or thin the yarn is.

purling (p) Forming rows of interconnecting loops in which the loops face away from you as you work.

reverse single crochet A stitch made by working a single crochet left to right, rather than right to left, across a row of stitches. Sometimes used as an edging.

reverse stockinette stitch (rev st st) The bumpy side of stockinette stitch.

ribbing A stitch made by combining knit and purl stitches to form an elastic fabric. Ribbing often begins and ends sweater projects, as well as hats, mittens, and socks.

ridges The bumps you see on both sides of garter stitch fabric. Each ridge represents 2 rows of knitting.

right side (RS) The side of a project that will be showing, such as the outside of a sweater.

ripping out Unraveling or pulling out stitches. You rip out when you find that you don't like the look or size of the knitted fabric, or when you find a mistake that you need to undo.

selvage The edge of the piece, generally the first and last stitch. Also spelled *selvedge*.

single crochet (sc) The most basic of crochet stitches. To complete a single crochet, insert the hook through a chain (or stitch); yarn over; pull the loop through the chain (or stitch); yarn over again; and pull through both loops on the hook.

single crochet decrease (sc 2tog) A crochet stitch that subtracts 1 stitch by combining 2 single crochets.

slip knot A knot that slips easily along the cord on which it's tied.

slip stitch (sl st) In crochet, a means of joining rounds or a way to move the yarn across part of a row without adding stitches. In knitting, a stitch that is moved from one needle to the other without being worked.

slip stitch patterns A color technique in knitting worked with one color per row. It involves knitting with one color and slipping stitches done in another color from a previous row.

slip stitch seaming Joining two pieces of work together with yarn and a crochet hook. This technique produces a strong, tight join that works well on flat seams.

stash   The inevitable squirreling away of pounds and pounds of yarn a knitter or crocheter doesn't immediately need but might use later.

stitch holders   Safety pin-shape accessories that hold knitting stitches you aren't currently using but will use later.

stitch markers   Little disks that slide onto your knitting needle or hook on crocheted fabric. Markers cue you where you should do something to the fabric, such as increase stitches or begin a new pattern.

stockinette stitch (St st)   A pattern created by alternating 1 row of knitting with 1 row of purling. Stockinette stitch creates a fabric that is smooth on one side and bumpy on the other.

stranding   Carrying the yarn not currently used for a stitch along the back of a piece, ready to be used.

Superwash wool   Specially treated wool that can be safely machine washed.

swatch   A sample you knit or crochet to determine whether or not your gauge is where it should be. It also allows you to preview what the project will look like.

tail   The extra yarn left after you do something in knitting or crocheting, such as casting on a stitch or changing colors.

triple crochet (trc)   A tall crochet stitch. To make this stitch, yarn over the hook twice; insert the hook into a stitch; yarn over again and pull through the first 2 loops (the 2 closest to the point); yarn over again and pull through the next 2 loops; yarn over one last time and pull through the remaining 2 loops.

Tunisian crochet   *See* Afghan crochet.

turning chains (t-ch)   Extra chain stitches made at the end of each row to accommodate the height of the stitch of the next row.

whip stitch   A seaming technique, often used to join squares or strips together for a decorative effect. Also called overcast.

wrong side (WS)   The side that faces inward in a project, such as the inside of a sweater.

yarn over (yo)   In knitting, winding the yarn around a knitting needle to increase 1 stitch and create a decorative hole in the fabric. In crochet, the movement of passing the hook under the yarn and then catching the yarn with the hook.

yarn winder   A tool that enables you to easily wind skeins of yarn into balls that pull from the middle. Also called a wool winder.

Index

Symbols

* (asterisk), 62
() (parentheses), patterns, 181-182

A

abbreviations
    decreasing stitches (crochet), 125
    increasing (crochet), 125
    patterns, 179
acrylics, fiber content, 14
Afghan crochet (Tunisian crochet), 23, 139-140
    creating, 140-141
    hooks, 23
alpacas, fiber content, 13
American method
    casting on, 44
    knitting, 49-51
angoras, fiber content, 13
Aran sweaters, 78
asterisks (*), 62
    patterns, 181
automation, 5-6

B

baby weight, 12
back loops (crochet), 129-130
back loops (tbl) (knitting), 75-76
    purling, 75-76
back post double crochet (bdpc), 131
backstitches, 159-160
bags, project, 24
balls, yarn, 9
bar increases, 68-69
bdpc (back post double crochet), 131
binding off, 55-56
    knitting, 56-57
    patterns, 184
    purling, 57
blocking, crochet finish, 163
    pinning, 164
    steaming, 165
    washing, 163-164
blocks, filet crochet, 134-135
    creating, 135-136
    decreasing, 137-138
    filling blocks, 136-137
    increasing, 137-138
    lace, 137
    reading chart, 139
bobbins, 25
    color crochet, 151-152

bobble stitches, 133
brand names, yarn label, 11
bulky weights, 12
buttonholes (knitting), 81
    cable cast on, 43
    horizontal, 81
    vertical, 81

C

c4b (cable 4 back), 77-78
c4f (cable 4 front), 78
cable 4 back (c4b), 77-78
cable 4 front (c4f), 78
cable cast on, 43-44
cable needles, 26-27
cables (knitting), 77
    cable 4 back, 77-78
    cable 4 front, 78
Campbell, Alan, 6
care instructions, yarn label, 12
cashmeres, fiber content, 13
casting off, 56
casting on, 39-40
    cable cast on, 43-44
    double cast on, 42-43
    single cast on, 41-42
    tight rows, 42
chain edge selvages, 169
chain stitches
    front, 113
    turning rows, 118
        next stitch, 119
    yarn over, 112-113
chains (crochet), 112
    left-handed crochet, 122
changing colors, crochet, 150-151
checkerboard patterns (knitting), 64
circles, crochet, 145
circular knitting, 91-92
    circular needles, 93-94

double pointed needles, 95-96
    joining, 93
    needles, 19-20
        round knitting, 93-94
    twisted stitches, 92-93
cluster stitches, 132
    bobble, 133
    popcorn, 132-133
    puff, 133-134
Cobey, Katherine, 180
colors
    changing, crochet, 150-151
    charts, 85
    contrasting, 83, 152
    crochet
        bobbins, 151-152
        changing color, 150-151
        stripes, 149-150
    knitting
        duplicate stitches, 87-89
        Fair Isle, 85-87
        intarsia, 85
        slip stitch patterns, 84
        stripes, 83-84
    names, yarn label, 11
    numbers, yarn label, 11
Colorado State University, Gustafson Gallery, 145
condo stitches, 102
cones, yarn, 10
Continental method
    casting on, 44
    knitting, 48-49
    purling, 52-53
contrasting colors, 83, 152
conversion charts
    crochet hooks, 22-23
    steel crochet hooks, 22
conversion tables, knitting needle sizes, 21
cotton dishcloths, knitting pattern, 187-188
cottons, fiber content, 14

counters, gauge, 33
crochet
  fundamental history, 5-6
  gadgets, 24
    bobbins, 25
    finishing accessories, 26
    measuring tools, 25
    stitch markers, 25
  holding hook, 109-110
    feeding yarn, 111-112
    slip knot, 110-111
  hooks, 21
    Afghan, 23
    conversion chart, 22-23
    dropped knit stitches, 103
    equivalent needle and hook size table, 24
    four parts, 21-22
    knitting needle comparison, 23-24
    size, 22-23
    types, 22-23
  patterns
    easy hat, 204-205
    felted crochet purse, 202-204
    simple scarf, 200-201
    Southwestern Stripes Afghan, 201-202
  purpose, 6
    creativity, 6
    family heirlooms, 7
    portable, 7
    stress reliever, 6
  stitches, practice examples, 119-120
  versus knitting, 7

D

dc (double crochet stitch) (crochet), 115-116
dec (decrease), 68
decreasing stitches (crochet), 126
  abbreviations, 125
  double crochet, 127
  single crochet, 126-127
  triple crochet, 127
decreasing stitches (knitting), 70
  abbreviations, 67-68
  evenly, pattern requirements, 183-184
  filet crochet, 137-138
  gull-wing lace, 73
  Knit 2 together, 70
  Knit 2 together through back loop, 70-71
  left and right slants, 73
  Purl 2 together, 71
  Purl 2 together through back loop, 71
  rows, pattern requirements, 183
  Slip slip knit, 71-72
  slip, knit, pass slipped stitch over, 72
double blocks, filet crochet, 135
double cast on, 42-43
double crochet stitch (dc) (crochet), 115-116
  decreasing stitches, 127
  practice, 120
  rounds, 145
double pointed straight needles, 19
  round knitting, 95-96
double spaces, filet crochet, 135
dropped stitches, correcting mistakes, 100
  crochet hooks used, 103
  purl stitch row below, 101-102
  row below, 100-101
duplicate stitches, 87-89
dye lot numbers, yarn label, 11

E

edgings, 167-168
  knitting crochet projects, 168
    seed stitch, 169
    selvage stitch, 168-169
  picot, 168
  reverse single crochet, 168
  slip stitch, 167

elastic fabrics, ribbing, 62-63
embellishments
    fringe, 171-172
    I-Cord, 174-175
    pom poms, 173-174
    tassels, 172-173
embroider scissors, 24
ending on WS rows, patterns, 182
English method
    casting on, 44
    knitting, 49-51
    purling, 53-54

F

Fair Isle knitting, 85-86
    purling, 86-87
    stockinette stitch, 86
    twisting stitches, 87
fdpc (front post double crochet), 130-131
felted purses
    crochet pattern, 202-204
    knitting pattern, 190-192
fibers
    content
        selection, 13-14
        yarn label, 11
    weight, selection, 15-16
filet crochet, 134-135
    creating, 135-136
    decreasing, 137-138
    filling blocks, 136-137
    increasing, 137-138
    lace, 137
    reading chart, 139
finishing
    accessories, 26
    binding off, 55-56
        knitting, 56-57
        purling, 57
    blocking, 163
        pinning, 164

steaming, 165
        washing, 163-164
    crochet edgings, 167-168
        knitting, 168-169
        picot edging, 168
        reverse single crochet, 168
        slip stitch, 167
    sewing seams, 158
        backstitch, 159-160
        grafting, 161-163
        mattress stitch, 158-159
        overcast stitch, 160-161
        slip stitch, 161
        whip stitch, 160-161
    weaving ends, 157-158
foundation chains, 112
    front, 113
    left-handed crochet, 122
    yarn over, 112-113
fringes, embellishments, 171-172
frogging, 104
front loops (crochet), 129-130
front post double crochet (fdpc), 130-131

G

gadgets, 24-26
    bobbins, 25
    cable needles, 26-27
    finishing accessories, 26
    measuring tools, 25
    point protectors, 27
    row counters, 26
    stitch holders, 26
    stitch markers, 25
garments, patterns sizes, 181
garter stitches, 54-55
    round knitting, 92
gauges, 29-30
    advantages, 34
    affects on size, 30-31
    counter, 25, 32-33
    importance, 32

measuring, 32
   length differences, 33-34
   tools, 32-33
   width differences, 33-34
  patterns
    requirements, 180
    specification, 31-32
  swatch uses, 34-35
  yarns
    label, 12
    weight, 15
German method
  casting on, 44
  knitting, 48-49
grafting (Kitchener stitch), 161-163
Granny Squares, 146-147
gull-wing laces, 73
Gustafson Gallery, Colorado State University, 145

H

half double crochet stitches (hdc) (crochet), 114-115
  practice, 120
hanks, yarn, 10
hats, crochet pattern, 204-205
hdc (half double crochet stitch) (crochet), 114-115
heirlooms, crocheting and knitting purpose, 7
history fundamentals, 5-6
hooks
  crocheting, 21
    Afghan, 23
    equivalent size table, 24
    four parts, 21-22
    knitting needle comparison, 23-24
    size, 22-23
    types, 22-23
  gripping, 109-110
    feeding yarn, 111-112
    slip knot, 110-111
  pattern requirements, 180
horizontal buttonholes, 81

I-J

I-Cords, embellishment, 174-175
"in, over, through, and off," 51
inc (increase), 68
increasing stitches (crochet), 125-126
  abbreviations, 125
increasing stitches (knitting), 68
  abbreviations, 67-68
  bar, 68-69
  even, pattern requirements, 183-184
  filet crochet, 137-138
  gull-wing lace, 73
  Make 1, 69-70
  rows, pattern requirements, 183
  yarn over, 68
intarsia knitting, 85

joining, round knitting, 93

K

k2tog (Knit 2 together), 68
  decreasing stitches, 70
k2tog tbl (Knit 2 together through back loop), 68
  decreasing stitches, 70-71
keeping to patterns, 184
Kitchener stitches (grafting), 161-163
Knit 2 together (k2tog), 68
  decreasing stitches, 70
Knit 2 together through back loop (k2tog tbl), 70
  decreasing stitches, 70-71
knit cast on (cable cast on), 44
knitting
  combining with purl stitch, 61
  fundamental history, 5-6
  gadgets, 24-26
    bobbins, 25
    cable needles, 26-27
    finishing accessories, 26
    measuring tools, 25
    point protectors, 27

row counters, 26
stitch holders, 26
stitch markers, 25
needles, 19
   circular, 19-20
   crochet hook comparison, 23-24
   equivalent size table, 24
   material, 21
   sizing systems, 21
   straight, 19-20
patterns
   cotton dishcloth, 187-188
   felted purse, 190-192
   scarf, 189-190
   short sleeved pullover, 194-197
   two needle hat, 192-194
purpose, 6
   creativity, 6
   family heirlooms, 7
   portable, 7
   stress reliever, 6
stitches, 47-48
versus crocheting, 7

L

labels, yarn, reading, 10-12
laces
   filet crochet, 135-137
   gull-wing, 73
left-handed crochet, 120-123
   basics, 121-122
   foundation chain, 122
   single crochet, 122-123
left-handed knitters, 57
   Continental cast on method, 44
   knitting, 57-59
   purling, 59
   single cast on, 44-45
lengths, yarn label, 12

M

M1 (Make 1), 68
   increasing stitches, 69-70
main colors, 83, 152
Make 1 (M1), 69
   increasing stitches, 69-70
manufacturers, yarn label, 11
marking crochet rounds, 145
materials, knitting needles, 21
mattress stitches, 158-159
measurements, gauge, 29-32
   advantages, 34
   affects on size, 30-31
   importance, 32
   length differences, 33-34
   patterns specification, 31-32
   swatch uses, 34-35
   tools, 32-33
   width differences, 33-34
measuring tapes, gauge measurements, 33
measuring tools, 25
mercerized cottons, 14
meshes, filet crochet, 134-135
   creating, 135-136
   decreasing, 137-138
   filling blocks, 136-137
   increasing, 137-138
   lace, 137
   reading chart, 139
methods
   casting
      cable cast on, 43-44
      double cast on, 42-43
      single cast on, 41-45
      tight rows, 42
   knitting, 48
      Continental method, 48-49
      English method, 49-51
      new rows, 51
   purling, 51-52
      Continental knitting method, 52-53
      English knitting method, 53-54

mistakes
    dropped stitches, 100
        crochet hooks used, 103
        purl stitch row below, 101-102
        row below, 100-101
    preventing, 99
    sloppy stitches, 103
    twisted stitches, 100
    unraveling, 104
        extra stitches, 104
        one stitch at a time, 104
        ripping out, 104
mohair, fiber content, 13
mosaic patterns, 84
multiple stitches (knitting), 62
    pattern requirements, 180

N

needles
    cable, 26-27
    circular, round knitting, 93-94
    double point, round knitting, 95-96
    finishing accessory, 26
    knitting, 19
        circular, 19-20
        crochet hook comparison, 23-24
        equivalent needle and hook size table, 24
        material, 21
        sizing systems, 21
        straight, 19-20
    pattern requirements, 180
novelty yarns, 14
numbers
    color, 11
    dye lot, 11
nylons, fiber content, 14

O-P

Orvieto Lace, 168
overcast stitches, 160-161

p2tog (Purl 2 together), 68
    decreasing stitches, 71
p2tog tbl (Purl 2 together through back loop), 68
    decreasing stitches, 71
packaging yarns, 9-10
parentheses, patterns, 181-182
Parker, Dorothy, 6
patterns
    asterisks, 62, 181
    basics, 179
        abbreviations, 179
        added materials, 180
        gauge, 180
        hook size, 180
        needle size, 180
        stitch multiples, 180
        stitch pattern, 180
        yarn requirements, 180
    charts, 184-185
    combining knit and purl stitches, 61
    crochet
        easy hat, 204-205
        felted crochet purse, 202-204
        simple scarf, 200-201
        Southwestern Stripes Afghan, 201-202
    duplicate stitch, 87-89
    Fair Isle knitting, 85-86
        purling, 86-87
        stockinette stitch, 86
        twisting stitch, 87
    garment size, 181
    gauge specification, 31-32
    intarsia knitting, 85
    knitting
        checkerboard, 64
        cotton dishcloth, 187-188

felted purse, 190-192
multiple stitches, 62
ribbing, 62-63
scarf, 189-190
seed stitch, 63-64
short sleeved pullover, 194-197
two needle hat, 192-194
parentheses, 181-182
schematics, 182
skipping instructions, 185
slip stitch (knitting), adding color, 84
terms, 182
bind off, 184
decreasing evenly, 183-184
decreasing rows, 183
ending on WS row, 182
increasing evenly, 183-184
increasing rows, 183
keeping to pattern, 184
multiple directions, 184
reverse shaping, 183
work even, 182
pc st (popcorn stitch), 132-133
pick up stitches (knitting), 78-80
picot edgings, 168
pictures, patterns, 182
pinning, 164
pins, finishing accessory, 26
plys, yarn labels, 12
points
crochet hook, 22
protectors, 27
polyamides, 14
polyesters, fiber content, 14
pom poms, embellishment, 173-174
popcorn stitches (pc st), 132-133
portability, 7
post stitches (crochet), 130
back post double crochet, 131
front post double crochet, 130-131
Post-it notes, 183
preventing mistakes, 99

project bags, 24
psso (Pass slipped stitch over), 68
puff stitches, 133-134
pull skeins, 9
Purl 2 together (p2tog), 71
decreasing stitches, 71
Purl 2 together through back loop (p2tog tbl), 71
decreasing stitches, 71
purling, 51-52
back loop, 75-76
binding off, 57
combining with knit stitch, 61
Continental knitting method, 52-53
dropped stitches, 101-102
English knitting method, 53-54
Fair Isle knitting, 86-87
left-handed knitters, 59
stitches, 47-48

Q-R

rayon, fiber content, 14
reverse sc (reverse single crochet), 132
reverse shaping, 183
reverse single crochet (reverse sc), 132
edgings, 168
reverse stockinettes, 54
ribbing (knitting), 62-63
right sides, knitting, 48
right-handed knitters, English cast on method, 44
rings, crochet, 143-144
working in center, 144-145
ripping out mistakes, 104
round knitting, 91-92
circular needles, 93-94
double point needles, 95-96
joining, 93
twisted stitches, 92-93
rounds, crochet, 143
circles, 145
double crochet, 145

Granny Square, 146-147
ring, 143-144
triple crochet, 145
tube, 145
working in ring, 144-145
rows
    casting on, 39-40
        cable cast on, 43-44
        double cast on, 42-43
        single cast on, 41-42
        tight rows, 42
    color crochet, 150-151
    counters, 26
    gauge, 29-30
        affects on size, 30-31
        importance, 32
        patterns specification, 31-32

S

sc (single crochet stitch) (crochet), 114
    left-handed, 122-123
scarves
    crochet pattern, 200-201
    knitting pattern, 189-190
schematics, patterns, 182
scissors, embroider, 24
seams, crochet finish, 158
    backstitch, 159-160
    grafting, 161-163
    mattress stitch, 158-159
    overcast stitch, 160-161
    slip stitch, 161
    whip stitch, 160-161
seed stitches (knitting), 63-64
    edges, 169
selvage stitches, crochet edges, 168-169
sewing, seams, 158
    backstitch, 159-160
    grafting, 161-163
    mattress stitch, 158-159

overcast stitch, 160-161
    slip stitch, 161
    whip stitch, 160-161
shanks, crochet hook, 22
sheep's wools, fiber content, 13
shell stitches (crochet), 134
short sleeved pullovers, knitting pattern, 194-197
silks, fiber content, 13
single cast on, 41-42
    left-handed knitters, 44-45
single crochet stitches (sc) (crochet), 114
    decreasing stitches, 126-127
    left-handed, 122-123
    practice, 120
single pointed straight needles, 19
sizes
    crochet hook, 22-23
    gauge, 29-30
        advantages, 34
        affects on pattern, 30-31
        importance, 32
        measuring, 32-34
        patterns specification, 31-32
        swatch uses, 34-35
    knitting needles
        conversion table, 21
        differing systems, 21
    pattern requirements, 181
    yarn label, 12
skeins, 9
sl (slip stitch), 68, 76
sl 1, k 1, psso, decreasing stitches, 72
sl st (slip stitch) (crochet), 117
slip knots (crochet), 40
    gripping hook, 110-111
Slip slip knit (ssk), 71
    decreasing stitches, 71-72
slip stitches (sl) (knitting), 76
    adding color, 84
slip stitches (sl st) (crochet), 117
    edgings, 167
    rounds, 144, 161

slip, knit, pass slipped stitch over (sl 1, k 1, psso), 72
    decreasing stitches, 72
slipped garter edges, 169
sloppy stitches, correcting mistakes, 103
Southwestern Stripes Afghans, crochet pattern, 201-202
spaces (crochet), 132
    filet crochet, 134-135
        creating, 135-136
        decreasing, 137-138
        filling blocks, 136-137
        increasing, 137-138
        lace, 137
        reading chart, 139
sport weights, 12
squares (crochet), 143
    circles, 145
    double crochet, 145
    Granny Square, 146-147
    ring, 143-144
    triple crochet, 145
    tube, 145
    working in ring, 144-145
ssk (Slip slip Knit), 68
    decreasing stitches, 71-72
steaming, 165
steel crochet hooks, conversion chart, 22
stitches, 7
    back loop (knitting), 75-76
        purling, 75-76
    backstitch, 159-160
    cable 4 back, 77-78
    cable 4 front, 78
    chain (crochet), 112-113
        front, 113
    checkerboards (knitting), 64
    closing, 150
    crochet, 113-114
        cluster, 132-134
        double crochet, 115-116
        half double crochet, 114-115

next row, 117-119
post stitches, 130-131
practice examples, 119-120
reverse single, 132
single crochet, 114
slip stitch, 117
spaces, 132
triple crochet, 116
variations, 129-130
decreasing (crochet), 126
    abbreviations, 125
    double crochet stitch, 127
    single crochet, 126-127
    triple crochet, 127
decreasing (knitting), 70
    abbreviations, 67-68
    Knit 2 together, 70
    Knit 2 together through back loop, 70-71
    lace, 73
    left and right slants, 73
    Purl 2 together, 71
    Purl 2 together through back loop, 71
    Slip slip knit, 71-72
    slip, knit, pass slipped stitch over, 72
dropped, correcting mistakes, 100-103
duplicate, 87-89
filet crochet, 134-135
    creating, 135-136
    decreasing, 137-138
    filling blocks, 136-137
    increasing, 137-138
    lace, 137
    reading chart, 139
garter, 54-55
gauge, 29-30
    affects on size, 30-31
    importance, 32
    patterns specification, 31-32
grafting, 161-163
holders, 26
increasing (crochet), 125-126
    abbreviations, 125

increasing (knitting), 68
    abbreviations, 67-68
    bar, 68-69
    lace, 73
    Make 1, 69-70
    yarn over, 68
knitting, 47-48
markers, 25
mattress, 158-159
multiples (knitting), 62
    pattern requirements, 180
overcast, 160-161
patterns, 32
    requirements, 180
pick up (knitting), 78-80
purling, 47-48
ribbing (knitting), 62-63
seed (knitting), 63-64
    edges, 169
selvage, 168-169
shell, 134
single crochet, left-handed, 122-123
slip (crochet), 161
slip (knitting), 76
sloppy, correcting mistakes, 103
stockinette, 32, 54-55
    Fair Isle knitting, 86
    twisting
        correcting mistakes, 100
        Fair Isle knitting, 87
    unraveling, 104
        extra stitches, 104
        one at a time, 104
        ripping out, 104
    whip, 160-161
stockinette stitches, 32, 54-55
    Fair Isle knitting, 86
storage devices, 24
straight needles, 19-20
stranded colors, 85
stress relief, crocheting and knitting purpose, 6

stripes
    color crochet, 149-150
    color knitting, 83-84
Stuart, King Charles, 162
substitutions, yarn, 16-17
superwash wools, 13
swatches, 32
    measuring gauge, 32
        length differences, 33-34
        tools, 32-33
        width differences, 33-34
    uses, 34-35

T

tackle boxes, 24
tails, casting on, 40
tape measures, 25
tapestry needles, 26
tassels, embellishment, 172-173
tbl (back loop), 75-76
    purling, 75-76
terms, patterns, 182
    bind off, 184
    decreasing
        evenly, 183-184
        rows, 183
    ending on WS row, 182
    increasing
        evenly, 183-184
        rows, 183
    keeping to pattern, 184
    multiple directions, 184
    reverse shaping, 183
    work even, 182
throats, crochet hook, 22
thumb rests, crochet hook, 22
tinks, 104
tools
    crochet hooks, 21
        Afghan, 23
        equivalent size table, 24

four parts, 21-22
knitting needle comparison, 23-24
size, 22-23
types, 22-23
gadgets, 24-26
bobbins, 25
cable needles, 26-27
finishing accessories, 26
measuring tools, 25
point protectors, 27
row counters, 26
stitch holders, 26
stitch markers, 25
knitting needles, 19
circular, 19-20
crochet hook comparison, 23-24
equivalent size table, 24
material, 21
sizing systems, 21
straight, 19-20
measuring gauge, 32-33
trc (triple crochet stitch) (crochet), 116
triple crochet stitches (trc) (crochet), 116
decreasing stitches, 127
practice, 120
rounds, 145
tubes, 145
Tunisian crochet (Afghan crochet), 23, 139-140
creating, 140-141
hooks, 23
turning chains (crochet), 118
next stitch, 119
twisted stitches
correcting mistakes, 100
Fair Isle knitting, 87
round knitting, 92-93
two needle hat, knitting pattern, 192-194

U–V

unraveling mistakes, 104
extra stitches, 104
one stitch at a time, 104
ripping out, 104

v-stitches (crochet), 134
vertical buttonholes, 81
viscose, 14

W–X

Walker, Barbara, 64
Warner House, 172
washing finished works, 163-164
weaving
ends, crochet finish, 157-158
needles, 26
weights, yarn label, 12
whip stitches, 160-161
wools
sheep's, 13
superwash, 13
winders, 10
work even patterns, 182
World War I, knitting socks for soldiers, 7
worsted weights, 12, 40
wrong sides, knitting, 48

Y–Z

yards, yarn label, 12
yarn over (yo), 68
crochet chain, 112-113
increasing stitches, 68
yarns
crochet, feeding yarn, 111-112
identifying without label, 11
label, reading, 10-12

novelty, 14
packaging, 9-10
pattern requirements, 180
selection
    fiber content, 13-14
    weight, 15-16
substitutions, 16-17
weights, recommended gauge, 15
winders, 10
yo (yarn over), increasing stitches, 68

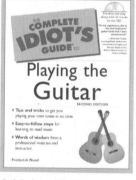

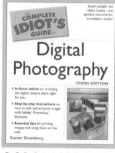
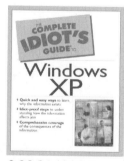